Primary Process Impacts and Dreaming the Undreamable Object in the Work of Michael Eigen

Primary Process Impacts and Dreaming the Undreamable Object in the Work of Michael Eigen examines Eigen's rich phenomenological work on becoming a welcoming object.

The contributors to this collection explore the core theme with reference to key Eigen works including *Feeling Matters* and *Contact with the Depths*. As a primary process psychoanalyst, Eigen's writing reflects a unique rhythm of faith that is able to "revivify" union-distinction body-affect-thinking potentialities within a creative psychoanalytic dyad. In this book, alongside its companion volume, *Toxic Nourishment and Damaged Bonds in the Work of Michael Eigen*, contemporary Eigen readers and writers articulate the various welcoming processes and attitudes needed to cultivate a "Hearing Heart," a central ingredient in reaching and touching those parts of self-deemed unwanted, unwelcomed, and even traumatized. *Primary Process Impacts and Dreaming the Undreamable Object in the Work of Michael Eigen* represents a wide range of psychoanalytic perspectives, and the chapters describe the genius of Eigen as well as contribute their own clinical and academic acumen.

Presenting a key aspect of Michael Eigen's transformational aesthetic, this book will be of great interest to psychoanalysts, psychotherapists, and all those with an interest in psychoanalytic and spiritual psychology.

Loray Daws is a registered Clinical Psychologist in South Africa and British Columbia, Canada. He is currently in private practice and is a senior faculty member at the International Masterson Institute in New York, USA.

Keri S. Cohen is a Licensed Clinical Social Worker and a Board-Certified Diplomate in clinical social work. She is a psychoanalytic psychotherapist in private practice in Pennsylvania, USA.

Primary Process Impacts and Dreaming the Undreamable Object in the Work of Michael Eigen

Becoming the Welcoming Object

Edited by Loray Daws and
Keri S. Cohen

Routledge
Taylor & Francis Group

LONDON AND NEW YORK

Designed cover image: © Melanie W. Cohen

First published 2024
by Routledge
4 Park Square, Milton Park, Abingdon, Oxon OX14 4RN

and by Routledge
605 Third Avenue, New York, NY 10158

Routledge is an imprint of the Taylor & Francis Group, an informa business

British Library Cataloguing-in-Publication Data
A catalogue record for this book is available from the British Library

ISBN: 9781032346052 (hbk)
ISBN: 9781032346045 (pbk)
ISBN: 9781003322993 (ebk)

DOI: 10.4324/9781003322993

Typeset in Times New Roman
by codeMantra

Contents

Acknowledgements

We are deeply indebted to Routledge, especially Susannah Frearson and Saloni Singhania, for their enthusiastic support to the two volumes and Michael Eigen's work in general.

Routledge for their permission to re-publish Jeff Eaton's *Becoming a Welcoming Object: Personal Notes on Michael Eigen's Impact*, previously published in *The Living Moments: On the Work of Michael Eigen* (2015), and a section taken from Eigen, 2011, (pp. 86–87), *Eigen in Seoul: Faith and Transformation (Vol. 2)* reproduced in Daws' *Welcoming the Psychotic Core*, Chapter 5 in this volume.

Thank you, Jeff Eaton, for your permission to re-publish *The Obstructive Object*, originally appearing in *A Fruitful Harvest: Essays after Bion*, by The Alliance Press, 2011. An earlier version also appeared in *Psychoanalytic Review*, Vol. 92, 2005. From us as editors, thank you for your generosity in contributing no less than three papers. Your writings on Eigen and Bion serve as an anchor and a backdrop for these volumes. We are grateful for your creativity of ideas and spirit. Like others in the volumes, your work greatly supports the field.

Phoenix Publishing House Ltd for granting permission to reproduce Louis Rothchild's chapter "Abraham's and Isaac's Fear and Silence" from his forthcoming book, *Rapprochement Between Fathers and Sons: Breakdowns, Reunions, Potentialities*.

Dr. Stephen Mosblech, Managing Editor of the *European Journal of Psychoanalysis*, for the republications of Adam Schechter's article *The Join and Distinction-Union: A Resonant and Complex Oneness*.

Dr. Klaus Ottmann, Editor and Publisher, Spring Publications, for the republication of Stephen Bloch's *Music as Dreaming*.

Ms. Melanie W. Cohen for the exquisite cover art for both volumes. Your felt sense is greatly valued.

To all the writers who contributed to the volumes: your love of Eigen, unique creativity, and psychic wisdom are valued and appreciated. Reading your work and including it in our vision has been a rare privilege. Thank you.

Concerning the included case material, all efforts have been made to ensure permission from the analysands as well as to disguise the material included.

As editors, and on behalf of all the writers included, we humbly and unreservedly acknowledge your contribution as the primal and vital background voices to the current work and the growth of psychoanalytic discourse in general. Although you will never be directly known, we extend our deepest gratitude for your presence.

Dr. Michael Eigen for his unending support and willingness to write the foreword to the volumes.

You remain our inspiration.

From Loray:

Keri Cohen for much support, humor, and creative perspective as we moved through the project over more than a year.

To my background of support: my family, many colleagues, too many to mention, and my analysts over 20 years (Drs. Assie Gildenhuys, A.C.N. Preller, and Janet Oakes). Autochthonous creation, inner freedom, and stepping forth are only possible through others. I remain deeply indebted and appreciative.

To the various analysands who graciously provided me with permission to include their inner work in this volume. Your work serves us all.

From Keri:

Thank you to Loray Daws for his vision and invitation to collaborate with him on these two volumes. His steadfast fortitude, generosity of spirit, and positivity accompanied this project with grace. I am very appreciative.

Thank you to Mike Eigen, who, at the beginning of the pandemic, predicted that there would be much creativity coming out of that world experience. These volumes are a testament to that prediction.

Thank you to my colleagues near and far, from whom I continue to learn and grow, including study, supervision, and dream groups, in which I am fortunate enough to be included. These welcoming spaces sponsor respite and growth.

Thank you to my husband and children. There are no words to describe the meaning and depth added to my life with all of you in it. You make it all possible.

About the Editors and Contributors

Rachel Berghash was born in Jerusalem. She has published a memoir, *Half the House, My Life In and Out of Jerusalem*, with Sunstone Press. Her poetry and poetry translations have appeared in numerous literary magazines, including *Chicago Review, Finalist in New Millenium Writings, Christianity and Literature, Forward, Psychoanalytic Perspectives, Colorado Review*, and in anthologies including *Living Moments* (Karnac) and *A Poet's Siddur*. In 2009, her poetry was nominated for the Pushcart Prize in poetry. Her book, *Psyche, Soul, and Spirit: Interdisciplinary Essays*, with co-author Katherine Jillson, has been published by WIPF & STOCK Publishers.

Stephen Bloch is a clinical psychologist and Jungian analyst in Cape Town, South Africa. He is both a Jungian Psychoanalyst and training analyst with SAAJA in Cape Town. He is a founding member of the Southern African Association of Jungian Analysts and has served on its Executive Committee, Assessment and Review, Ethics, and Library Committees. Stephen has given training seminars on transference and countertransference, dream interpretation, Klein, Winnicott, Bion, and Eigen, the psychoanalytic frame, music and psychoanalysis, embodiment, psychotherapy, and the meditating patient. He has published papers and reviews, and co-edited with Paul Ashton Music and Psyche (Spring Publications, 2010) and with Loray Daws of a festschrift for Michael Eigen entitled *Living Moments: Papers in Honor of Michael Eigen* (Karnac, 2015).

Marian Campbell is a clinical psychologist and Jungian analyst living and working in Cape Town, South Africa. After many years at Red Cross War Memorial Children's Hospital and the University of Cape Town, she is currently in full-time private practice. She is a member of the South African Association of Jungian Analysts, currently serving on the Executive Committee; a member of the Cape Town Psychoanalytic Self Psychology Group; and an associate member of the Independent Group of Analytical Psychologists, UK. Her interests include psychic aliveness, poetry, psychoanalysis, and climate psychology.

Keri S. Cohen, LCSW, is a Board-Certified Diplomate in clinical social work. She is a psychoanalytic psychotherapist in private practice in Lancaster, PA.

Her work is with adults, adolescents, and children. She is a graduate of the University of Pennsylvania's School of Social Policy and Practice, and holds a certificate from the William Alanson White Institute's Online Intensive Psychoanalytic Psychotherapy Program. She has presented papers at national and international conferences on Bion, Ferenczi, and Eigen, and is a co-moderator of the international online Studying Eigen group. She teaches a private seminar and has attended Michael Eigen's Tuesday New York seminars for more than 15 years. Cohen is the co-editor of the 2021 Routledge book *Healing, Rebirth, and the Work of Michael Eigen* and has written published papers which include the works of Eigen, Ferenczi, and Bion. Cohen was asked to write the introduction to *Eigen in Seoul Volume Three: Pain and Beauty, Terror and Wonder* (Routledge 2021) and the foreword to Eigen's forthcoming Routledge book *Bits of Psyche: Selected Seminars of Michael Eigen*.

Loray Daws is a registered clinical psychologist in South Africa and British Columbia, Canada. He is currently in private practice and serves both as a senior faculty member at the International Masterson Institute and as a board member at the Object Relations Institute in New York. Loray specializes in psychoanalysis and daseinsanalysis, and he is the editor of six books on psychoanalysis and existential analysis.

Paul DeBlassie III is a depth psychologist and writer living in his native New Mexico. For the past forty years, his clinical practice has specialized in treating individuals in emotional and spiritual crisis. Essays on trauma, spirituality, and archetypal phenomena have been included in *Depth Insights: Journal of Depth Psychology* and *Quadrant: Journal of Jungian Psychoanalysis*. His metaphysical novels have explored the dark side of religion and psychic transformation and won numerous awards, including the Independent Press Award and the International Book Award. His memberships include the International Association of Relational Psychoanalysis and Psychotherapy, the Depth Psychology Alliance, and the International Association for Jungian Studies.

Jeffrey L. Eaton is a graduate and faculty member of the Northwestern Psychoanalytic Society and Institute, a member of the IPA, and a Board-Certified Psychoanalyst (CIPS). He received the Frances Tustin Memorial Lecture Prize in 2006 and has been the Beta Rank Memorial Lecturer at the Boston Psychoanalytic Society, the Margaret Jarvie Memorial Lecturer at the University of Edinburgh, a presenter at The Tavistock, London, and the 2017 International Guest Lecturer for the Australian Psychoanalytic Society. He has also been a frequent guest speaker at the International Frances Tustin Trust meetings as well as at International Bion meetings. For over a decade, he was Senior Consulting Child Psychotherapist for the Gunawirra Foundation in Sydney, Australia, a project providing intervention for at-risk Aboriginal mothers, children, and infants. He was also the founder of The Alliance Community Psychotherapy Clinic, a project of The Northwest Alliance for Psychoanalytic Study. For over a decade, he participated in INSPIRA, the International Seminar on Psychoanalytic Intervention and Research into Autism, and is currently on the board of the Frances Tustin Trust, now based in Israel. He is the author of *A Fruitful Harvest: Essays after Bion* and several chapters in edited collections. Information about his writing and practice can be found at www.jleaton.com. He provides consultation to psychotherapists and psychoanalysts around the world and is in private practice in Seattle, WA.

Ofra Eshel is a faculty, training, and supervising analyst at The Israel Psychoanalytic Society and Institute and a fellow IPA. She is an Honorary member, The New Center for Psychoanalysis (NCP), Los Angeles. She is the Former vice president, The International Winnicott Association (IWA). She is the Founder and head of the postgraduate track "Independent Psychoanalysis: Radical Breakthroughs" at the advanced studies of the Program of Psychoanalytic Psychotherapy, Faculty of Medicine, Tel-Aviv University. Her papers have been published in psychoanalytic journals and book chapters, translated into eight languages, and presented at national and international conferences across four continents. She is the recipient of several grants, honors, and prizes, including the 2021 Robert Stoller Lecture Speaker (Los Angeles, 2021), the 2013 Frances Tustin International Memorial Prize and Lecture, the 2017 Symonds Prize, and the 2022 Leonard J. Comess Award. She is the author of *The Emergence of Analytic Oneness: Into the Heart of Psychoanalysis* (Routledge, 2019), translated (in 2023) into Chinese.

Isolde Keilhofer is a psychoanalyst in private practice in New York City and beyond. She is a training analyst and supervisor with the National Psychological Association for Psychoanalysis (NPAP), the Metropolitan Institute (MITPP), and the China American Psychoanalytic Alliance (CAPA). With a background in literature, she teaches courses on Freud and writes about traumas amidst generational, cultural, and geographical displacements and the intersection of languages. Her papers have been published in Other/Wise, the *On-Line Journal of the International Forum for Psychoanalytic Education* (IFPE). She is a longtime participant in Michael Eigen's Bion seminar.

Alitta Kullman is a psychoanalyst and psychotherapist in private practice in Newport Beach, CA. Dr. Kullman specializes in the treatment of eating disorders and is the author of the highly regarded *Hunger for Connection: Finding Meaning in Eating Disorders*, published by Routledge in 2018.

Shalini Masih is a Psychoanalytic Psychotherapist registered with the United Kingdom Council for Psychotherapy. She has taught Psychoanalysis at institutions like Ambedkar University, Delhi, India, and Birkbeck College, University of London, UK. She has written and published on various psychoanalytic, clinical, and cultural themes. She received the prestigious Scholar Award from Division 39, APA, in 2020. Her clinical thinking and psychoanalytic writing have received a lot of appreciation, including one of her papers nominated for the Gradiva Awards 2020 under the Best Article Category. Currently, Masih is living with her partner, daughter, and dog and practicing as a Psychoanalytic Psychotherapist in a quaint town in the West Midlands, England.

Ebru Salman is a psychologist in Izmir, Turkey. She met Bion's work during her master's degree in comparative literature and has been writing a series of papers on his work. Some of her writings were published in Turkish in *Suret*, a bi-annual psychoanalytic journal. She has attended Michael Eigen's seminars for four years. She is the Turkish translator of the books *Women and Sexuality in Muslim Societies*, *Creative Movement–The Plevin-Garcia Method*, *The Art and Science of Dance/Movement Therapy*, and *Listening to Hanna Segal*, and various psychoanalytic articles published in the issues of *The Turkish Annual of the International Journal of Psychoanalysis*.

Epsita Sandhu is a psychodynamic psychotherapist working in a holistic health clinic and in private practice in Bengaluru, India. She holds a Master's degree in Philosophy in Psychoanalytic Psychotherapy from Ambedkar University, Delhi, where she also completed her clinical training. She was presented with the prestigious Scholars Award from Division 39 of the American Psychological Association in 2023 for her thesis work on perinatal grief.

Adam Shechter is a psychoanalytic psychotherapist who works with individuals, couples, and groups. He specializes in the intersection of Hyman Spotnitz's Modern Psychoanalysis and Michael Eigen's style of clinical work and theory. Adam explores this meeting point along with other therapeutic areas in his private practice, including expository writing and conference presentations. He co-authored, with Daniel Y. Harris, the chapbook *Paul Celan and the Messiah's Broken Levered Tongue: An Exponential Dyad* (2010). Also, he formerly edited the interdisciplinary poetry journal, *The Blue Jew* Yorker.

Willow Pearson Trimbach is the director of clinical training and associate professor of the Clinical Psychology Department at the California Institute of Integral Studies in San Francisco. A psychologist, psychotherapist, and music therapist, she has a private practice in Oakland, California (drwillowpearson.com), seeing adults online who reside in California and Washington. Dr. Pearson Trimbach is also a singer and songwriter, with six albums of original music and a seventh album of Tibetan Buddhist songs of realization (lionessroars.org). She is co-editor and contributing author of *The Spiritual Psyche: Mysticism, Intersubjectivity and Psychoanalysis*, published by Routledge in 2021.

Introduction to *Primary Process Impacts and Dreaming the Undreamable Object in the Work of Michael Eigen*

Becoming the Welcoming Object

Loray Daws and Keri S. Cohen

> A therapist is a kind of specialist in letting the other in, feeling the impact of the other, staying with images and thoughts to which the feel of the other gives rise. (Eigen, 2001, p. 5)

After reading parts of Eigen's *Damaged Bonds* (2001), an analysand reflected with deep emotion,

> Eigen is the soul's manna... my soul manna... This week, reading Eigen's work provided me with a way to think about parts of my experience in a way ... I don't know how to describe it... it's all still there, but open... an opening....

As she read the paragraphs, I felt relief for us as an analytic couple, my heart opening to a mutual sharedness – a shared transitional evocative object and space. Eigen's psychoanalytic work is known for nourishing its readers, just as it has done for countless analysands and practicing clinicians for over five decades. Eigen has steadfastly carved a singular psychoanalytic vision and language, further contributing to our ever-growing wisdom literature within psychoanalysis. More specifically, Eigen's writing and analytic vision invite the reader as a witness to the primordial language of *coming- into- being*, the lifelong struggle to remain "faith"-"fully" open, welcoming, and supportive to our most obstructive and obdurate experiences with a sense of loving kindness. Furthermore, rarely does one currently find a psychoanalyst able to creatively and seamlessly traverse the fields of psychoanalysis, philosophy, religion, and spirituality with grace and compassion,

> Explorations of soul damage, survival, and regeneration take many forms. Therapy is a kind of slow-motion action painting with emotions and thoughts within and between people. The taste and feel or quality of personal presence is at stake. In therapy we have a chance to slow things down, to chew on moments of injury/regeneration, and to taste and partly digest what ordinarily sweeps us

along. We get a chance to test out, absorb, and work with what we fear (often rightly so) may be annihilating about life-giving bonds. An ancient mystery renewed in therapy involves, reciprocally, learning undergoing certain forms of annihilation can add to life. (2001, p. xi)

Soul damage, ontological shocks, rips, and tears meet Eigen as an agent of faith, soul incubator, and auxiliary dream-worker. In the language of Virgil, Eigen works to revivify and resurrect lost and unborn capacities of the beleaguered psyche,

What can therapy offer? Therapist, among other things, may be auxiliary dream-workers who support personality in order to let dream-work dream. We enable people to dream the undreamable and draw growth-stopping damage into dream-work that connects one with oneself. Dream-work is steeped in infinite heartbreak and terror, but there are, too, infinities of beauty that break the heart, *like bread, in joy, which dream-work tastes, chews, digests, celebrates, crumb by crumb.* (2001, p. 61) (Italics added)

What supports a dream supports a person. The ability to create a dream, to see an experience through, to process affects, to support a self- such generative work can suffer immense degradation. Damaged bonds damage unconscious processing. Unconscious processing tries, in part, to work with its damage. Such a circle can spiral- damage adding to damage. What damages a dream damages a person. (2001, p. 27)

With its compendium volume, it is the wish of this volume to introduce the reader to two essential vertices in Eigen's work – serving as a welcoming other and holding and transforming the obstructive object (1986, 1992, 1993, 1995, 1996, 1998, 1999, 2001, 2002, 2004, 2005, 2006, 2007, 2009, 2011, 2012, 2013, 2014a&b, 2016, 2018, 2020). In the evocative writing and introductory chapter of Eaton (Chapter 1), titled *'be'-'coming' a welcoming object*, Bion's autobiography, *All My Sins Remembered: Another Part of a Life* (Bion, 1985), serves as an introductory vertice to Eigen's *primary process impacts and dreaming the undreamable object*. Eaton reminds the reader of Bion's painful recounting of his seeming inability to comfort his infant daughter – his astonishment to find "such depth of cruelty in myself" (Bion, 1985, p. 70), his ability to remain with such a painful self-awareness. Eaton sensitively reflects on Bion's and Eigen's unique psychoanalytic sensibilities in

how we can face pain, tolerate it, explore it, and communicate about it. We can try to *reverse* the habit of rejection by *welcoming experience*. If we can cultivate, expand, and sustain a disciplined and compassionate attention to the truth of our own suffering, we might learn to observe how pain can keep transforming in unpredictable ways. However, none of this is possible without first resolving to welcome experience. (This volume)

Turning to Eigen's work concerning the welcoming of experience, Eaton further writes,

> It's impossible to briefly describe the dozens of different strands of Eigen's work that cumulatively create a vision of human resilience, faith, and creativity. But to make a concise formulation, Eigen encourages his readers to grow the capacity to welcome *any* kind of experience. (This volume)

Evoking the imaginary, Eaton reflects on the poem by Rumi, *The Guest House*, formulating a sensible psychoanalytic ethic of welcoming. As a psychoanalytic host, Eigen clearly possesses the unique capacity

> for following the phenomenological trail of different flavors of emotional experience. He will wonder why something is so present, or so missing, so intense, or barely detectable. He notices slight shifts in qualities of experience and encourages new spaces for speaking as well as for silence. In this way Eigen becomes a kind of midwife creating space for surprises, for welcoming a new idea, exploring new energies, and dabbling in novel perceptions. Eigen not only tracks how bodily impulses in the patient might emerge, he freely draws on his own bodily aliveness simultaneously, opening up space to explore the impacts of mind-to-mind and body-to-mind encounters, expanding a generative transforming field. (This volume)

Not only as host to the Psychoanalytic Guest House, able to house those in need of rest, ever sensitive to each wanderer's psychic palette and taste buds, Eigen further serves as a psychological midwife, courting spaces for all kinds of experience thereby welcoming the "dabbling of novel perceptions," evoking the potential for growing psychic equipment able to transform primary process impacts and shocks (Eigen, 1996),

> Throughout his work Eigen reminds the reader that part of being human involves growing the equipment to process the experience of being human. We can never process everything, sometimes not even enough. One way to define trauma involves the impact of experience that damages or disables emotional processing equipment. Eigen believes in *a basic rhythm, a rhythm of breakdown and repair*. (This volume)

Throughout Eigen's work, emotional overwhelm and storms are not to be related to as 'pathologies' in need of 'confinement' but as a natural reality in human interaction in need of a welcoming approach. As such,

> We need to grow with impacts, or around them, and let a sense of what it feels like to be together to develop. The sense of what it feels like to be together is

what makes us—all of us—partners. To not cultivate the feel of another is a kind of soul murder. The evolution of the human race depends on not aborting the feeling of another. (2005, p. 21)

Primary emotional storm, vulnerability, permeability. The first thing to do is to acknowledge it. Grant it space, time, recognition, honor. Note it: we are in and part of an emotional storm. It is us and we are it—partly. Don't pull the plug by violence or collapse. It is enough to begin with a sense that emotional storm is happening. The simple fact: impact is happening, impact is happening, impact is happening. *No need to sanitize or soundproof it. We are struggling to build our capacity to bear being with another human being, to bear to build one's own responsiveness, reciprocal responsiveness.* (2005, p. 19) (Italics added)

Struggling to build our capacity to bear others finds the welcoming of our *Sensitive Self* in Toxic Nourishment (1999, chapter 1 and 8) and the various unwanted states that arise in ourselves and others without trying to find a Bug Free Universe (1999, chapter 4) or Soundproof Sanity (1999, chapter 10). In Eaton's writing,

> Part of the difficulty in welcoming a patient's unwanted experience is linked to the pain of welcoming unwanted states that arise in ourselves, states that are often troubling, even shocking, but that nonetheless record the emotional impact of our 'contact with the depths' evoked by another person's suffering. (This volume)

Given such an ethic, Eaton describes the treatment of a young autistic child with sensitivity and clinical Eigenesque wisdom – reaching and welcoming experiences often described/felt as unreachable or relegated to mastery-control models of mind.

Building on Eaton's T-ego contribution (welcoming the transcendental mind ego) to the body-ego, Chapter 2 finds the *welcoming heart psychoanalysis* of Ofra Eshel. Specifically, in the *Hearing Heart* and *The Vanishing Scream of Being*, Eshel continues her work as a primary process psychoanalyst by asking, "How can a heart hear?," writing poignantly,

> The marvel of a "hearing heart" has followed me over the years into my psychoanalytic work, becoming a fundamental aspect of my clinical thinking when facing the "voice" of trauma or breakdown, together with essential ideas of Winnicott, Tustin, and Eigen ... I have suggested that the 'hearing heart' can be attained only through *a willingness to dare to open one's heart and soul to another human being*. It is thus at the core of the analyst's difficult, sometimes exceedingly difficult, struggle to give himself/herself over — with all one's heart, soul, might, in Eigen (1981) words— to being there within the troubled emotional experience of the patient's world, staying open and attuned, sensing, hearing, and feeling the 'voice' of the patient's trauma or breakdown that cries out. (This volume)

Through countless contributions, Eshel (2015, 2016, 2019) has come to view that in every treatment, "in its deepest essence, there is a cry, pleading, even screaming, or else stifled, silenced, vanishing, annihilated (Winnicott, 1974), which seizes and grips the analyst/therapist, necessitating their 'hearing heart' (Eshel, 2015, 2016, 2019)" (this volume). Building on Winnicott's notion and writing on "hope and the last scream," the signifier of original failure and the long-buried hope that the original frozen situation can be re-found and related to, Eshel presents Ben's psychoanalytic treatment as educator. Similar to Tustin's "heart-break" and Eigen's "vanishing SOS scream," the reader is allowed to experience firsthand Eshel's astounding clinical acumen and primary process sensibilities. Eshel, by sculpting a creative Tustin-Eigen couple, feels compassionately 'with' and 'into' various heart agonies – our perennial heart-brokenness,

[**Tustin**].... these patients threaten to break therapists' hearts because they themselves are 'heartbroken.' The 'heartbreak' goes beyond what we usually mean by the term. The feeling of brokenness goes into the very fabric of their being.... Their sense of 'being' was felt to be threatened. Annihilation stared them in the face, and very desperate steps had to be taken to combat it. This concretized experience of encapsulation spells death to the psyche ... Understanding their sense of agony helps us. (Tustin, 1990, pp. 155–157)

[**Eigen**] ... The bits and pieces of exploded personality floating in the [therapy] room might not be redolent with meaning so much as flotsam and jetsam of an extended SOS signal, like a thinning, vanishing scream over time... Even so, the vanishing debris might have value as passing signals of a catastrophic process that began long ago and still goes on... Feel the impact... something like: I am catastrophe in process. My personality is catastrophic. Something awful has happened, is happening. I am undergoing a state of disintegration... Maybe part of what needs to happen is to sit with the explosion, hear the SOS; listen, hear the scream. *There is a scream inside...* Stay with the scream, an inaudible scream of your patient's being... The scream is a sign of distress that cannot be addressed by the screaming one. A distress the adult or baby cannot solve, an unsolvable disturbance... But you are prepared to stay with the scream for decades, to sit with the unsolvable disturbance, providing a background support for something to grow over time.... (Eigen, 2012, pp. 19–21, italics mine)

For Eshel as a psychoanalyst,

I see the 'hearing heart' as an essential part of the analyst's increased receptive capacity, and emphasize the crucial necessity of the analyst/therapist's *openness of heart*. And adding Tustin's idea of 'broken-heartedness,' and Winnicott's and Eigen's hearing of the patient's vanishing scream, it is the analyst/therapist's heart that *hears and experiences the unthinkable emotional situation itself,* especially when the patient's transmission is unthinkably broken. In the Hebrew verse 'With all one's heart, with all one's soul, and with all one's might' (Eigen, 1981; Deuteronomy, 6:5), the word 'heart' is spelled with a double letter *beit* ב — בבל *levav* — rather than the usual בל *lev* (that does not find *expression* in the English translation). It is this double 'heartedness' that I put forward here. This very vital quality of the *analyst's hearing and experiencing 'broken-heartedness'* and the vanishing scream engenders a different possibility for reaching and meeting – psych-to-psyche, heart-to-heart – the painful immensity of the brokenness of a human psyche. (This volume)

This vital quality of the analyst hearing and experiencing the broken-heartedness speaks directly to Eaton's second contribution, entitled *Welcoming Suchness* (Chapter 3). In *Welcoming Suchness*, Eaton explores and describes two patterns that are both basic and complex, patterns that are the product of, and informed by, an intricate, continuously transforming relationship held by a *matrix of pain* and a *matrix of contact*, the confluence of both *welcoming objects* and *obstructive objects*. The creation of meaning and the psychological apparatus able to hold such meaning naturally evolve in the oscillation between welcoming and obstructive forces, as well as the capacity to welcome such experience. Eaton's own unique Bion-Eigen dialectic. To articulate the dialectic, Eaton divides his essay into three sections, i.e., "A Matrix of Pain: Welcoming an Echoing Darkness," briefly exploring Bion's ideas on obstructive object relations, followed by "A Matrix of Contact: Becoming a Welcoming Object," exploring elements of an analyst's internal workspace for listening, and finally, in "Welcoming Suchness," Eaton describes how becoming a welcoming object allows an analyst to "welcome suchness," a Buddhist term for "that which is," principally denoting a moment of direct experience free from conceptual elaboration or ascription of judgment, i.e., Bion's notion of O;

> In this essay, I describe some patterns that are both basic and complex. An intricate, continuously transforming relationship between *a matrix of pain* and *a matrix of contact* unfolds in some way in every life. This can be seen in individuals, couples, families, and groups. The relationships between stasis, growth, and destruction of meaning evolve or devolve according to many complex variables. Two important variables are the influence of *welcoming objects* and *obstructive objects*. The creation of meaning evolves in the oscillation between obstructive forces and the capacity to welcome experience, explore experience, share experience, and learn from experience. (This volume)

In the section *A Matrix of Pain: Welcoming an Echoing Darkness*, Eaton familiarizes the reader in the most gentle, caring way with the vagaries of becoming:

> To be born into this life involves vulnerability to experiences of helplessness, dependence, sickness, cruelty, injury, loss, separation, change, betrayal, violence, aging, and ultimately death. Becoming aware is painful. Welcoming experience inevitably discloses the pain of being alive. (This volume)

Although being alone with one's pain could be agonizing (matrix of pain), disclosing such suffering to another (matrix of contact) may bring its own complexities, vulnerabilities, and, at times, without the necessary equipment for the experience of goodness, failures. Situations representing a *crisis of connection* are central to Eaton and his reading of Eigen and Bion, and reversals are ever-present. Concerning the presence of the obstructive object (see Cohen and Daws, 2024b), the human couple perennially faces emotional catastrophes serving as the basis for the ego-destructive Sphinx-like internal object:

> This catastrophe becomes internalized and personified as an ego-destructive Sphinx-like internal object. A background of emotional catastrophe can be partially represented and appears in dreams as frightening intrusive persecutory figures and uninhabitable environments. Or emotional catastrophe may remain largely unrepresented but perdures as an ego-destructive background unconsciously stimulating anticipated annihilating impingement. (This volume)

Various adaptations are possible: *a relentless withdrawal, the interruption of contact*, or *a tenacious attack on contact with links to reality*, leading to states of nameless dread. Holding such intimidating states of mind may also welcome new experiences for the analytic couple, even in the midst of damage. Such an attitude is based on an enduring approach of Eigen – that of analytic Faith: "The most precious gain is the evolution of openness toward experiencing, or, as Bion writes 'experiencing experience'" (Eigen, 1993, p. 133). Eschewing memory, desire, and understanding, combined with sincere curiosity, discipline, and compassion, may foster the creation of an "enhanced alpha function capable of sponsoring a matrix of contact and of welcoming a matrix of pain" (This volume).

These exceptional three chapters serve as foundation to the various chapters to follow, i.e., the cultivation of a hearing heart for the Other and the self, following the rhythms of contact-pain and coming through, surviving various modes of withdrawal, the interruptions of contact, and the tenacious attacks on links to reality (i.e., psychosis – see Daws, this volume), all by relying on Eigen as mystic and sage. Eigen's 30 volume works may be read as a faithful rendering of the developmental movement from the transcendental and body ego concerns in dual union to the capacity to bear with another as the dyad navigates union-distinction demands. Such creative duality holds the transformation of the psychotic core, welcoming toxic nourishment and damaged bonds in emotional storms, thereby cultivating a sensitive self able to sustain "Faith" in all its vicissitudes.

In *The Join and Distinction-Union: A Resonant and Complex Oneness* (Chapter 4), Shechter poses a creative integration between Spotnitz's joining technique (matrix of contact) and Eigen's distinction-union structure. Both Spotnitz and Eigen have, with psychoanalysts such as L. Bryce Boyer, Harold F. Searles, Peter L. Giovacchini, and Vamik D. Volkan, opened the so-called narcissistic transferences, enlivened the field of psychoanalysis, and supported countless analysands with pre-Oedipal difficulties. Shechter provides a concise description of what is meant by Spotnitz's concept "joining." as well as Eigen's distinction-union structure psychoanalysis,

> By joining a patient, their ego is spared the intrusion of a new idea via an interpretation or explanation. Instead of going against or in some way mentally exceeding the patient's conscious state, the therapist goes with the flow of the patient's psyche and defenses, protecting them from foreign infringement. On the developmental level, as will be explored below, the join primarily addresses the patient at the symbiotic phase with its inferred next phase of separation. The distinction-union structure reframes this early relational bond both inside the traditional analogy of the therapist as mother and the patient as infant, and all the while conceptualizes that mode of therapeutic relation as rooted and flowing from a primordial psychic essence that is both ineffable and tangible to clinical work. (This volume)

By "linking" "joining" with Eigen's "union-distinction" concept, if not the theory of "resistance," the analyst is able to join and support the analysand's much-needed protection against damaging stimuli as they navigate the demands of (symbiosis) union and separation-individuation, themes evident in Eigen's writing since 1973. More specifically, "joins" support vital resistances "through fostering a union and the associated insulation needed to naturally strengthen the ego" (this volume). Shechter artfully mentions that "resistance" here is not meant as a willful act of defiance in need of undoing by the analyst, but rather,

> Here, resistance is taken as a structure just as indigenous to the life of the psyche, as is distinction-union. We can even theorize that it is resistance that drives the distinction-union structure. Or vice versa. Psychic life viewed as a state of ongoing adaptive changes that uses unions and distinctions to manage the ego's relationship to the object. (This volume)

Similar to the work of Thomas Keating (as for Eigen), Schechter creates a language more focused on the *transfiguration* (rather than dismantling) of the adaptive/defensive/false self. Eigen's unique use of union-distinction structure scaffolds the analysand to suspend false distinctions of the self, similar to the writings of Winnicott, enabling the analysand to enter a more "undifferentiated state" with the aim of birthing "genuine distinctions" (Eigen, 2004, p. 307). Joining as a psychic womb, an open-ended container (Eigen, 2004), as a creative at-one-ment, may transform "false distinctions; parse them, break them down, and make them embryonic, so that the raw elements of the personality are accessible to new growth" (this volume). Eigen (2004) also puts forth that therapeutic work is primarily done by the therapist functioning as an "open-ended container," who conveys that in "psychic life almost anything is possible, and at the same time that a sense of limits deepens and sharpens the search" (p. 310) and [t]endencies to link together and hold apart permeate our psychic field with variable antagonisms and complementarities"

(2004, p. 211). Schechter thickens the latter in deepening Spotnitz's and Eigen's unique understandings of working with fragmenting/cohering movements in the therapy, especially when psychotic anxieties abound, and can be read in the case of Kurt (2011) and discussed in greater detail by Loray Daws in Chapter 5.

In Nomad to NO-MAD, Daws writes on Eigen's unique primary process psychoanalysis. Since Eigen's first publication in 1973, Eigen has sculpted a psychoanalytic language and understanding for those exposed to the heartbreaking experience of being unwanted, unwelcomed, and symbiotically traumatized (matrix of contact mainly bringing toxic nourishment). Eigen's primary process psychoanalysis scaffolds the sensibilities needed to accompany the psyche in returning (an immersing-emerging dialectic) to its indestructible generative core, "revivifying" the union-distinction body-affect-thinking potentialities and storms within a *dyad* held by a unique *rhythm of faith*. Through a close reading of *A Basic Rhythm* (2002) and *Tears of Pain and Beauty: Mixed Voices* (2011), Eigen's *welcoming primary process psychoanalysis*, the language of Virgil, traces the lived world of both psychotic and deeply schizoid analysands. That is, Eigen's primary process writing as an emotional grid informs a unique sensibility in working with analysands in need of an organizing experience (Eigen, 1986, Hedges, 1994a&b), where psychological development has been exposed to both lack (privation and deprivation) and exposure to Winnicott's Z-dimension. Surviving petrification, impingement, engulfment, and appropriation brings forth the bare-life environment of moral violence, of epistemic and ontological insecurity, and D.W. Winnicott's *moral sin*, the unthinkable catastrophe when one seeps into another's core and "steals him from himself."

Caught in an unimaginable catastrophe, that is, living 'in' or 'between' two worlds, one characterized by *deadness* and the other unable to *support rebirth*, many psyches were prematurely exposed, if not brutalized, by unthinkable and unmitigated hatred, rage, fright, and shock traumas – Eigen's *disaster anxieties* (1996). The complex relationship between disaster anxiety and chronic broken-down-ness is discussed by exploring three case studies and possible ways to welcome such chronic areas of broken-down-ness. It is held that a *rhythm of faith, with its affirming maternal values*, holds to the possibility that the infant-adult may be "saved," even "resurrected" from such tormenting anxiety and despair through the (m)other's "merciful intervention" (Elkin, 1958, p. 68), akin to a "*spiritual resurrection*" (Elkin, 1958, p. 69). With the merciful Other as background support, spiritual darkness, *the* primordial sense of betrayal and despair evoking *primordial injury rage as well as the Diabolic Mother-Frightened Child archetype*, may be held so as to lime the possibility of *transfiguration* over time.

As mentioned, welcoming areas of broken-down-ness, the matrix of pain, and the difficulties in joining within the matrix of connection given such pain demand much from the analyst (see Eigen's Wounded Nourishment Concept, chapter 2, 2001). Control and mastery models, although helpful and needed at times, mainly serve as psychic short-circuits to the evolution of the sensitive and traumatized self. Holding to the *Area of Freedom* (Eigen, 1996, chapter 7) as one navigates the reality of broken-heartedness within the matrix of obstruction-contact can be more than the heart can bear (Eigen, 1996, see pp. 82–84 in detail):

> Psychophysical equipment may be damaged from birth or from something lacking in the environmental provision. It may suffer from immaturity that in some way remains chronic. Depth psychology tries to enable growth of psychic equipment as much as possible and develop better compensations to the extent that the equipment is irreparable. One does not help another individual find or grow equipment for creative living without sacrifice. Winnicott repeatedly speaks about the importance of the analyst growing the capacity to wait (responsive waiting, waiting-in-aliveness). The analyst must outgrow cleverness for his own satisfaction and cultivate the silence that let the ***core of core do its work***. At the same time the analyst must act naturally, like the ordinary good-enough mother who, for a time, spontaneously molds herself (Schechter's joining) along the infant's developmental lines. Such paradoxical demands permeate analytic work. The analyst must bear and enjoy the tension of paradoxical living, as paradoxical truths shift from stage to stage. (1996, p. 83)

Kullman's chapter (Chapter 6), *The Welcomed Object*, continues the concept of the welcoming object in a deeply *felt and personal way*, inviting the reader to witness various meditative moments distilled from her own sensibilities and holding of Eigen's thinking-feeling rhythms. Responding to an unexpected health crisis, Eigen served as a welcoming object of solace, enabling Kullman to *think-feel* the unthinkable (fear):

> After several days in shock, I decided to reach out to Michael Eigen—whom I had 'known' for more than a decade online in various iterations—in the hopes that he could help me figure out how to *think* the unthinkable... He made me laugh and let me cry. He listened, opined on my rational fears, and walked me through the irrational ones. He helped divide and dissect terror and was so sure I would survive that I suspect even God Himself would not have dared crossing him. Mike was with me—the partner, the witness—I needed to contain that terror. If there was an upside to such a traumatic event, it was to have been blessed with 'meeting' Michael Eigen from the inside out. In Mike's care, I felt myself becoming a 'welcomed object.' But this was far from unique to me. Putting out the welcome mat for the human soul and psyche infuses all of Michael Eigen's contributions.... (This volume)

Not surprisingly, to many Eigen readers, the contact generated a most creative approach and interest in Kullman's weekly contact with Eigen's reading group, which has been ongoing for more than five decades. After COVID-19 necessitated the group to move online and Eigen made his recording available, Kullman "*spontaneously* began transcribing them—perhaps in an effort at holding on to the 'moonbeam' in my hand—the mysterious 'kernel' of Michael Eigen's wisdom that so nourished me" (This volume, italics mine). In doing so, Kullman provides the reader with a collection of quotes, "the tiniest sliver of thoughts, ideas, and brilliance put forth in his works and Seminars," in the hope that she can offer,

> a taste of the 'psyche/soul' experience that is Michael Eigen ...I may succeed in awakening your 'psychic tastebuds,' as Mike would put it, and that the following quotes may entice you to further sample his work, to explore with him 'the challenge of being human' while simultaneously making contact with his depths. (This volume)

As with Eaton's *Becoming a Welcoming Object* (Chapter 1), moving inwards and making use of our psyche's creativity, Pearson Trimbach's paper, *Welcoming Dreams* (Chapter 7), provides a rare glimpse of a depth psychotherapist's inner matrix of pain and matrix of contact and the product of such internal work (via the medium of the dream) – the birth of a song. Dreaming the very obstructive forces represented in dreams finds an aesthetic moment. For Pearson Trimbach, welcoming our dreams,

> ... is the welcoming of the spiritual psyche in all her dimensions. Welcoming our dreams is a profound expression of welcoming ourselves in all our complexity. This welcoming is a *never-ending and ever-renewing lifework*. For this lifework, we need ambassadors—those who have welcomed us in all our shadow and light—emanating from and continuous with the pregnant void. And this is the welcoming generosity that Michael Eigen extends in his being through his writing and his teaching. (This volume) (Italics added)

Throughout the welcoming and working through of her "birthday dreams," Eigen serves as a faithful inner sage, supporting Pearson Trimbach's creative unfolding of welcoming the *unwanted (dreams)*. Welcoming and opening to the unwanted is rewarded, as seen by the experience of an ecstatic dream, enlivening Pearson Trimbach's "unbounded artistic psyche" and birthing a song. For Pearson Trimbach,

> Singing and recording this dream song is a way to keep *dreaming the dream*, to keep feeling the dream, to open to the dream continually, to welcome the dream repeatedly, and to be in an ongoing relationship with the dream. Every time I sing or play the song, there is a quality of original artistry's further emergence. *As dreaming is a kind of original artistry* (Pearson, 2021a), singing the dream is to carry that artistry into Psyche's living room, into Psyche's expanse. (This volume) (Italics added)

The analyst's inner working, as evident in Pearson Trimbach's creation of a lucid object (Bollas, 2013) as *a kind of original artistry* with the help of Eigen as internal welcoming other is also evident in chapters such as 'Ah, *Strawberries!* by Shalini Masih (Chapter 8), *Welcoming the Eye/I of the Storm: A Homecoming Story* by

Epsita Sandhu (Chapter 9), *Listening in with Michael Eigen* by Isolde Keilhofer (Chapter 10), *Faces of the Welcoming Object: Musings on Midlife, Madness, and Mysticism* by the Jungian analyst Marian Campbell (Chapter 11) and *Music as Dreaming - Welcoming Absence through Music* (Chapter 12) by fellow South African Jungian analyst and Eigen scholar Stephen Bloch.

In a deeply felt personal-clinical paper, and returning to the importance of Eigen's writing of letting the "*core of core do its work*" (1996, p. 83), Masih invites the reader into a crucial phase of her clinical journey where personal losses (due to COVID-19) encapsulated the capacity for being with an analysand and her own sensitive self. Reflecting from the echo chamber of the supervisory space with Eigen, Masih artfully explores Eigen's gentle soul midwifery and his welcoming attitude towards the pain of being fully human during pandemic stress,

> He invites his students for creative waiting and a chance to expand the thinking apparatus by delaying succumbing to intensities. He balances his steadfast exploration of psychic reality with a special brand of passivity - *'pure resonant passivity expressively waiting.'* (Eigen, 2018) Not only is Mike never in a rush, he avoids it. (This volume)

Poignantly observed by Masih, Eigen's possesses a life-sustaining ability to see those parts of the self-invisible in plain sight, even more so: "My experience of learning from Mike has been an answer to a question that has often plagued my mind – How does one recognize a person's Otherness without making them an Other to oneself?" (This volume). Through aesthetic reveries and unstructured ideas, those psyche elements of self and others creating recoil can now be welcomed. Eigen's sensibilities for Masih nourish (manna) the clinical encounter and its natural difficulties, revivifying the sensitive self as well as welcoming the "tyrant," a theme evident in a beautifully written chapter by Epsita Sandhu, *Welcoming the Eye/I of the Storm: A Homecoming Story* (Chapter 9).

In *Welcoming the Eye/I of the Storm*, Sandhu reflects on a psychotherapy process with a male analysand who experienced both relational and sexual trauma as a child and a youth. Despite such experiences, a lifetime of "catastrophic" encounters,

> …his focus remained on the problems of not being able to build a stellar career, not being able to do the work he could feel proud of, not being free enough of the pendulum of anxiety and numbness that kept him suspended yet afloat. An endless flagellation of *nots*. He also felt *not* in enough trouble to be able to go any deeper. He had done all the narrativizing he needed to do about his 'past' trauma. He did *not* see how talking about any of that could help him. (This volume)

With deep compassion and analytic fortitude, both analysand and analyst revisit *Home*, as it is, in essence, *where the Heart aches*, the primal site of "Knots after knots after knots, [and as psychoanalysts] we welcome them all," (this volume) working through a painful mourning process (*Rudhali – welcoming mourning*) so to regain access to desire, the vitality needed for further separation-individuation. Throughout the clinical presentation, the reader also comes to appreciate the impact of culture, gender, and transgenerational pain on personal grief, which may finally give way to creative possibilities in living while accepting the fall-out of painful and tragic knots (+K and 'nots'- +Knots).

Both Masih's and Sandhu's chapters serve as welcoming reminders of Eigen's way of listening to the supervisee and the analysand, articulating in vivid clinical process Isolde Keilhofer's unique contribution to Eigen's way of listening. More specifically, in *Listening in with Michael Eigen*, Keilhofer explores Eigen's distinctive contributions to the art and practice of psychoanalytic writing and listening. As Eigen himself declares,

> I've spent my life listening to others, keenly aware I am listening to myself as well, that the other is me, that we are working with damage we share and inflict. My writing is a kind of listening as well as a longing to be heard. I've been touched to find my voice touches others who need it. They hear the wound the writing comes from. (Eigen, 2007, p. 89)

For Eigen, psychoanalysis is both a *talking-listening cure* as well as a *writing cure*, a "voice for the excluded" (Eigen, 2001a, p. 12), a voice as part of a "… deeply felt message that the pain you speak of is real, more real than you or anyone, so far, can bear" (Eigen, 2002a, p. 10). Throughout the chapter, Keilhofer also creates a psychoanalytic listening genealogy, from Freud, who emphasized receptivity, i.e., likening the analyst's listening attunement to a telephone receiver, the analyst forever adjusting to the frequency of the transmission, to the great Wilhelm Reich, who wrote on listening beyond conscious perception, *Listening with the Third Ear* (1948). Eigen, in his creative way, adds in his Seoul seminar (2010), "I love the big ears of the Buddha … I think that's what psychoanalysis ought to use for its logo. Like a new way of listening, a new way of hearing oneself" (Eigen, 2010, p. 16). So many *ways of hearing* are part of Eigen's writing, but significantly so is the type of psychoanalysis Eigen serves as a modern founder – that is, a psychoanalysis known for its radical shift from epistemological psychoanalysis to an ontological psychoanalysis. Keilhofer writes that epistemological psychoanalysis involves knowing, understanding, and interpreting. In contrast, ontological psychoanalysis involves being, becoming, and waiting, echoing Eigen's psychoanalytic approach: "I'm not a theorist. For me it's all expressive. Phenomenological. (Eigen, 2016, p. 128).… my desire is not to 'solve' anything, but to open fields of experiencing" (Eigen, 2007, p. 130). For Ogden,

> From the perspective of ontological psychoanalysis, it is not the knowledge arrived at by patient and analyst that is the central point; rather, it is the patient's experience … in which the patient is engaged not predominantly in searching

for self-understanding, but in experiencing the process of becoming more fully himself. (Ogden, 2019, p. 665)

Epistemological listening-hearing and ontological listening-hearing, or listening and hearing how another knows, comes to know, and wants to be known, to listening and hearing our innermost '*be'-ing*.

Following a most transformative contribution, *Living Moments*, published in 2015, and reflecting the ontological turn, Marian Campbell writes in her chapter, *Faces of the Welcoming Object: Musings on Midlife, Madness, and Mysticism,*

> … it is to Eigen I turn for comfort and encouragement, for rest and hope- where my soul breathes a sigh of relief in the complex simplicity that there is impact and coming through, where the how is more important than the why, where I find the fine tracings of my own inner psychoanalytic mystic and where I am inspired by his deep commitment to welcoming, opening to experience- even when the experience is of being unable to be welcoming or to be unwelcomed. (This volume)

For Campbell, Eigen as "psychoanalytic mystic" and Eigen as the "welcoming object" are intertwined, "a kind of constant conjunction, crucifixion-resurrection" (Eigen, 2011, p. 110). With this conjunction in mind, Campbell circumambulates Eigen's *rhythm of faith*, Buber's I-Thou/ I-IT thinking, Bion's O, and Jung's Godhead as she explores the biblical figure of Job: "There is something wild and elemental, yet so intimately personal, in this story of Job, in this faith in O." Campbell relies on this powerful and transformational myth in her evolving sense of the welcoming object, and for the aim of the current chapter, understanding the vicissitudes of midlife, "as many of my patients and I find-lose our selves in the throes of middle age." How to creatively not only welcome midlife but also remain welcoming in midlife with its diverse and, at times, rather disruptive-eruptive energies remains a challenge. Campbell turns to Eigen as an educator,

> So the question isn't 'Am I going to die?' I am going to die and not too long from now. The question is 'Am I alive now?'- and what would that mean, to be alive now? That's the real question. (Eigen, 2011, p. 62)

Midlife as invitation and catalyst – the reintroduction and reimagining of Eigen's dual union-distinction dilemmas, all in service of our relating to 'O.' Returning to the writings of the great James Hollis (2006) and Sharon Blackie's work entitled *Hagitude* (2022), the archetypal can serve as an organizing principle to contemporary menopausal women's mythopoetic needs. In this liminal space, greater understanding can be given to the body and psyche as they undergo relentless transformations in midlife, supporting the *Emerging I beyond object usage* and creatively reimagining Ann Ulanov's work *Finding Space* (Ulanov, 2005) and Grotstein's (2000) "transcendent position."

Eigen's primary process as *songline* serves as the basis for Stephen Bloch's artful paper *Music as Dreaming*, and in a somewhat similar position to Pearson Trimbach's chapter, Bloch regards music a primary process organizer, the acoustic object able to perform alpha work on raw undigested affective experience. For Bloch,

> Music can be regarded as dreaming, in this sense of it performing alpha work on raw emotional experience. Indeed, Bion described beta-functioning in musical terms when he wrote: 'It is as if the word is a counterpart of the pure note in music, devoid of undertone/overtones.' (Bion,1992, p. 53) Moreover, Bion regarded alpha elements as also operating in auditory (and olfactory) domains, and wrote of the 'auditory system with which is linked transformations such as music noise'. In *Different Trains* and *Jesus' Blood*, one can see the action of musical dreamwork-alpha on undigested experience, allowing it to be thought, remembered, and mourned.

As with Keilhofer's chapter, reading Bloch's chapter calls for a specific capacity to hear – an ear that can serve as a psychic singing bowl, an *alpha ear*, creating a form of sound medicine, Bloch's *musical dream-work- alpha*. To illustrate music as a form of dreaming,

> two twentieth-century minimalist musical works are used as a basis for exploring how an acoustic symbol may develop. The Music has been selected for several reasons. Firstly, as will be shown, minimalist Music has particular points of convergence with the analytic experience. Secondly, the works are significant because of how they explore the interface of words and Music. Thirdly, in the sense that they concern themselves with the experience of absence, they allow insight into the earliest origins of the symbolic process.

Through such minimalistic music and scaffolding of the acoustic object in the work of Bion, Winnicott, Ogden, and Eigen, a deeper appreciation is given to the pre-linguistic importance of acoustic resonance between analyst and analysand. For Eigen, deeply injured analysands "reach" for the musical in the therapist, and

> There is soul music, inner music, akin to the music of the spheres. You can hear it. Yet it has no sound at all. Profoundly silent. Yet this silence sounds. It is deeply musical. Keats writes 'spirit ditties of no tone'. There are moments when this no tone is the inaudible tone of the universe. Poets often use words to communicate wordless realities. We speak of vibrating to one another, or a bell ringing inside, or my bell ringing your bell, or yours ringing mine. What is it that rings? You can hear it or almost hear it —by what sense? (Eigen, 2011, p. 118)

This volume concludes with two conceptually rich chapters-Ebru Salman's *Moving to Inner Lights* (Chapter 13) and Paul DeBlassie's chapter (Chapter 14), *Seer, Sage, Mystic: Luminous Presence in the Work of Michael Eigen*. As transcendental works, the aforementioned writers add and find creative expressions in Eigen's T-ego (transcendental) and body-ego concepts, limed by Eigen's *welcoming spirit*. Although a rather lengthy description from Salman's chapter, Eigen's transcendental work, as also found and described by writers such as Plato and Bion,

> posits *an awareness of self and other at the emergence of the self*, and he sees a constant oscillation of 'distinction-union' with an 'anonymous I,' an 'I-yet-not-I,' an 'otherness' constitutive to human subjectivity, which is experienced in infancy as a primordial experience of merger and separation with the mother. He describes the 'distinction-union structure' as 'a kind of DNA-RNA of experience. Every micro-moment or 'cell' of experience is made of distinction-union tendencies.' (Eigen, 2011, p. 1) Semi-permeable boundaries *between* self and other, *between* psyche and body, *between* parts of the personality, *between* the finite aspect of human subjectivity and infinity are marked by this 'distinction-union structure' (Eigen, 1986). His conceptualization has in its background, as well as many psychoanalytic formulations and his clinical experiences, the triune doctrine of Holy Trinity (three-yet-one in communion), other ancient texts with the idea of many-in-one or one-in-many, and physicist David Bohm's implicate-explicate orders (Eigen, 2011, pp. 2–3). In Eigen's view, the 'co-constitutive' nature of distinction-union tendencies supports the basic rhythm of breakdown-recovery and affect processing. In psychosis, due to very early trauma, basic trust that sustains the distinction-union oscillation is maimed; the rhythm of faith gets damaged or jammed, and is replaced with an 'interlocking of rigidity and fluidity' which permits neither unintegration (union), nor being defined (distinction) (Eigen, 1986). For Eigen, in healthier functioning, the basic rhythm is the 'pulse' of the living psyche, the psyche 'breathes' (2002), and the distinction-union structure enables a communication and communion with a 'boundless, unknown support.' (2009, 2011). (This volume) (Italics added)

This very rhythm of faith that experiences damage, replaced with an "interlocking of rigidity and fluidity" permitting neither unintegration (union) nor being defined (distinction), as opposed to a breathing, pulsating psyche wherein the distinction-union structure enables communication and communion with a "boundless, unknown support," is central to the chapter of DeBlassie.

An intimate work mapping the pain of spiritual transformation, if not rebirth, underscoring Eigen's concept of "shock of grace" (Eigen, 1998, p. 118) as well as Eigen's soulful writing as part of his deep attunement to the *mundus imaginalis*, the world of spirits - our archetypal and Orphic dimensions in being. For DeBlassie, so clearly and vividly presented in his own transformative process after a crisis of faith, depth psychotherapy should rely on spiritually transformative moments, and as such,

> … for a therapist as a devotee of soul healing, rigid and dogmatic understandings of unconscious drives, objects, and relational nuances must be shed in order to *invite transformative mystic encounters, luminous presence/s that provide entrance into higher and deeper orders of meaning, healing, and transformation – an infusion of grace.* (This volume) (Italics added)

Tracing depth psychology as a soul/spiritual sensitivity, DeBlassie revisits psychoanalytic luminaries such as Sigmund Freud, William James, James Grotstein, the archetypal figure Demeter, and many more to accentuate Eigen's *shocks of grace* able to support the necessary transfigurations and transmutation of the psyche. More specifically, and central to DeBlassie's thinking,

> Thus, the illuminative realm of seer, mystic, and sage opens psychic senses to a 'mystic-genius aspect of self' (Eigen, 1998, p. 16), welcoming illuminative objects (Eaton, 2015), Bion's godhead (Bion, 1984, 1995), and the 'infinite presence at one with O' (Grotstein, 2007, p. 77). Psychoanalytic mystic openness nourishes the subtle sensitivities of the seer's third eye, the sage's third ear, and the psychoanalytic therapist's openness to the mystic unknown (Eigen, 1998, p. 11). Ever evolving, the work of Eigen explores complexities of psychoanalytic understanding of self, other, and everyday life that coalesce into '. . . the great light and creative darkness, pointing to experience that uplifts and transforms' (Eigen, 2016, p. 25). (This volume)

DeBlassie explores through various vignettes and self-experience the "hard work miracle" of the psychoanalytic process as a spiritual invitation/initiation, accentuating the importance of crisis as a signifier to presencing the illuminative mind. A crisis may find a dream or dreams, highlighting a path to be taken, even if arduous. Even as a psychoanalyst, finding one's calling or path within psychoanalysis can be daunting,

> How much struggle, ups and downs, and all-arounds there are in forever discovering one's illuminative path. Walking my own path of truth to the unconscious has meant remaining a depth psychologist and not a psychoanalyst. After completing my residency in clinical psychoanalysis at Northwestern University School of Medicine, an illuminative nightmare shook me to the core. It dramatized the horror ahead for me in adhering to one psychoanalytic school and becoming a card-carrying zealot of a particular ideology … Shocked, I awakened knowing that the path of what the Greeks called *psyche therapeia*, a life of devotion to the soul, was my calling, but not as an ordainee. I remain, now forty years later, an independent depth psychologist on my own path of practicing devotion

to and healing for the soul. To this day, archetypal inspiration from illuminative dreams resonates and lingers. (This volume)

DeBlassie passionately describes "finding" the work of Eigen and taking to heart the importance and difficulty of the mystical path – the impact not only on growth but its more frightening aspects. Despite the impacts of finding one own path, DeBlassie weaves the importance of *welcoming this luminous presence*, Eigen's "mystic light," that may awaken "riches lying dormant within" (this volume). A radiant invitation, a *luminous welcoming*, for us all.

Finally, the poetic works of Rachel Bergash accentuate the luminous, welcoming quality of Eigen's work, and each volume will commence and end with Bergash's Eigenesque vision. As editors, we also sincerely hope this book welcomes your own "Eigen" in the most meaningful way.

Namasté

The divine light in me bows to the divine light within you.
I honor the place in you where the entire universe dwells.
I bow to the place in you that is love, light, and joy.
When you and I bow to our true nature, we are one.
My soul recognizes your soul.
We are the same, we are one.
I honor the place in you that is the same as it is in me.

Bibliography

Bollas, C. (2013). *Catch Them Before They Fall: The Psychoanalysis of Breakdown*. London & New York: Routledge.

Eigen, M. (1986). *The Psychotic Core*. Northvale, NJ: Jaon Aronson, Inc.

Eigen, M. (1992). *Coming Through the Whirlwind*. Wilmette, IL: Chiron Publications.

Eigen, M. (1993). *The Electrified Tightrope* (A. Phillips, Ed.). Northvale, NJ: Jason Aronson, Inc.

Eigen, M. (1995). *Reshaping the Self: Reflections on Renewal in Psychotherapy*. Madison, CT: Psychosocial Press.

Eigen, M. (1996). *Psychic Deadness*. London: Karnac.

Eigen, M. (1998). *The Psychoanalytic Mystic*. London, UK: Free Association Books.

Eigen, M. (1999). *Toxic Nourishment*. London: Karnac.

Eigen, M. (2001). *Damaged Bonds*. London: Karnac.

Eigen, M. (2004). *The Sensitive Self*. Middletown, CT: Wesleyan University Press.

Eigen, M. (2005). *Emotional Storm*. Middletown, CT: Wesleyan University Press.

Eigen, M. (2006a). *Lust*. Middletown, CT: Wesleyan University Press.

Eigen, M. (2007). *Feeling Matters*. London: Karnac Books.

Eigen, M. (2009). *Flames from the Unconscious*. London: Karnac Books.

Eigen, M. (2011). *Eigen in Seoul: Faith and Transformation (Vol. 2)*. London: Karnac Books.

Eigen, M. (2012). *Kabbalah and Psychoanalysis*. London: Karnac Books.

Eigen, M. (2013). *Contact with the Depths*. London: Karnac Books.

Eigen, M. (2014a). *The Birth of Experience*. London: Karnac Books.

Eigen, M. (2014b). *Faith*. London: Karnac Books.

Eigen, M. (2014c). *A Felt Sense: More Explorations of Psychoanalysis and Kabbalah*. London: Karnac Books.

Eigen, M. (2016). *Image, Sense, Infinities, and Everyday Life*. London: Karnac Books.

Eigen, M. (2018). *The Challenge of Being Human*. Abington: Routledge.

Eigen, M. (2020). *Dialogues with Michael Eigen* (L. Daws, Ed.). London & New York: Routledge.

Eigen, M., & Govrin, A. (2007). *Conversations with Michael Eigen*. London: Karnac Books.

Elkin, H. (1958). On the origin of the self. *The Psychoanalytic Review*, 45: 57–76.

Elkin, H. (1966). Love and violence. *Humanitas*, 2: 165–182.

Elkin, H. (1972). On selfhood and the development of ego structures in infancy. *The Psychoanalytic Review*, 59: 389–416.

Eshel, O. (2016). The vanished last scream: Winnicott-Bion-Eigen. *IJP Open – Open Peer Review and Debate*, 3: 1–32.

Eshel, O. (2019). *The Emergence of Analytic Oneness: Into the Heart of Psychoanalysis*. London & New York: Routledge.

Grotstein, J. S. (2007). *A Beam of Intense Darkness: Wilfred Bion's Legacy to Psychoanalysis*. London & New York: Routledge.

Ogden, T. H. (2019). Ontological Psychoanalysis or "What Do You Want to Be When You Grow Up?". *Psychoanalytic Quarterly*, 88: 661–684.

Reik, T. (1948). *Listening with the Third Ear: The Inner Experience of a Psychoanalyst*. New York: Farrar, Straus.

Foreword

Michael Eigen

The tendencies and states explored in these two volumes have a history going back to the beginnings of human beings' attempts to make contact with, communicate, and express themselves. Many vocabularies have been developed to deal with what it feels like to be a human being, and this current work's concern with obstructive and welcoming tendencies are a welcome addition to use one of our vocabulary partners or siblings. I'm tempted to write obstructive-welcoming with a hyphen, the two are so much part of our makeup, and we will see in these chapters many angles, mixes, dissociations, and communions between them. The writings here open possibilities of human experience, relationships to ourselves, quandaries, and wonders.

To be welcoming, to be obstructive, to be welcomed, or to be obstructed – how many ways can you think of that you personally have felt these throughout a day? If you kept a diary even for a short time about feelings of welcome-obstruction, you would be touched by the realization of the ways and myriad moments they enter our psychosocial tapestry. If you make it even more personal and reflect on ways you welcome and/or obstruct yourself throughout the day and even moment-to-moment, awe as well as chagrin about our beings may grow.

I think of a car having an accelerator and brake – both needed for safety and speed. I learned very early that cars may be modeled on the human body in significant ways. And when I think of animals speeding up-slowing down depending on hunger and safety needs, a sense of having so much in common with all life spreads. One of the beautiful things of grammar school was learning about the needs of plants as well as people. Life everywhere – what will or can happen?

Obstruction is often associated with trauma, but it can also play a positive role making room for waiting, detour, and alternatives. One of the fun subjects in the first psychology class I took some sixty-five years ago was learning how an infant can grow by going around a blockage rather than going through it, especially when the latter was impossible. I once wrote (Eigen, 2018) about protecting our home from destructive squirrel invasion, and one time a squirrel caught in a cage kept banging its head against the bars until it perished. All other squirrels in that situation explored and waited and were left free in faraway parks. What different ways can we react to blockages and what diverse functions can they have?

Both welcoming-obstructive can have positive and negative consequences. There is even a long history of humanity welcoming and promoting destructive behavior. Positive and negative vary in so many ways.

Freud linked death anxiety with birth anxiety. You can image and dramatize this in many ways. Will I survive being born? Going through a tight tunnel – does suffocation fear begin even before breathing? Winnicott felt when trauma hits as the self begins to form we can be left with fear of beginnings all lifelong. A lifelong fear of the self's existence. He places much emphasis on how the caretaking other responds to the baby's survival dreads. Can we be? How? With what quality?

Loray Daws and Keri Cohen have done a great service focusing on qualities of welcome and obstruction in growth. My work is used as an occasion to assemble significant explorations of these tendencies that are part of our basic makeup. The authors do much more than explore aspects of my work but use the former to stimulate, add, and open their own. It is a welcome compliment that one's own voice can help catalyze the creative voices of others.

Bion wrote of an "obstructive object," and Jeffrey Eaton contributed a growing dialogue with a "welcoming object" as well. Dualities have been with us ever since human beings tried to give expression to their multiple tendencies, an expressive momentum that, to my mind, has helped stimulate evolution of experience in many keys and dimensions. I am more than hopeful that these two books touch obstructive-welcoming aspects of our psyche and humanity in ways that enable many readers to find more of their own voice and being as well. We are engaged in processes that can add to our appreciation of who we are and can be as we grow in learning how to support our lives and life itself.

Living Moments

Rachel Berghash

After "Living Moments," On the Work of Michael Eigen

When it befalls me to have a living moment—
to hear leaves vibrate to the breeze,
when my kids are well in these turbulent times,
and my husband speaks tenderly to me
as the sun blushes among grey clouds,
when pain is gone,
and calm settles in my bone,
I stretch the arms of my soul
and hug the world thrice,
I am alive, I cry,
and privileged in this tumultuous
dawns and late nights
to love you, and you, and you … and you.

Rachel Berghash 2022

Chapter 1

Becoming a Welcoming Object

Personal Notes on Michael Eigen's Impact

Jeffrey L. Eaton

Becoming a Welcoming Object

At the end of his autobiography *All My Sins Remembered: Another Part of a Life* (Bion, 1985), the English psychoanalyst Wilfred Bion describes an extremely painful memory. He is sitting in his garden with his infant daughter. His wife has died in childbirth. His daughter calls out to him, and feeling "numbed and insensitive", he refuses to answer her or go to her. She begins to cry and crawl toward him across the lawn, but he ignores her. He even feels angry that she is persecuting him. Finally, the child's nanny picks her up and comforts her. Bion feels, he reports, astonished "to find such depth of cruelty in myself" (Bion, 1985, p. 70).

Hatred of pain is spontaneous and often deeply entrenched for many unconscious reasons. By rejecting pain, we inevitably amplify it. The habit of rejecting pain spreads it moment by moment, person to person, family through family, creating patterns of suffering that can last for generations. Bion seems to be warning that rather than finding relief when we go dead to pain, we open a door to even deeper forms of pain, like cruelty inflicted upon innocent others.

Bion's work inspires another way of being with pain. Instead of turning away from it, we learn how to turn toward pain. Bion questions how we can face pain, tolerate it, explore it, and communicate about it. We can try to reverse the habit of rejection by welcoming experience. If we can cultivate, expand, and sustain a disciplined and compassionate attention to the truth of our own suffering, we might learn to observe how pain can keep transforming in unpredictable ways. However, none of this is possible without first resolving to welcome experience.

One of the main inspirations I have found for the plausibility of becoming a welcoming object is Michael Eigen's example. There are many beautiful themes in Eigen's twenty-some books. It's impossible to briefly describe the dozens of different strands of Eigen's work that cumulatively create a vision of human resilience, faith, and creativity. But to make a concise formulation, Eigen encourages his readers to grow the capacity to welcome *any* kind of experience.

Perhaps what impresses me most is Eigen's constant recognition of the complexity of forms that life forces take. He is somehow consistently able to describe in

DOI: 10.4324/9781003322993-1

vivid personal language the myriad ways life impulses evolve, get tangled or even strangled, and yet continue to grow in sometimes undreamable and unthinkable suffering.

Rumi's poem *The Guest House* provides a model for the attitude inspiring my reflections on becoming a welcoming object. Rumi beautifully evokes an ethic of "welcoming". There is perhaps no deeper need than to be welcomed by another and no greater pain than to be rejected, ignored, or exiled. Every lifetime involves the never-ending oscillation, lived out moment by moment, of the tension between welcoming and rejecting, being welcomed and feeling exiled. We are always searching for shelter in welcoming spaces and the relief and promise of contact with other welcoming hearts and minds.

A deep commitment to the power of welcoming runs like an underground river through all of Eigen's work. Welcoming is the action that openness to experience makes possible. Eigen's sensibility is infectious because he helps to welcome so much and because he shares so much of the harvest of his own experience. He really seems to believe in the presence of "the guides from beyond" who arrive with necessary messages for those willing to clear a space and learn how to listen.

Eigen's welcoming attitude helps me to recognize these guides from beyond as communications from my own "sensitive self". The unconscious is not a thing but a living, flourishing process that touches and shapes everything. Eigen describes unconscious momentums and intensities. He opens a space to pay attention to life's embryonic aspects. He makes room for complexity and does not shy away from describing the arrogant, prickly, grimy, poisoning processes that can kill awareness from the inside out.

Here there is always another side, always another view. Take another look, Eigen encourages. Destructive influences have their place amid sun, seed, soil, and rain. Life survives and keeps renewing—or "coming through", as he likes to say. We struggle toward the light, spreading thoughts like seeds along the way.

At a basic level, the capacity for welcoming, if it is to foster sustainable creativity, must involve opening beyond interpersonal concerns. After we have learned how to begin to be open to others and to the world, we must learn how to turn back again, move inward more thoroughly, and rediscover shattered, scattered, and alienated aspects of ourselves. We impact ourselves as much as we impact others. We need new ways of sensing, tracking, and exploring self ↔ world intercourses that are embedded in self ↔ Self expansion and evolution.

At the core of Eigen's work, in conjunction with his attention to destructive forces, is a luminous affirmation of the wonder of human experience, especially emotional experience. Over decades, his work has drawn attention to and celebrated a deep feeling that Buddhists call the preciousness of human embodiment.

Inspired by openness, we can ask, in an honest and compassionate way and with a practical spirit: How well do I welcome my own experiences? What quality of relationship do I offer to my own thoughts, intuitions, emotions, fantasies, wishes, desires, and dreams? How well can I play with my own life experiences? How free am I to meet myself? In my view, Eigen's "welcoming" is part of the function of the mystic part of the personality, ultimately opening to welcoming the presence of what Bion terms O and all its turbulent reverberations.

Welcoming the Breath

In 1977, Eigen published a short paper titled *Breathing and Identity* (Eigen, 1993, pp. 43–47). In it, he makes several intriguing observations. For example, he suggests that "the therapeutic use of the body in the West has largely been assimilated to the paradigm of appetite" (1993, p. 43). Eigen says that our conception of the self as based on the model of appetite is quite different from a view of self that could be derived from paying attention to the experience of breathing.

"Appetite … is a more ambivalent experience", writes Eigen. "The rise of appetite involves more acute and insistent sensations than [does] the flow of breathing". In contrast to appetite, "Breathing goes on constantly at a fairly steady pace with momentary and periodic variations … it is not experienced as a disturbance under normal circumstances" (1993, p. 45).

A psychology looking only at what interrupts is incomplete or unbalanced. Eigen shifts attention from what intrudes (sensations of lack or wanting) to what sustains (the background flow of the breath, a sense of plenitude, even gratitude). He highlights the intriguing question of what a psychology that placed breathing in the foreground would feel like.

Breathing is one of our first unconscious linking devices. Breathing links inside and outside, mind and body, and even self and other. Breathing creates a basic rhythm. This basic rhythm emerges and is elaborated unconsciously in the body's experience of self, other, and world. As Eigen says, breathing is "*a bodily form for communion and relatedness in life*" (1993, p. 45, my italics).

Dreaming is to the mind what breathing is to the body. Dreaming involves other forms of linking and like breathing dramatically sustains and enhances different qualities of experience. Without the capacity to dream, we slowly suffocate emotionally. A shallow relationship to dream life is like not knowing how to breathe from your belly. One strand of a basic rhythm, then, is how mind dreams the body and how affective bodily life energizes mind and dream.

Welcoming the Body

A body exists in time against a dual background of sensation and infinity. Sensation orients us and, according to Bion, traps us in the familiar moment. Our identification with our bodies makes us believe that the moment has tangible boundaries or shapes. In fact, the moment has no edges. Instead, every moment is like the universe itself, a moment of growth, constantly expanding. Our senses, however, cannot register this sort of space, or, if they do, we might feel a kind of panic, like the person whom we call psychotic.

Intuiting the radical openness of the moment brings us into touch with another aspect of basic rhythm: the fear of breakdown, the too-muchness of experience that is felt both in mind and body.

Attention to any moment reveals how many rhythms can evolve. In his book *Kabbalah and Psychoanalysis* (2012), Eigen mentions the "in-out rhythm of the breath" (p. 6), which he links with Taoist ideas and a larger theme of expansion

↔ contraction. Breath is linked with life and death. Breathing in, expanding, links with life energy, while breathing out, contracting, evokes an eventual "last breath" and the inescapable reality of death.

Of course, it is not just the lungs that expand; minds expand and contract too; perceptions widen or become narrow; tolerance deepens or stays shallow. Pictures of the world change and transform with a fluidity that rides on the rhythm of a breathing ↔ dreaming process in experiences of body-mind-self.

From his earliest work, Eigen has emphasized the relationship between self-other and body-mind dynamics. In *Coming Through the Whirlwind* (1992), Eigen writes:

> Either mental or physical aspects of life may be more or less prominent in experience at any time. They may interweave and blur but they are never identical. The "I" may distinguish itself from or identity with either mind or body at a given time ... Their relationships are typically subtle and complex, since each is apt to be experienced as both self and other in a variety of ways. The boundaries between shift, so that there is latitude in what may be considered mind or body as conditions change. [p. xiv].

Eigen tracks what he calls "a kind of biography of body self/mental self in heart-to-heart, mind-to-mind encounter" (1992, p. xv). Perhaps because much of my clinical work is spent with difficult-to-reach children, I've become attuned to the creaturely expression of encounters with others. I long ago started to pay attention to what Eigen calls a "basic pathological psychic structure of our day" (*ibid.*). He describes this as "a detached, covertly transcendent, steel-like mental ego vis-à-vis an explosive-fusional body ego" (*ibid.*). This formulation has opened a lot of windows for me in my work with autistic states in children.

One of Eigen's special qualities as a writer, supervisor, or therapist seems to be how much room he makes *to play* with experience. Play, according to Winnicott, has its origins in the freedom to express deep bodily aliveness. In my own training (mainly Kleinian), it was hard to imagine interpretation as a form of "spontaneous gesture" or play. Eigen's example, among others, helped soften a certain kind of rigidity that can influence both body and mind.

Eigen has a knack for following the phenomenological trail of different flavors of emotional experience. He will wonder why something is so present, so missing, so intense, or barely detectable. He notices slight shifts in qualities of experience and encourages new spaces for speaking as well as for silence. In this way, he becomes a kind of midwife making space for surprises, for welcoming a new idea, exploring new energies, and dabbling in novel perceptions. He not only tracks how bodily impulses in the patient might emerge, but he also freely draws on his own bodily aliveness too. He creates space to explore the impacts of mind-to-mind and body-to-mind encounters, expanding a generative, transforming field.

Welcoming Emotional Storm

Few analysts are more creative than Eigen in describing the turbulence of self-other and self-to-self impacts that emerge through the evolving adventure of psychoanalytic dialogue.

Some of Eigen's most moving writing comes through exploring the theme of impact as it emerges from "emotional storm". Throughout his work, Eigen reminds the reader that part of being human involves growing the equipment to process the experience of being human. We can never process everything, sometimes not even enough. One way to define trauma involves the impact of experience that damages or disables emotional processing equipment.

Eigen believes in a basic rhythm, a rhythm of breakdown and repair. He writes:

> The sense of trauma-recovery and breakdown-repair is a basic emotional sequence that informs and colors our lives. It is part of a basic faith and trust that meets many challenges. Nevertheless, even when the sequence comes out well—on the side of repair, recovery, reconciliation—something inside of us does not altogether let go of the breakdown. We keep one of our many inner eyes on it. The fact that we are beings subject to emotional breakdown does not go away. [Eigen, 2005, p. 18]

We are creatures that must contend with catastrophe. Some people are more sensitive, while some are more resilient. Some people turn away, while others plunge into the black hole. Eigen keenly describes how we need each other to help grow the capacities for making sense and meaning of our lives, even as these same human relationships can be the sources of so much psychological wounding and even emotional crippling.

Eigen writes that "Emotional storm is not pathology. It is part of reactivity, permeability, responsiveness—part of what happens when people meet". He continues:

> We need to grow with impacts, or around them, and let a sense of what it feels like to be together to develop. The sense of what it feels like to be together is what makes us—all of us—partners. To not cultivate the feel of another is a kind of soul murder. The evolution of the human race depends on not aborting the feeling of another. [2005, p. 21]

Bion, Buber, and Levinas, among others, are in the background of this ethical sensibility. I find the attitude of the welcoming object epitomized in Eigen's voice in passages like this:

> Primary emotional storm, vulnerability, permeability. The first thing to do is to acknowledge it. Grant it space, time, recognition, honor. Note it: we are in and part of an emotional storm. It is us and we are it—partly. Don't pull the plug by violence or collapse. It is enough to begin with a sense that emotional storm is happening. The simple fact: impact is happening, impact is happening, impact

is happening. No need to sanitize or soundproof it. We are struggling to build our capacity to bear being with another human being, to bear to build one's own responsiveness, reciprocal responsiveness. [2005, p. 19]

Welcoming a Sensitive Self

Though Eigen does not write about autism in any great detail, I have nonetheless been inspired by his way of working and have used his ideas to develop a space in myself to welcome the emotional storms that inevitably emerge in the psychoanalytic process when treating children with autism.

Autistic children are among the most sensitive selves in certain kinds of ways. I regard the analyst's attitude as a crucial variable in creating a setting with an atmosphere that makes communication with a difficult-to-reach child eventually possible.

Eigen's example has helped me to open my imagination to getting-to-know and sometimes even "becoming" my patient's experience. I strive to embody a new and tolerable presence in each encounter so that we can discover each other and begin to interact, in whatever form may be possible.

Without lively interaction, we cannot build and expand what Frances Tustin called "a rhythm of safety". Discovering an interactive rhythm of safety helps to consolidate a sensory floor for experience. With a sensory floor for experience, a child can begin to attend to the world around him. When this is possible, the capacity to harness emotional interest and invest those emotions in actual others begins to emerge.

Finally, a sensitive self with many different aspects begins to be expressed through the analytic process, and it becomes possible to explore all sorts of emotions and impulses together. This shared experience involves tolerating intensities, recognizing and describing patterns, and ultimately fosters symbolization of personal experience. A whole new kind of learning process begins to take center stage from session to session.

The process of discovering a sensitive self coming alive amid autistic defenses often involves a literal movement from screaming to dreaming. The complexity of this process is impossible to describe briefly. However, I would like to evoke something of this movement by sharing a "moment of growth", one of many, in my experience with a boy who I will call Steven.

I met Steven when he was seven. He had been diagnosed with autism at the age of three. His parents were struggling now with his violent meltdowns, which could last as long as an hour. These events involved screaming, hitting, kicking, biting, and, on some days, smearing his feces on his bedroom walls.

Early in our work, I was lucky to discover that Steven was able to draw. The complexity of Steven's experience as he drew was fascinating to observe. For a long time, he didn't say much to me. But he made many kinds of sounds as he drew.

His noisemaking was often very animated. He oscillated between excited nonsense sounds, squeals, musical jingles, snatches of cartoon narratives, and occasional very polite sculpted statements. I began to realize that each "scene" that he was drawing was accompanied by a kind of emotional soundtrack. There were also long stretches of concentrated silence.

Over time, Steven tolerated my sharing feelings and questions evoked by the impact of his drawings and sounds upon me. At some point, he confided that there was "a secret movie inside" that was completely private that no one could ever know about.

The moment of growth I want to describe occurred over a series of sessions in our third year of twice-weekly meetings. By this time, Steven had decided to allow me to become an audience and to share in the elaboration of his secret movie.

Steven had created an entire world externalizing and developing his secret movie. He made paper figures, cut them out, colored them, named them, and then staged interactions among the different characters.

He created different worlds by making scenes, like movie backgrounds and stage sets. Gradually, these worlds evolved into three-dimensional productions. For example, he drew a swirling portal that looked like a Jackson Pollock picture and, not satisfied with the effect, cut a door in the paper so that it could actually fold open. Then he could move a paper character through the portal into a new dimension.

One day, Steven introduced the character of a giant monster dog. This dog was much larger than the paper children, who were the heroes of his secret movie. The dog had mean eyes, sharp fangs, and a giant scar over half its body. I was told he was sent to terrorize the children by an evil figure who dominated a parallel universe called "the shadow world".

The atmosphere I felt during this unfolding drama made a deep impact on me. I felt in a new and different way how Steven's screams were now becoming dreamt through the materialization of this mean dog and his *sharing* it with me.

I said to him, "I think by sharing your secret movie you are letting what used to be screams becomes dreams now, like this monster dog". I also said, "I think you used to feel such a pressure to keep this all to yourself because you were afraid that to let it out would ruin everything". Steven searched my face with his eyes, almost like an infant trying to fathom the expression on his mother's face.

In our next session, Steven said, "Remember the monster dog?" He said, "I want to do something to it". He took the figure of a little boy, an important character in his secret movie, and he made the monster dog eat the little boy. Then he showed me how the boy traveled through the insides of the monster dog. I thought of Jonah being swallowed by the whale, but didn't say so.

Then Steven began to hum "All You Need Is Love" by the Beatles. Then he sang the words to "All You Need Is Love". He turned the monster dog over and began to color the blank back side of the paper.

He made a heart with the word "Love" written inside. He then drew a picture of a tree and two flowers. He then drew a bubble right behind the dog's eye and filled it with a rainbow, a sun, and a smiling moon. Then he drew a peace sign. In the dog's feet, he drew a heart, a tear, a girl's face, and a math equation. In the dog's tail, he drew a devil's face, an angry face, a swastika, a lightning bolt, and then a lock with a key.

Instead of fangs, he made the dog's teeth smooth. The creation of this drawing took the entire session, and we did not talk about it as he was making it. Throughout the whole session, I had many intense feelings, including suspense, anticipation, and even a sense of dawning awe.

In the next session, Steven said, "Do you still have the dog?" "Yes", I said. "And I'm very curious to find out about all the changes you made in the dog during our last meeting". "Yes", said Steven, "they are very important".

When he looked at the dog again, he began to literally shiver with excitement. He started to sing "All You Need Is Love" again. I noted out loud how excited he was to see his creation again. I said it stirred up so much in his mind and in his body. He took this comment, I guess, as a shaming one and tried to pull himself together. I said that he seemed to feel I was criticizing him, which I said I had not meant to do.

He said he would tell me about the dog. The little boy, he said, had gone inside the dog to bring him love. At first, the dog had wanted to either spit the little boy out because he was poison, or else to chew him up completely and poop him out. The evil master in the shadow world did not want the boy to stay inside and change the dog from evil to loving.

But the little boy had refused to be stopped. His job was to save the dog and to change the dog from the inside out. The little boy sang to the dog, "all you need is love" and the love began to spread out inside the dog, first changing his heart.

As the love spread through the dog, connecting his eyes and brain with his heart and legs, new things appeared. There was a new heart for the dog that changed the way he could feel. A new brain changed the way he could see. A peace sign calmed the dog down.

I asked Steven what the symbols on the dog's feet meant. The heart meant more love to help the dog move. The tear represented the dog's sadness, which he could now feel because he had been so evil. The girl's face represented the dog's love for his mother. And the equation represented the dog's new-found confidence in being able to learn.

I was deeply moved by all this and said so. Then, I asked about the dog's tail. Steven explained that you can't make evil, anger, and meanness just go away. He said that was how the dog was born and that is just how it is. It can't be changed. But, since the dog has love inside of him now, those things can be locked in the tail so they can't get out and spoil the love that connects everything else.

Steven turned the dog over again and showed me how a rainbow was reflected in the dog's tail because the evil was safely confined. He said, "What you see from the outside is the love".

Welcoming the Unwanted

My experience with Steven provides one example of how psychotherapy can sponsor a surprising process of transformation that begins with welcoming unwanted experiences.

Welcoming unwanted experience has been a strong theme in Eigen's work from his earliest writing. His essay *Working with 'Unwanted' Patients* (Eigen, 1993, pp. 25–42) impressed me deeply when I read it many years ago. The essay describes some of the challenges of working with patients that others might consider not only undesirable but also untreatable. Eigen offers this reflection on working with difficult patients. He writes:

> Perhaps one of the most far-reaching contributions of psychoanalysis to the concept of human relations is its theory of the way in which the helper uses the full range of his thoughts and feelings to further his understanding of the one he helps. The analyst learns to become sensitive to his positive and negative states as a source of intelligence about himself, the patient, and the varied forms their relationship assumes. If this is difficult with people with whom one easily feels good, how much more so with someone whose type of ego deformation is seriously off-putting. [Eigen, 1993, p. 39]

Part of the difficulty in welcoming a patient's unwanted experience is linked to the pain of welcoming unwanted states that arise in ourselves, states that are often troubling, even shocking, but that nonetheless record the emotional impact of our "contact with the depths" evoked by another person's suffering.

In looking over Eigen's many books, it is my sense that few analysts have sustained such a continuous concern in their writing with the forces of affirmation and growth alongside a deepening exploration of factors that combine to destroy awareness and truncate lives. One of the powerful lessons derived from Eigen's example is that he never turns his back on the reality of human destructiveness.

I register a generosity of spirit, as well as the toughness and courage, demonstrated by Eigen's willingness to focus so much attention on multiple forms of suffering. It is hard to really appreciate, much less to describe, the myriad forms of darkness, violence, perversion, and damage that can emerge within an individual, a couple, a family, a group, or a nation. Violence demands attention, yet there is nothing easier or more common than to turn away from it.

Evidence of destructiveness is everywhere in daily life. Violence can be so intimidating that it becomes unspeakable. Daring to speak is one of the most important acts in re-establishing a human dimension otherwise often crushed in the aftermath of violence.

Eigen helps find words for violence, trauma, damage, and forms of extreme distress. The value of this dimension of his work can't be underestimated. We need real language to sustain the possibility of thinking, exploring, fathoming, and working through violence and the suffering that it sows.

Eigen describes many intensities and pathways of destructive impulses, actions, thoughts, wishes, and deeds. Over the years, he has introduced a new lexicon to help think about such unwanted experience. He speaks, for example, of psychic deadness, toxic nourishment, damaged dreamwork, and annihilated selves. Naming and describing painful states of unwanted experience, as well as sharing detailed and moving stories about people he has worked with, helped, and learned from, encourages his readers to risk noticing, approaching, contacting, and listening deeply and carefully to the violent others alive within ourselves and our own experiences.

Eigen has written movingly about what he calls "killers in dreams" (2005, pp. 120–153). He writes, "Not all people survive themselves. Killers in dreams portray aspects of the pressure that personality exerts against itself, that life exerts against itself" (p. 137). He also observes:

> To kill, not to kill, to kill *and* not to kill, a kind of unconscious pulse gives rise to the feeling that life is threatened, precarious, saved in the nick of time. We escape the knife—once more, but not always, not forever. Relief after fright creates a powerful rhythm in emotional life. Shock, fear, threat, danger—coming through, survival, renewal. A basic rebirth sensation partly involving living through dangers, especially our own dangerous natures. When this works decently enough, the destructive urge adds spice to life, makes for drama and suspense. [Eigen, 2005, p. 137]

Eigen encourages an improbable conversation with the bullies inside. Anyone who welcomes their dreams over decades will notice the presence of delinquents, sadists, firestarters, serial killers, murderers, and psychopaths. Not only do these figures populate newspapers, films, novels, and television programs, but they also enter our dreams and, by doing so, disturbingly color the perceptions of our daily lives.

Some people turn off the nightly news because it is so disturbing to watch. How much more troubling, then, is it to refuse the news of your own dream life because it feels too traumatic, violent, and wounding.

According to Eigen, we should seek to know and work on some of the annihilating aspects within ourselves. After a while, as we adjust to the atmosphere of a nightmare or accept the presence of a fragment of a very bad dream oddly coexisting with brighter emotions, scenes, and images, we become gradually familiar with a congregation of destructive and damaged objects seeking an audience within.

Letting our demons bring news from dream life helps to diminish our fears in the long run. Such figures frighten us when they first arrive, but that is perhaps because they feel so unwanted, and we refuse to welcome them. There is a beautiful story about the Tibetan saint Milarepa. A great master, he was still plagued by demons who arrived to destroy his quiet mountain retreat. Then, instead of fighting the demons or fleeing from them, Milarepa invited them to sit with him and to have tea. As soon as he sincerely welcomed them, their power over him disappeared, and they vanished.

Properly welcomed, our negative emotions no longer arrive as alien, split-off, denied, or disowned threats. Doing the work of welcoming the unwanted in ourselves is a vital practice to prepare to welcome the unwanted that others so urgently need to speak about and find an audience for.

By welcoming unwanted aspects of experience, we break the spells we have lived under for sometimes very long periods of time. We emerge into new relational spaces as well as into new qualities of mental space. One may even begin to harvest the fruits of a darker wisdom from those inner experiences of violence, cruelty, and murder-dread. Eigen gives a creative example of this in his chapter on "Killers in Dreams". He asserts:

> Rising energy vis-à-vis a lower energy threshold can be translated into killers in dreams, and, vice versa, a fall of energy after adaptation to a higher energy level can be represented as a threat to life. On the other hand, too much control, toning down, cutting off energy flow can find expression as a killer in dreams. Dream killers spontaneously give expression to changes in energy (from high to low, low to high) or control (too much, too little along a severity-diffusion continuum). [Eigen, 2005, pp. 124–125]

Such insights are stunning. They seem possible because Eigen is willing to get-to-know unwanted states of mind and is not hypnotized by the cobra-like aura of destructiveness. Nor does he concretize destructiveness and treat it as an unchanging or unchangeable power. He's keenly attuned to the flux and flow of process, and this kind of attention to the many-colored strands of experience leads to a de-concretizing attitude that slowly expands possibilities for thinking and feeling, lessening intimidation and anxiety.

The Buddhist teacher Stephen Levine often said that if the pain of the world made a sound, we would all be deafened by its roar. Fear of pain and hatred of it spreads and amplifies misery, isolation, helplessness, and hopelessness. Eigen writes extensively about the necessity of comprehending how and why psychic numbness and deadness appear as outcomes of living in a damaging world.

Eigen respects the way people take paths of numbness, deadness, denial, and self-attack. His method, though that is probably too formal a word, is to show up as a beacon of auxiliary awareness, encouraging the gradual expansion of attention, welcoming faint signals of life, hope, interest, novelty, desire, truth, rage, as well as any of the many kinds of aliveness that can emerge from the inertia of living within long-established bunkers of psychic survival.

Most of all, Eigen encourages a keener witnessing of the mystery of constantly changing experience itself. Paying attention to mystery, suffering, not-knowing, getting-to-know, becoming—these are all factors in the way healthy growth can be detected in what otherwise appear to be barren or poisoned psychic landscapes.

It is a tall order to learn to play with destructiveness! But that is the sort of evolution that Eigen suggests is possible. Such transformations arise from the deep faith Eigen has in the possibilities of communication with unwanted aspects of experience. His radical generosity has been to share so much of his own experience in the form of writing and teaching in a way that cracks open ordinary psychoanalytic knowledge.

Welcoming the Future

I still remember the excitement I felt stumbling onto a copy of Eigen's early book *Coming Through the Whirlwind* (1992) while browsing one day at a local bookstore on my lunch hour. I could barely put the book down to return to my work. Today, I think Eigen's books will remain small, potent, largely hidden treasures, expressions of his unique sensibility that others will continue to discover and value over time.

By writing as fully and openly as he has, Eigen's work has become a meaningful act of resistance to the corrosive effects of the widespread denigration of meaning in our culture. By his own assessment, Eigen sees the emergence of what he calls "an age of psychopathy" (2007). He defines this as the intentional manipulation of psychotic anxieties for the purpose of gaining, consolidating, and exploiting power. It is one thing to offer information, and quite another to risk sharing your own critical wisdom. Such openness is a much-needed antidote to the superficial flood of images that saturate daily life as well as to the claustrophobic states of mind that people can become trapped in through their many unconscious identifications.

Eigen's work offers countless glimpses into the amazingly complex and idiosyncratic processes that can evolve between patient and analyst. He evokes the many ways analysts and patients sometimes triangulate O, bringing body, mind, heart, and soul together to expand consciousness of self-other, mind-body, and God-world.

In my own work, Eigen has helped me to begin to recognize that over time, screams are able to be dreamt. The silent scream can eventually be heard, and the scream that never stops screaming can become part of a larger rhythm of breakdown, repair, discovery, and gratitude.

Our dreams take us beyond what we believed we could tolerate. Gradually, we learn to work with the oscillation of opening and closing, welcoming and rejecting, screaming and dreaming. Each day, with the encouragement of others, we grow a little beyond what was thinkable or bearable yesterday. Without encouragement like this, we would be lost.

In his book *Rage*, Eigen writes:

> Let us pray for a safe, healthy, productive life for all. But we can be sure that whoever and wherever we are, the same old human problems will rise to greet us, and we will have ourselves to face not just at the end or the beginning of the day, but throughout our lives.
>
> It is one of the great paradoxes of living that we do change when we focus on what can't change. Sometimes we will hold hands. Sometimes we will travel alone. But we will never stop moving toward a beginning when it comes to what we do with ourselves and each other ... We have a lot of evolving to do. [2002, pp. 178–179]

Chapter 2

The "Hearing Heart" and the Vanishing Scream of Being

Ofra Eshel

The poet Paul Celan, tormented by catastrophic reality [of the Holocaust], longing desperately to reach out to an Other, "goes with his very being to language. Stricken by and seeking reality ... Toward something standing open, occupational, perhaps toward an addressable Thou, toward an addressable reality." A poem, he cries out, "can be a message in a bottle, sent out in the — not always greatly hopeful — belief that somewhere and sometime it could wash up on land, on heartland perhaps" (1958, p. 596). Despairing and inconsolable, Celan drowned himself in the frozen waters of the Seine in 1970.

But his powerful words on hope and belief, on reaching out "toward an addressable Thou" and "heartland," resound powerfully within me. They connect to the peculiar biblical combination of a "hearing heart"—"עמוש בל"—which has captured my imagination and thinking and carved out a space in my clinical understanding over many years. As a child in primary school, I studied the biblical story of King Solomon asking God to give him a "hearing heart" to be able to judge the people (I Kings 3:9), and I was perplexed by this peculiar combination—how can a heart hear? The marvel of a "hearing heart" has followed me over the years into my psychoanalytic work, becoming a fundamental aspect of my clinical thinking when facing the "voice" of trauma (Caruth, 1996) or breakdown (Winnicott, 1974), together with essential ideas of Winnicott, Tustin, and Eigen (Eshel, 1996, 2004, 2012, 2004, 2015, 2016, 2019).

I have suggested (2004, 2015, 2019) that the "hearing heart" can be attained only through *a willingness to dare to open one's heart and soul to another human being*. It is thus at the core of the analyst's difficult, sometimes exceedingly difficult, struggle to give himself/herself over—with all one's heart, soul, and might, in Eigen's (1981) words (based on Deuteronomy 6:5)—to being there within the troubled emotional experience of the patient's world, staying open and attuned, sensing, hearing, and feeling the "voice" of the patient's trauma or breakdown that cries out. For trauma "is always the story of a wound that cries out, that addresses us in the attempt to tell us of a reality or truth that is not otherwise available" (Caruth, 1996, p. 4). I have come to think during the years that within every treatment, in its deepest essence, there is a cry, pleading, even screaming, or else

DOI: 10.4324/9781003322993-2

stifled, silenced, vanishing, annihilated (Winnicott, 1974), which seizes and grips the analyst/therapist, necessitating their "hearing heart" (Eshel, 2015, 2016, 2019).

On a Brief Note of Fiction

Before continuing, I would like to relate to another text from early times, carried deep within me over many years. For "a message in a bottle," "hope," "heartland," and "the heart"[1] are linked to very meaningful images from books of my childhood. In my childhood reading, I encountered the image of sending an SOS message in a bottle thrown into the sea out of a desperate hope to be found and rescued. In particular, my imagination was captured by Jules Verne's book *In Search of the Castaways* (English)/*The Children of Captain Grant* (French and Hebrew), which describes, in six illustrated volumes, a wide-ranging journey in search of Captain Grant and two sailors who survived a shipwreck. The search was undertaken after a bottle containing an SOS message written in English, German, and French was retrieved from a shark's stomach. However, it was nearly impossible to decipher the message because the sea had badly damaged the papers. Only one thing was clear: the survivors were somewhere on the 37th parallel in the southern hemisphere. Lord Glenarvan of Scotland volunteers to undertake this search, for it was on the maiden voyage of his yacht, the *Duncan*, that the bottle was found. Together with his young wife, Captain Grant's two children, a geographer named Paganel who boards the ship by mistake, and the crew of the *Duncan*, Lord Glenarvan sets out on a long, difficult, and dangerous rescue mission, searching for the survivors all along the 37th parallel throughout South America, Australia, and New Zealand. During their journey, they encounter natural disasters and wild beasts, great generosity, courage and love, cruelty, and evil treachery. In the end, after almost giving up hope and barely surviving themselves, they arrive quite by chance at a desert island, where they find Captain Grant and the two sailors.

The six tattered volumes of *The Children of Captain Grant* are still on my bookshelf today. And within me, I still carry the imprint of this enchanting story about an SOS letter that indeed found its way to a heartland, and the felt sense of SOS messages that drift for years, seeking an addressee with a "hearing heart."

I will now return to the analytic texts and expand on these ideas by relating to the writings of Winnicott, Tustin, and Eigen, all of whom have featured at the heart of my clinical thinking over the years. I will then offer a clinical illustration.

Winnicott—Hope and the Last Scream

Winnicott's fundamental model of therapeutic regression in the 1950s is closely related to belief and hope: "A belief in the possibility of a correction of the original failure," and especially "the hope of a new opportunity" (1954). He describes the individual's early need to defend the self against the maternal "environmental failure by a freezing of the failure *situation*," along with a hope "that opportunity will occur at a later date for a renewed experience in which the failure situation will be able to be unfrozen and re-experienced, with the individual in a regressed state, in an environment that is making adequate adaptation … In the very ill person there is but little hope of new opportunity" (p. 281). This is realized by providing in treatment "a new and reliable environmental adaptation which can be used by the patient in correction of the original adaptive failure [of the early maternal environment]" (p. 293). Hence, the critical importance of the analyst/therapist who now carries "the hope of a new opportunity for an unfreezing of the frozen situation and a chance for the environment, the present-day environment, to make adequate though belated adaptation" (p. 283)—a hope that from this point on will reverberate throughout Winnicott's thinking and writings about therapeutic regression (Eshel, 2021).

Winnicott further relates hope to screaming. The stifled scream, rooted in the early child-mother relationship, is not screamed or experienced because the patient's crying went unmet in childhood, and "*hope was abandoned.*" The emergence of the patient's scream "only becomes possible as a result of the analysis, in which hope about screaming returned and is recaptured from the time before [the patient] became ill … it is the only way to correct the failure of [her] last scream to work … screaming again, this time with hope" (Winnicott, 1969. pp. 116–118, italics in original).

Winnicott (1953) also recognizes the SOS call for help or rescue that the child needs to send out through psychiatric symptoms. Fourteen years later (1967), he speaks about the antisocial tendency as a sign of hope and hears an SOS that is a signal of hope in the antisocial act—the SOS of a deprived child that "has usually become lost" (pp. 90–91).

Eigen (2012) too writes about the vanishing SOS, as I will describe later. Again and again, the quest is for the stifled scream and the desperation to be heard, for only in this way can the lost hope return.

Tustin's "Heart-Break"—Or, "Who Needs a Heart When a Heart Can Be Broken?"[2]

Then Frances Tustin's "heart-break" entered into my "heart" thinking. In the early 1990s, I became acquainted with Tustin's writings, and although I did not work with autistic children, her ideas influenced the way I thought of and practiced psychoanalytic treatment, especially with severely disturbed patients. In particular, I was touched by her words regarding "the heart-break which is at the centre of human existence" (1972). She wrote about it powerfully in her first book, ending on a somewhat enigmatic note:

Distribution of largesse may seem like sympathy and kindness. Manipulation of materials, often of an extremely capable and skillful kind, may seem like creative activity. But these are not the works of creative imagination or caring. *For this to occur, the heart-break which is at the centre of human existence has to be experienced again and again in ever-widening contexts of developing maturity. The care of psychotic children demands people who have experienced this.* (1972, p. 83, my italics)

"*Who needs a heart when a heart can be broken?*" The words of Tina Turner's song resounded while I was reading Tustin's words. But Tustin, who over the years (1991, 1994) discarded some of her early key ideas, retained the idea of "broken-heartedness"—from her first book in 1972 to her last, eighteen years later, in 1990. And in her final book, she writes that as a result of what she has learned from autistic children, she understands:

> … that these patients threaten to break therapists' hearts because they them-selves are 'heartbroken.' The 'heartbreak' goes beyond what we usually mean by the term. The feeling of brokenness goes into the very fabric of their being…. Their sense of 'being' was felt to be threatened. Annihilation stared them in the face, and very desperate steps had to be taken to combat it. This concretized experience of encapsulation spells death to the psyche…. Understanding their sense of agony helps us. (1990, pp. 155–157)[3]

Furthermore, writes Tustin, "I have called upon poets and writers to help me in this task … we need to be encircled by their integrating aesthetic embrace" (1986, p. 12).

Eigen—the Heart and Hearing the Patient's Vanishing Scream

I have called upon Mike Eigen, thus adding to the biblical "hearing heart" and to Frances Tustin's "heart-break" the concluding sentences of his book *The Electri-fied Tightrope* (1993), written in his own unique way:

> I wonder if all therapists feel the sacred element of this work. I suspect many do, in one way or another. In this business we deal with broken lives and heartbreak, and we do so with our own broken hearts. Yet we discover, within our patients and ourselves, *heart within heart within heart* … what a breathtaking experi-ence to discover such richness at the null point, always more than we can take. (pp. 277–278; my italics)
>
> "The intuited suffering of a broken heart is something that needs … well, to be suffered," writes also Hinshelwood (2018), emphasizing that this "'know', from inside as it were," is "the true nature of psychoanalytic evidence". (p. xviii)

I have further added Stefan Zweig's (1939) powerful words, written many years ago at the beginning of his book Ungeduld des Herzens/*The heart's impatience* (German and Hebrew)/*Beware of Pity* (English), also stemming from the depths of a broken reality:

> There are two kinds of pity. One, the weak and sentimental kind, which is really no more than the heart's impatience to be rid as quickly as possible of the pain-ful emotion aroused by the sight of another's unhappiness, that pity which is not

compassion, but only an instinctive desire to fortify one's own soul against the sufferings of another; and the other, the only one that counts, the unsentimental but creative kind, which knows what it is about and is determined to hold out, in patience and forbearance, to the very limit of its strength and even beyond. (1939, *The heart's impatience* (German and Hebrew)/*Beware of Pity* (English), p. 1)

I follow Zweig's powerful sentences with Eigen's remarkably beautiful and telling words about hearing the patient's vanishing SOS scream, so that the scream does not die out and become lost. It is, indeed, the hearing of the heart:

In psychosis, Bion (1970) depicted an explosion (trauma), with bits and pieces of personality floating in space at accelerating velocity, going further and further away from each other and further from the point of explosion ... The bits and pieces of exploded personality floating in the [therapy] room might not be redolent with meaning so much as flotsam and jetsam of an extended SOS signal, like a thinning, vanishing scream over time ... Even so, the vanishing debris might have value as passing signals of a catastrophic process that began long ago and still goes on ... Feel the impact ... something like: I am catastrophe in process. My personality is catastrophic. Something awful has happened, is happening. I am undergoing a state of disintegration...

Maybe part of what needs to happen is to sit with the explosion, hear the SOS; listen, hear the scream. *There is a scream inside* ... Stay with the scream, an inaudible scream of your patient's being...

The scream is a sign of distress that cannot be addressed by the screaming one. A distress the adult or baby cannot solve, an unsolvable disturbance ... But you are prepared to stay with the scream for decades, to sit with the unsolvable disturbance, providing a background support for something to grow over time... (Eigen, 2012, pp. 19–21, italics mine)

Hear – heart – here.

Tustin's understanding of the "broken-heart," and Winnicott's and Eigen's hearing the silenced scream of the patient's being have converged with my years-long journey regarding the significance of the "hearing heart" in psychoanalysis, becoming now *a meeting of hearts*.

Freud writes that the analyst "must turn his own unconscious like a receptive organ toward the transmitting unconscious of the patient. He must adjust himself to the patient as a telephone receiver is adjusted to the transmitting microphone" (1912, pp. 115–116). And Bion writes, "If the analyst is prepared to listen, have his eye open, his ears open, his senses open, his intuition open, it has an effect upon the patient who seems to grow" (1990/1974, p. 131). I see the "hearing heart" as an essential part of the analyst's increased receptive capacity and emphasize the crucial necessity of the analyst/therapist's *openness of heart*. And adding Tustin's idea of "broken-heartedness" that has to be experienced, and Winnicott's and Eigen's hearing of the patient's vanishing scream, it is the analyst/therapist's heart that *hears and experiences the unthinkable emotional situation itself*, especially when the patient's transmission is unthinkably broken. In the Hebrew verse "With all one's heart, with all one's soul, and with all one's might" (Eigen, 1981; Deuteronomy, 6:5), the word "heart" is spelled with a double letter *beit* ב—לבב *levav*—rather than the usual לב *lev* (that does not find *expression* in the English translation). It is this double "heartedness" that I put forward here. This very vital quality of the *analyst's hearing and experiencing "broken-heartedness"* and the vanishing scream engenders a different possibility for reaching and meeting—psych-to-psyche, heart-to-heart—the painful immensity of the brokenness of a human psyche.

Clinical Illustration: The Gate of Tears

I will now describe, by using a case illustration, my critical struggle to hear, experience, and stay within the patient's "broken-heartedness" of early breakdown, when the patient in treatment repeatedly points to its endless, massively traumatic impact without the ability to go through it.

Ben, a very tall, athletic, and strikingly handsome young man of twenty-eight, came to me for psychoanalytic psychotherapy because of a prolonged depressive crisis over the preceding two years, centering on a girlfriend who had betrayed and left him. He had already been through two failed psychotherapies, which had terminated with a recommendation for medication.

Ben vacantly described what had happened with the girl in response to my questions. There were always girls who had been interested in him, who had "come on to him," but after a night or two, they would leave. Only this girl, Julie, had stayed, insisting on continuing the relationship, saying that she loved him. After three months together, she decided to go abroad. Ben did not object and even felt relieved. She left, and about a month later, the tone of her letters changed; the letters became more sporadic until they finally stopped. On her return three months later, she told him that, while abroad, she had had a relationship with someone else. Although it had ended, she categorically refused to go back to Ben, despite his repeated requests that she return and try again. From her point of view, Ben was a closed issue, she said. He began calling her day and night, sometimes speaking, pleading with her to come back, feeling humiliated but unable to stop, and other times not speaking at all. Each night, he hung around her house for hours, drunk, drugged, in a daze, tracking her movements: Was she at home? What time did she switch off the light? What time did she go to bed? Did she have someone else?

Despite enrolling in a university, Ben barely attended lectures and repeatedly failed all his examinations throughout those two years. He sometimes did random, simple work, mainly at night, to partially cover his expenses. It was a major, all-encompassing emotional and functional crisis.

Having told me this, and after asking him a few more informational questions and receiving informational answers in the first sessions, there appeared to be nothing else to say, talk about, or relate to. Any effort of mine to ask and encourage him to talk always ended up in the same meaningless, empty, futile place. "Does zilch for me," Ben would repeatedly respond to anything, his words addressed to no one. There was no area that interested him. Studies? "Zilch"; he had no interest in what he was studying and no interest in any other field either. The long trip around the world he had taken after his military service and the places he had visited? "Zilch." Going out with friends? "Zilch." Work? "Zilch." The treatment? "Zilch," and they'd told him everything in his previous treatments, which "also did zilch for me." When I gave up on my attempts to ask questions and encourage him to talk, a silence that was no less hollow and dreary reigned. It was not non-speaking, but this "Zilch" that crept into speech and silence, into every corner, everywhere, limitless, with no way out; it was as if there was an irreparable fault in the aliveness of his psychic apparatus. "Zilch." A desolate emotional wasteland. There was only the nocturnal, disconnected, ceaseless, and despairing hanging around Julie's house, perhaps because she, by leaving him, was the only one who had broken through this nothingness.

After about two and a half months of this, I thought that perhaps if Ben were in treatment with a younger female therapist, one closer to him in age and his world, something more libidinal and alive might evolve. And perhaps I had also become weary; thus, I offered him this alternative. But Ben immediately replied that he had no intention of going to any other therapist, neither younger nor older, that this was the last treatment he was ever going to try, and besides, he didn't know why he was still trying at all.

And so we continued treatment for another month. Gradually, there was a significant diminishing of his nocturnal wanderings. And then, after being in treatment for almost four months, Ben told me that he saw no point in continuing; nothing had changed, it was end-of-year-exam time, and it would be better to spend his time studying. After one further session, I accepted his decision, asking him only to call me if matters deteriorated. Ben called about three weeks later. He told me that he had failed all his exams, hadn't even sat for some of them, and resumed his nocturnal wanderings around Julie's house.

We resumed treatment.

During this period in treatment, Ben tried something different. He brought the letters Julie had written him from abroad and read them to me, trying to seek and discover with me what had happened and when, when had she stopped loving him, what had gone wrong, and why. He brought photographs of them that had been taken before she went abroad; they showed a handsome couple, with Julie looking at him very affectionately.

During these months, Ben's wanderings around Julie during treatment replaced his nocturnal wanderings around her house. He struck up a relationship with a new girl, but she, too, terminated it after two weeks. Once again, the relationship was terminated abruptly. Once again, there was this terrible gap between his remarkably attractive appearance and the incomprehensible and unavoidable collapse of any relationship.

After about three months into this stage of treatment, Ben came to a session looking very tired. He said he had hardly slept that night because he had been with a woman several years older than him, whom he had met at a pub, but did not want to continue the relationship with her. He did not want to hurt her because she wanted something serious. She was as desperate as he when he wanted someone. Perhaps he would go out with her a few more times when he was lonely and drunk. Ben added that he was not attending lectures; he didn't feel like it or want anything. Ben asked if he could lie down on the couch in my room. He lay down and asked, "Can't see you?" Then he lay silent and motionless until the hour was up, utterly inert on the couch; he looked very long and stiff. I thought (although I did not know for sure) that he had closed his eyes. He awoke just before the session was over and left.

In the following session, he did not utter a single word. I felt that he had been frightened by his letting go at the previous session. Ben called the day before the next session to say he would not be coming. He did not want to continue treatment. I asked him to attend so that we could talk about it, A.

Although Ben did come, he was adamant that he didn't want to be in treatment any longer. It ran counter to the macho image he had been raised to assume, and it annoyed him. Then he fell silent. Later, he said that he had called Julie that week, and she had told him that she didn't want to speak to him, that he was no longer part of her life, and then she had hung up on him. He didn't want to be in treatment. I said that he couldn't leave treatment like this, without something improving for him, in some area—in his studies, at work, in love. "It doesn't matter, I'll go somewhere or other," he said. But I felt that he could not go in this state. And in stark contrast to the previous time he had wanted to leave treatment, now I was fighting for this failed treatment with a stubbornness incomprehensible to me, telling him that I couldn't let him go like that, to nowhere, despairing and destructive, that this ran counter to my professional and human responsibility. And as I spoke, I felt tears coming into my eyes.

He looked at me, seeing my distress, and said, almost feelingly (I thought), "You're the only one who cares about me, of all the psychologists. I know it's not a matter of ego with you. But you just don't understand—I'm lost. I'm lost. There's no chance. No chance at all."

"Give me, give the treatment, a year," I said. "You came to treatment at the beginning of April. So stay in treatment until next April, and if it doesn't help you, I won't say another word if you want to go."

"I came at the beginning of April?" Ben asked. "That's when I was born." We checked my appointment book and found that he had come for the first time one day after his birthday.

Something in this new, surprising, and tangible feeling of time, which had thus entered the treatment, drew my attention to the fact that every three or four months, a crisis would arise in treatment. Julie, too, had gone abroad after three months with him and had betrayed him after four. As he had come to therapy at the time of his birth, had something happened during his first year of life, after four months? Had something been stopped and cut off at that time? But what?

I suggested something that I do not usually do—that he ask his mother what had happened when he was about four months old. At first, he refused, saying, "What would be the use of my asking? And anyhow, what's the use of my telling you things?" I told him that *now* I know him differently and have thus come to know his suffering and distress after seeing the letters and getting to know the recurrent and incomprehensible collapse of every relationship.

He said he "had scenes in his head" that he could not relate to. But when I asked him what was on his mind, he could not stand it; I should not ask him, I should say what *I* think, and he will correct me. We agreed to this.

Ben came to the following sessions without having asked his mother. I waited. "How can I ask questions like that [to mother]? It is weird; what would I say to her?" he finally said. I suggested he say to her, "The therapist asked me to ask." When Ben did ask her, he came back and said that his mother had been astonished by his question and told him that, at that time, terrible things had happened that she had never spoken about. She wanted to tell Ben about that period, but he did not want to hear it. So his mother requested that if Ben and I gave permission, she would tell me directly. Ben gave his consent, and I gave mine. I subsequently received a long, poignant letter from her in which she recounted that when Ben was three months old, he had contracted spastic bronchitis. Ben's mother spent nights walking around holding him in her arms, frightened for his life, while he struggled to breathe, wheezing, almost suffocating. A month later, when he was four months old, his brother, who was a year older, contracted meningitis. His condition was critical, and she sat at his bedside in the hospital for three weeks without going home or seeing Ben during that entire period. When she finally returned home, Ben neither cried nor was happy; he was not ill but completely quiet, and she thought everything had passed satisfactorily. And, she added, she herself had been too tired to think about anything. During the subsequent months, she underwent a period of terrible fatigue and depression, unable to bear anything more.

I read the letter and realized that it was here that Ben had given up forever, had emotionally died out and had become this "Does zilch for me." But when I related and read to Ben what she had written, he sat there with a blank, immobile face. "I see that this moves you," he said at the end, "but it makes no difference to me. It was a long time ago. It's nothing. It does zilch for me."

However, things flowed a little more freely during the treatment that followed. He spoke more, bringing up "the idea of self-destruction—to hurt yourself in order to hurt the person who had hurt you, that you're angry at them, that they should feel bad, that they should feel that it's their responsibility." At the end of March, toward the end of the four-month extension that had been granted, he gradually withdrew and shut down; his words dried up, and at the beginning of April, he told me that a year had gone by, there was no change, and he was stopping treatment.

This time, I did not argue. "You kept to the agreement, and I am thankful for that," I said, and added softly, "I am very sorry that despite the great effort we both made, I did not manage to help you."

The treatment was terminated.

About five months later, Ben called to tell me he was taking the university's summer semester. At first, I did not grasp the significance of this, but then he added that he was taking the summer semester because he wanted to *complete* his studies by March of the following year, as this time, he had passed all of his end-of-year exams. I realized that a change was taking place.

He called again three months later. He told me that he had successfully completed the summer semester and would finish his studies in March. He called again in March after passing all his final examinations. He had begun a relationship with a new girl, and again she terminated it a week later. He thought he should resume treatment. We arranged to begin again in April, this time on the day before his (thirtieth) birthday.

At the first session back at treatment, he quietly recited and sang a song by Ehud Ba'nai [an Israeli singer] that I had not heard before—*Please hurry*: "The boy is thirty, he's got a high fever, he's out of work and love." And when he reached the chorus, there were tears in his eyes:

> Please hurry, put a bandage on my heart
> Before you lay me down to sleep
> And tell me of the child I once was,
> How joyful I was at the first rain.

The treatment has continued ever since for years (after another year, it turned into analysis, at his request)—heavy, complex, draining, but surviving, enduring, and becoming, with time, truly transformative.

To conclude, I will return to Eigen's captivating words:

> "Wherever you find yourself with a patient, you have to go. We wish things could be otherwise, could be easier, but we have little choice when light shines through the ruins of injury." (Eigen, 2005, p. 41) Perhaps only such being-there, within the unbearable emotional experience of the patient's psychic reality with a hearing and experiencing heart could stand a chance. In this way, the catastrophic impact turns into a catastrophic change (Bion, 1965) that *becomes-with the analyst a catastrophic chance*. Patient-with-analyst are given a new chance to relive and experience it t(w)ogether.

Notes

1 In those years, I also read the book *The Heart* ("Cuore" in Italian) by Edmondo de Amicis, a moving children's book which includes the well-known story *From the Apennines to the Andes*, the tale of Marco, a courageous young boy who travels with his pet monkey from Genoa in Italy to Argentine in search of his mother, who had gone to Argentine to work and suddenly stopped writing to her family.

2 From "What's love got to do with it" (Tina Turner, 1984).

3 Tustin's words about the agony of the "heartbroken" patients who developed the plaster cast of autism to cover their brokenness relate closely to Winnicott's ideas on early breakdown or madness (1974, 1965). Tustin herself refers to the "Fear of breakdown" thinking of Winnicott (1990, pp. 154, 156).

References

Bion, W.R. (1965). *Transformations*. London: Maresfield Library/Karnac.

Bion, W.R. (1970). *Attention and Interpretation*. London: Maresfield Library/Karnac.

Bion, W.R. (1990/1974). *Brazilian Lectures: 1973 Sao Paulo, 1974 Rio de Janeiro/Sao Paulo*. London & New York: Karnac Books.

Caruth, C. (1996). *Unclaimed Experience: Trauma, Narrative, and History*. Baltimore, MD & London: Johns Hopkins University Press.

Celan, P. (1958). Speech on the occasion of receiving the literature prize of the Free Hanseatic City of Bremen. In *Selected Poems and Prose of Paul Celan*. J. Felstiner (Tran). W. W. Norton, pp. 395–396.

Eigen, M. (1981). The area of faith in Winnicott, Lacan, and Bion. *Integrated Journal Psychoanalysis*, 62: 413–433.

Eigen, M. (1993). *The electrified tightrope*. A. Phillips (Ed.), Northwale, NJ & London: Jason Aronson.

Eigen, M. (2005). Interview with Micha Odenheimer. *Another Country (Eretz Acheret)*, 26: 36–42.

Eigen, M. (2012). *Kabbalah and Psychoanalysis*. London: Karnac.

Eshel, O. (1996). Story-telling in the analytic situation. *Sihot – Dialogue, Israel Journal of Psychotherapy*, 10: 182–193.

Eshel, O. (2004). Let it be and become me: Notes on containing, identification, and the possibility of being. *Contemporary Psychoanalysis*, 40: 323–351.

Eshel, O. (2012). In the dark depths "Beyond the pleasure principle": On facing the unbearable traumatic experience in psychoanalytic work. *Sihot – Dialogue, Israel Journal of Psychotherapy*, 27: 5–15.

Eshel, O. (2014). On intersubjectivity and beyond. *Sihot – Dialogue, Israel Journal of Psychotherapy*, 28: 260–269.

Eshel, O. (2015a). The "hearing heart" and the "voice" of breakdown. In L. Aron, L. Henik (eds.), *Answering a Question with a Question: Contemporary Psychoanalysis and Jewish Thought, Vol. II: A Tradition of Inquiry* (pp. 133–152). Boston: Academic Studies Press.

Eshel, O. (2016). The "voice" of breakdown: On facing the unbearable traumatic experience in psychoanalytic work. *Contemporary Psychoanalysis*, 52: 76–110.

Eshel, O. (2019). *The Emergence of Analytic Oneness: Into the Heart of Psychoanalysis*. London & New York: Routledge.

Freud, S. (1912). Recommendations to physicians practising psychoanalysis. *S.E.*, XII: 109–120.

Turner, T. (1984). What's love got to do with it? Britten, T. & Lyle, G. [Recorded by Tina Turner] *Private Dancer*. Capitol Records.

Tustin, F. (1972). *Autism and Childhood Psychosis*. London: Hogarth Press.

Tustin, F. (1986). *Autistic Barriers in Neurotic Patients*. London: Tavistock.

Tustin, F. (1990). *The Protective Shell in Children and Adults*. London: Karnac Books.

Tustin, F. (1991). Revised understandings of psychogenic autism. *International Journal of Psychoanalysis*, 72: 585–591.

Tustin, F. (1994). The perpetuation of an error. *Journal of Child Psychotherapy*, 20: 3–23.

Verne, J. (1867–1868). *The Children of Captain Grant* (Hebrew), Tel Aviv, Joseph Simoni Publishing, 1960.

Winnicott, D.W. (1953). Symptom tolerance in paediatrics: A case history. In D.W.Winnicott (ed.), *Through Paediatrics to Psycho-Analysis* (pp. 101–117). London: Karnac Books, 1992.

Winnicott, D.W. (1954). Metapsychological and clinical aspects of regression within the psycho-analytical set-up. In D.W. Winnicott (ed.), *Through Paediatrics to Psycho-Analysis* (pp. 278–294). London: Karnac, 1992.

Winnicott, D.W. (1965). The psychology of madness: A contribution from psychoanalysis. In C. Winnicott R. Shepherd, M. Davis (eds.), *Psycho-analytic Explorations* (pp. 119–129). Cambridge, MA: Harvard, 1989.

Winnicott, D.W. (1967). Delinquency as a sign of hope. In C. Winnicott, R. Shepherd, M. Davis (eds.), *Home Is Where We Start from* (pp. 90–100). London: Penguin Books, 1986.

Winnicott, D.W. (1969). Additional note on psycho-somatic disorder. In C. Winnicott, R. Shepherd, M. Davis (eds.), *Psycho-analytic Explorations* (pp. 115–118). London: Karnac Books, 1989.

Winnicott, D.W. (1974). Fear of breakdown. *International Review of Psycho-Analysis*, 1: 103–107.

Zweig, S. (1939). *Ungeduld des Herzens/The Heart's Impatience* (Hebrew). Or Yehuda: Kinneret Zmora-Bitan, Dvir – Publishing House, 1986.

Chapter 3

Welcoming Suchness

Jeffrey L. Eaton

Introduction

In Franz Kafka's short story *"Before the Law,"* a man from the country approaches an open gate where a doorkeeper meets him. Upon arrival, the doorkeeper explains that the man cannot be admitted through the gate. The doorkeeper says that he is only the first, and the least intimidating, of many doorkeepers who the man will have to face should he attempt to enter the gate before he is granted permission. Perplexed, the man decides to wait for an indefinite time rather than test the doorkeeper's warning. The man chooses a passive solution, waiting until he is too old to enter the gate. Kafka's dramatization involves both an interpersonal encounter with the doorkeeper and an internal stalemate. This pictures a variation on an obstructive object scenario. The man's curiosity is not welcomed; his desire is thwarted. Discouraged, he gives up the impulse to explore. He becomes his own doorkeeper, forbidding change.

Many years ago, after reading *A Theory of Thinking*, I had the strong intuition that the writings of the English psychoanalyst W.R. Bion (1897–1979) might open an important gate for my development as a psychoanalyst. While Bion's writings can be hard to assimilate, I was motivated to go through the ominous gate. I have continued to study Bion's work for two decades. Bion's writings offer a vision of the complexity of human experience. He explores creativity and destructiveness at interpersonal and intrapsychic levels. Through clinical work and self-reflection, over time, I have assembled scattered clues about how to understand the hidden dynamics of frustrating obstructive situations dramatized poetically by writers like Kafka.

In this essay, I describe some patterns that are both basic and complex. An intricate, continuously transforming relationship between *a matrix of pain* and *a matrix of contact* unfolds in some way in every life. This can be seen in individuals, couples, families, and groups. The relationships between stasis, growth, and destruction of meaning evolve or devolve according to many complex variables. Two important variables are the influence of *welcoming objects* and *obstructive objects*. The creation of meaning evolves in the oscillation between obstructive

DOI: 10.4324/9781003322993-3

forces and the capacity to welcome experience, explore experience, share experience, and learn from experience.

This essay is divided into three sections. The first section is titled *A Matrix of Pain: Welcoming an Echoing Darkness*. I briefly explore and elaborate on Bion's ideas about what can be called obstructive object relations (Eaton, 2011). In the second section, titled "A Matrix of Contact: Becoming a Welcoming Object" (Eaton, 2015), I explore elements of an analyst's internal workspace for listening. I speculate about some of the factors that might open a *matrix of contact* in an analytic process. A brief clinical vignette from a child case illustrates some of the links between pain, contact, and suchness. Finally, in a section titled "Welcoming Suchness," I describe how becoming a welcoming object sometimes allows an analyst to "welcome suchness." Suchness (Tathata in Pali) is a Buddhist term for "that which is." It denotes a moment of direct experience free from conceptual elaboration or ascription of judgment. In Bion's work, suchness is a moment of becoming O or an evolution (in contradistinction to experience saturated with memory, desire, or familiar understanding and sensory satisfaction). In lived experience, obstructive and creative welcoming forces always seem to be complexly interdependent. They unfold together as twin movements between the fate of pain and the possibilities of psychic growth and realization.

A Matrix of Pain: Welcoming an Echoing Darkness

A Buddhist teacher named Stephen Levine once said that if the amount of pain in the world made a sound, we would all be deafened by the roar. To be born into this life involves vulnerability to experiences of helplessness, dependence, sickness, cruelty, injury, loss, separation, change, betrayal, violence, aging, and ultimately death. Becoming aware is painful. Welcoming experience inevitably discloses the pain of being alive. Sometimes what emerges from allowing contact with experience is a wordless echoing darkness. Sometimes a patient and analyst can be faced with an intimidating reality that the emotionally immediate experience of a session feels like a matrix of pain.

In a poem called "A Poisoned Tree," William Blake (1986, p.) writes:

> *I was angry with my friend:*
> *I told my wrath, my wrath did end.*
> *I was angry with my foe:*
> *I told it not, my wrath did grow.*

Blake's poem shows a link between emotional pain *and* communication. When pain can be shared and talked about, it tends to ease or diminish. On the other hand, when pain cannot be shared, it tends to grow in intensity. This simple observation is at the heart of much agonizing human suffering.

It can be agonizing to be left alone with your pain. But, for some people, it can be even more awful to feel exposed, showing your suffering to another. The possibility of communication and of sharing experience can evoke a matrix of contact within a matrix of pain, or vice versa. Many people inhibit communication because they anticipate that it will amplify their pain. Emotional contact is equated with violent emotional impingement. Blake's poem captures the difference between an obstructive object (foe) and contact with a welcoming object (friend). Contact with a welcoming object makes communication possible, including risking expressing difficult emotional realities. On the other hand, an encounter with an obstructive object thwarts communication and amplifies pain.

Bion knew this in his bones. In his autobiography, *The Long Weekend*, he tells a story about receiving a prestigious military honor, the Distinguished Service Order (DSO). While on leave from fighting at the front during World War I, Bion met his mother in London. She had come to visit her nineteen-year-old son when he received the medal presented by King George V. Describing the aftermath of the ceremony, Bion (1991, p. 191) writes:

> *We walked slowly along Green Park to our hotel. It was hopeless to pretend; my mother was no fool. It was simply a matter of compelling our face muscles to do their drill.*
>
> *By eight that evening I felt neither of us could stand any more. Pleading the excuse of an early morning and a long day I suggested we should go to bed. She agreed—like an automaton.*
>
> *As I entered the bedroom and closed the door, I felt I had entered hell…*
>
> *The next morning when I saw my mother's white powdered face, I recognized misery. We did not talk; we had withdrawn. We said good-bye in the hotel and a taxi took me to Waterloo.*

This is an example of a deeply personal moment of suffering. In it, an overlap between a matrix of pain and a matrix of contact can be clearly seen.

The experiential origins of Bion's ideas on the obstructive object are found in his autobiographies, though they are not explicitly named as such. The theoretical origins of the idea are explored in his "schizophrenia papers," which are collected in *Second Thoughts: Selected Papers on Psycho-Analysis* (Bion, 1993). A complete sketch of the development of Bion's obstructive object concept is beyond the scope of this essay. Instead, I select a few relevant aspects to highlight the obstructive object experience and how it creates a matrix of pain that thwarts emotional contact.

In *Notes on a Theory of Schizophrenia*, Bion (1993) emphasizes how language can be used as an action to evacuate painful experience. The violence of evacuation damages language use as a communicative link. Bion describes how thoughts begin to feel like omnipotent actions when action substitutes for thought. Language fails to function as a communicative link, and communication between patient and analyst breaks down. Furthermore, a patient can lose the ability to communicate within himself. The ability to express himself is thwarted precisely when he is most vulnerable and in need of emotional help.

The intensity of psychotic suffering leads to an intolerance of pain and contact with reality, which is felt to stimulate pain. Splitting processes accelerate, leading to psychic fragmentation. Projective identification functions as a form of violent evacuation amplifying feelings of fragmentation and persecution. This terrible process culminates in attacks on the organs of perception. This is just the beginning of a complex phenomenology Bion tries to describe and that I call a matrix of pain.

According to Bion (1993, p. 38), there are four features of what he names a psychotic personality:

> *(1) a conflict that is never decided between the life and death instincts (2) a preponderance of destructive impulses (3) hatred of external and internal reality (4) a tenuous but tenacious object relationship.*

An obstructive object is a specific configuration associated with a psychotic part of the personality. This obstructive figure refuses to acknowledge the reality of pain. Bion highlights how in the transference, a patient can feel that his analyst refuses to know about the patient's suffering. This transference prediction becomes concretely reified by the analyst rejecting the need of the patient to communicate in raw, primitive ways. An inability to use projective identification as a form of communication characterizes the breakdown in the communicative link between patient and analyst. An external object is experienced as unable to welcome communication of distressing experience and lend potential meaning to it. According to Bion, the consequences of such a pattern show that some patients have internalized an *ego-destructive object* that attacks links on awareness of experience and thwarts communication both within and between others.

This situation represents *a crisis of connection* and is a key element of a matrix of pain. Making an emotional connection is felt to be intolerably frustrating, even dangerous. Connection is both fragile (tenuous) and stubbornly clung to (tenacious). Every attempt to communicate feels repeatedly interrupted or thwarted. Both patient and analyst become caught up in a perfect storm of communicative breakdown. It is a crisis of connection, not only for the infant (or patient) but also for the mother (or analyst). In other words, the possibility of communication as a link breaks down *between* participants. A matrix of contact becomes equated with a matrix of pain.

In the presence of an obstructive object, mounting frustration and nameless dread suffuse a tenuous link, creating an emotional catastrophe *for the couple*. This catastrophe becomes internalized and personified as an ego-destructive Sphinx-like internal object. A background of emotional catastrophe can be partially represented and appears in dreams as frightening intrusive persecutory figures and uninhabitable environments. Or emotional catastrophe may remain largely unrepresented but perdures as an ego-destructive background unconsciously stimulating anticipated annihilating impingement.

In this scenario, the patient demonstrates acute hypersensitivity, appearing almost allergic to awareness of experience of any kind.

I recall a psychotic patient who thought he heard screaming coming from inside my consulting room while he was waiting for his session. When he entered my room, he walked anxiously around, looking for something. Eventually, he was able to tell me that he was searching for evidence that I had been burning my previous patient alive. He expressed the belief that I wanted to help, but he said, "I do not want to be burned alive." He told me he suspected my method was trying to "fry off" each patient's illness. He believed that I had a blow torch hidden somewhere in the room. He said he wanted no part of such a treatment. This man believed that I was caring, stupid, and arrogant. Making emotional contact with me felt both life-giving and murderous.

In an obstructive object scenario, a matrix of pain can be pictured as involving three intimidating interdependent forms. The first form involves *a relentless withdrawal* from contact because contact with another is felt to evoke emotional catastrophe. The second form involves *the interruption of contact*, when the tenuous connection to a yearned-for good object is traumatically lost, creating an abject tear in the fabric of going on being. The third form involves *a tenacious attack on contact with links to reality*, leading to states of nameless dread. There are probably many more possible variations.

In obstructive object relations, the terror of making an intimate link is felt to evoke emotional catastrophe. An obstructive object *field* constellated by the interaction of patient and analyst reveals a background of ego-destructive shame (Eaton, 2021). One aspect of the patient desperately wants to communicate intense emotions while, at the same time, a different unconscious force forbids communication as a form of self-preservation. Such scenarios involve abject states of feeling no right to exist, no right to belong, and no right to interact creatively. The challenge for the patient is that as he allows himself to communicate, to come alive emotionally, and to make intimate emotional links to experience, he also vividly feels shame, pain, and anxiety more intensely. If he risks expressing this pain, he predicts that this will destroy him and whoever else he is related to.

A Matrix of Contact: Becoming a Welcoming Object

When I visited Michael Eigen several years ago in his office in New York City, he greeted me by saying, "Tell me *everything.*" His communication embodied an energetic transmission of a welcoming experience. I palpably *felt* Eigen's sincere generosity of spirit as well as his curiosity about getting to know me. Rather than directing the session in any specific way, he was open to what might happen between us. Conversation was an invitation to make emotional contact and to share experience. Eigen could play, affirm, question, and respond spontaneously. I rapidly recognized how free he was to wait, to relax into uncertainty, and to see what might evolve. Eigen offered a space for *meeting*. His focus seemed to be characterized by an openness to what each next moment might call forth.

Eigen was deeply influenced by Bion. When Bion recommended that an analyst make it a practice to eschew memory, desire, and understanding at the beginning of each session, he was seeking to open less saturated experiential space both within the analyst and between analyst and patient. When an analyst can treat a session like a blank page, he creates conditions to welcome surprise, discovery, and transformation. An unsaturated attitude registers repetitions based on memory, desire, and habits of conceptual understanding without becoming too identified with them. If an analyst can welcome experience without clinging to meaning, this attitude creates an atmosphere that makes it possible for a patient to risk contact with his or her own deeper emergent unconscious experience. Out of this matrix of contact, an evolution in a session might occur—a sudden glimpse of a pattern that connects or a significant insight that shifts awareness of experience in unpredictable ways.

Toward the end of his life, Bion highlighted the need to welcome intuition and imagination as significant qualities of a disciplined analytic attitude. His emphasis shifted from the interpretation of meaning (as unconscious content) to the awareness (registration) and description (notation, attention, and inquiry) of emergent experience. He increasingly focused on the process of how meaning is ascribed to experience (theory of transformations). The notation O is not about a mystical elsewhere state of being. It is, instead, an empty symbol pointing to moments of direct experience, what Buddhists call the "suchness" of a moment.

In *The Italian Seminars*, Bion (2005, p. 13) says:

> ... *what you have to do is to give the germ of a thought a chance. You are sure to object to it; you are sure to wish it conformed to some cherished psychoanalytic theory ... you have to dare to think and feel whatever it is that you think or feel, no matter what your society or your Society thinks about it, or even what you think about it.*

Bion valued the freedom to register, tolerate, explore, and express personal realizations. He did not think that an analyst could look back in time to uncover the origins of experience or make definitive causal links. Psychoanalysis, for Bion, was about exploring experience, not explaining it. Instead, he suggested that with the assistance of an analyst's disciplined attention and imagination in gathering the details of the experience of each session, a patient could get to know him- or herself better through analytic investigation of the complexity of the present moment. This temporal complexity includes the way that the past and future impinge on the experience of being now-here together with another.

Writing in the British Independent tradition, in an article titled "Raiding the inarticulate: The internal analytic setting and listening beyond the countertransference," the English analyst Michael Parsons (2007, p. 1453) describes:

> ...*the internal analytic setting as being the kind of inward space that is needed for the analyst to be truly an analytic listener to herself ... The idea that unconscious aspects of the analyst's psyche stirred up by the analytic encounter may not impede the analysis but bring fresh creativity into it brings us beyond the usual conception of countertransference ... The analytic situation may also evoke capacities, and functions, in an analyst's psyche of which he was not previously aware.*

Analytical work over many years with children on the autism spectrum and with some psychotic adults has involved an immersion in learning how to welcome suffering. Self-awareness, self-observation, and self-reflection are necessary capacities to learn from intimidating emotional experience. When encountering a matrix of pain, an analyst may need to realize capacities and functions that have not previously been available. This implies welcoming new experiences and, sometimes, tolerating what Bion called catastrophic change. Catastrophic change means tolerating disorientation and reorientation, as part of absorbing and making space for the impact of a new experience. For an analyst to do this, he must be free to welcome his own emergent experience. Clinging to familiar concepts obstructs welcoming a new experience. Listening to yourself listening to another is an ongoing practice. Over time, it gradually helps to open an *internal workspace for welcoming experience.*

Eigen (1993, p. 133) has emphasized the role of faith in the analyst's attitude of facing uncertainty (O): "The most precious gain is the evolution of openness toward experiencing, or, as Bion writes, "experiencing experience," a process in which something more is always happening (or about to)." Patience was one quality that Bion emphasized as necessary to allow such an opening. He also, infamously, advocated eschewing memory, desire, and understanding. In my experience, there are qualities that support an analyst's greater openness. These qualities include sincere curiosity, discipline, and compassion. These interdependent aspects can combine to create an enhanced alpha function capable of sponsoring a matrix of contact and of welcoming a matrix of pain (Gooch, 2002).

An internal workspace for welcoming experience can be pictured as a field constellated by the relationship between a matrix of pain and a matrix of contact. A matrix of pain is characterized by withdrawal from experience, interruption of experience, or attacks on the awareness of experience. A matrix of contact makes possible tolerating being with painful experience rather than withdrawing. A matrix of contact also supports the possibility of reaching out after painful interruptions of contact. Additionally, a matrix of contact welcomes limits to destructive attacks so that a space for new experience is not permanently destroyed or saturated by patterns of a rigidly fixed mindset.

In what follows, I will offer a sketch of how some of these elements make up this complex internal mental workspace. I will anchor these ideas with a clinical vignette, a brief description of work with a young boy, whom I will call Ernie. This vignette portrays the discovery of a capacity to welcome and *share* experience.

Ernie, aged 10, was diagnosed on the autism spectrum. The sessions I will describe came after about a year of twice-weekly psychoanalytic psychotherapy. During the first several months, Ernie had been either silently withdrawn or angrily resistant. He showed little interest or willingness to communicate. My attempts to understand Ernie's experience all seemed to be received as impingements that aggravated him. During this period, I repeatedly reminded myself of a supervisor's advice: *you must be patient.* Significant internal work went into tolerating and containing Ernie's negativity. The sessions I will describe show, I hope, how Ernie's matrix of pain finally begins to open into a tenuous matrix of contact.

One day Ernie began to play with Legos. He sat on the floor and built silently. I sat on the floor near him. When I tried to speak, he turned his back to me.

I understood something then. I realized that I needed to shift my attention to *welcoming experience itself*, not trying to make meaning of Ernie's experience. I shifted my attention from explanation to *being with* Ernie. I tried to observe his experience as it unfolded. This shift involved finally accepting my helplessness to make an emotional link with Ernie. It freed me to be more receptive and open.

Now I will present moments from two consecutive sessions. In the first session, Ernie made a series of Lego objects. I watched in silence as he built. He placed each object carefully on the carpet. His actions seemed full of intent. He was clearly creating a scene of some kind. I kept my curiosity in check. This was the first time he had built anything in a sustained way and the first activity that felt remotely like imaginative play. I did not ask him to tell me anything about what he was doing. Instead, I paid close attention to my own emotions as the scene unfolded.

I felt a sudden sense of enormous sadness. I sat quietly, registering, tolerating, and observing this sadness within. After some time, I felt a strong sense that the scene Ernie had made needed a witness. But I knew that talking to Ernie about this was not the answer.

Spontaneously, I decided to make a little figure out of Legos. Ernie did not seem to care that I had started to build too. Once I had made a little person-like figure, I waited until what felt like a pause, then I placed my figure into Ernie's scene:

> Ernie looked at the figure. There was a moment of suspense between us. It felt like he was weighing his options. Finally, he said, softly, "what's that?"
>
> I answered, "This is an observer, someone to find out what is happening."
>
> Ernie was quiet. I could almost feel how he was making an internal choice of some kind. Then he said, "Apple trees".
>
> "Apple trees"? I asked.
>
> Ernie explained that the figures he had built were apple trees.
>
> This was a surprise.
>
> I waited.
>
> Ernie said, "The apple trees are full of fruit but most of the apples are on the ground and are going to rot."
>
> I said, without thinking, "the good apples need to be collected".
>
> Then, I made a little wheelbarrow out of Legos.
>
> Ernie watched as I built. We were both silent. When I had finished, I placed the wheelbarrow in the imaginary orchard.
>
> I said, "The good fruit can go in here".
>
> Ernie seemed deep in thought. The atmosphere felt poignant.

In the next session, Ernie began to build again. He was silent as he built. He placed the little Lego observer I had made the previous session near him. It took him most of the session to build a new scene. I watched silently, listening to myself internally as I observed him. It felt like there was a link between us, and it felt calm to me. Ernie repeatedly stopped what he was doing and started over, undoing then rebuilding.

I wondered silently if he was being interrupted by something. But this didn't feel quite right to me. I imagined then that Ernie was trying to realize something that he had in his mind's eye. Perhaps, I thought, he felt a lot of resilience. He stayed with his task until he had constructed what felt right to him. I continued to wait. I didn't say any of this to Ernie.

In *The Challenge of Being Human* (Eigen, 2018, p. 73), Mike Eigen writes:

> *...I often reach a deep point of not knowing, a kind of creative waiting, that shifts the ambience in the room. As time goes on, a person with me begins to sense something further, perhaps a still point of her own that is a little freeing. It is less a matter of solving problems on their own terms as shifting the center of gravity, allowing something more to grow.*

My feelings and thoughts, though unspoken, were real experiences for me. When he had finished, Ernie placed a new Lego object in front of me. It was a large, flat square. Part of the square was yellow, and the other part was blue. The two colors met in a jagged line in the middle. Now it was my turn to wonder "what's that?" Ernie did not tell me. He said I should guess. All my guesses were wrong. Finally, Ernie said, "It's the sea." Pointing at the jagged line, he said, "This is where the sea meets the shore. And there is a wave coming in."

I felt deeply moved. I thought: "this is how we meet, like the sea meeting the shore." I said, "This is what making contact feels like when it can be tolerated." Later, I said, "One of the biggest mysteries is about what happens in your mind and in my mind when we are away from each other and when we are together again." Ernie did not speak. He made direct eye contact and then started to build something new.

Welcoming Suchness

In Buddhism, in the Pali language, the word *Tathata* means suchness. Suchness denotes the way things are, free of conceptual elaboration or the ascription of meaning. Suchness evokes a feeling of immediate, direct experience. I experienced moments of Ernie's play as opening brief shared moments of suchness. Moments of suchness are often new experiences. They don't promote change, but they are change.

Experience precedes meaning. A quality of sincere curiosity allows an analyst to become interested in a patient's picture of the world. How does experience look, feel, sound, taste, and smell to a person? How does experience move a person, both in body and in mind? Does a patient turn toward experience or away? Does she stand still or seek or retreat? What direction do her thoughts and feelings travel in? Do they move together or apart?

Compassion and discipline deepen an experience of analytic listening. Compassion welcomes suffering, and discipline contains it. Discipline means a commitment to try to stay with difficult experience, rather than evading it. Eigen has advised that therapists learn to welcome a rhythm of opening and closing to experience. We open a bit, then recoil, then open and try again. Gradually we gain more faith in letting in, letting be, and letting go.

The combination of curiosity, discipline, and compassion fortifies analytic attention. This is what Bion called a K-link, a willingness to get-to-know experience. The K-link opens the realization of an internal workspace. Listening after Bion implies a willingness in the analyst, and eventually in an analytic couple, to realize and grow the capacity to welcome whatever a moment might call forth.

A matrix of contact, supported by curiosity, discipline, and compassion, involves trying to pay attention to *everything* a person might communicate. Compassion involves welcoming the first-person embodied testimony of an experiencing subject. Discipline involves welcoming the data of a psychoanalytic session before trying to select what is significant. This includes what a person says, how they say it, and how this communication impacts a listener. Curiosity involves a sincere openness to the patient's picture of the world, including how different that experience might be from the analyst's own.

Listening with a welcoming attitude involves sincere curiosity about the detailed particulars of the experience of another person as they are narrated or experienced *in real time*. Listening after Bion does not start by decoding or asserting meaning. It starts with registering experience and how that experience is either tolerated or rejected. Being with experience is the place to start, over and over.

Welcoming moments of suchness sponsor awareness of a matrix of contact gradually capable of developing within a matrix of pain. The practice of eschewing memory, desire, and understanding helps an analyst to welcome moments of suchness. An analyst's capacity to combine curiosity, compassion, and discipline as a complex growth mindset increases her ability to register, tolerate, reflect upon, and reply to moments of suchness. These combined qualities characterize an analyst's internal workspace. Augmented alpha function can gradually change the atmosphere of the analytic field. Sharing moments of suchness creates a dynamic interaction between a matrix of pain and a matrix of contact in the direction of psychic growth.

References

Blake, W. (1986) *Songs of Innocence and of Experience: Shewing the Two Contrary States of the Human Soul*. Oxford: Oxford University Press.

Bion, W.R. (1991) *The Long Weekend: Part of a Life*. London: Karnac.

——— (1993) *Second Thoughts: Selected Papers on Psycho-Analysis*. Northvale: Jason Aronson.

——— (2005) *The Italian Seminars*. London: Karnac.

Eaton, J.L. (2011) "The Obstructive Object" in *A Fruitful Harvest: Essays after Bion* (17–33). Seattle: The Alliance Press.

——— (2015) "Becoming a Welcoming Object: Personal Notes on Michael Eigen's Impact" in *Living Moments: On the Work of Michael Eigen*. Ed. Bloch, S., & Daws L. (131–148). London: Routledge.

——— (2021) "On Caesura, Temporality, and Ego Destructive Shame: Ominous Transitions in Everyday Life" in *Temporality, Shame, and Social Crisis: Ominous Transitions*. Ed. Hinton, L., & Willemsen, H. (27–39). London: Routledge.

Eigen, M. (1993) "The Area of Faith in Winnicott, Bion, and Lacan" in *The Electrified Tightrope* (109–138). Northvale: Jason Aronson.

Eigen, M. (2018) *The Challenge of Being Human*. London: Routledge.

Gooch, J. (2002) "The Primitive Somatopsychic Roots of Gender Formation and Intimacy: Sensuality, Symbolism, and Passion in the Development of Mind" in *Primitive Mental States Volume II: Psychobiological and Psychoanalytic Perspectives on Early Trauma and Personality Development*. Ed. Alhanati, S. (159–174). London: Karnac.

Parsons, M. (2007) "Raiding the inarticulate: The internal analytic setting and listening beyond the countertransference". *International Journal of Psychoanalysis*. 88: 1441–1456.

Chapter 4

The Join and Distinction-Union

A Resonant and Complex Oneness

Adam Shechter

Introduction

Infinite.
Finite.
Union
Distinction

One investigates such opposing immeasurables in order to grasp how fundamental and elusive relations work. Going for a jog along the beach in the early morning highlights the contrast of a defined point of self in an unbound environment. Through feeling this smallness in relation to a vast largeness, one begins to infer the infant's diffuse comprehension of the early object.

Therapy challenges us to use our intellects to create a frame out of what seems like a natural geometry of the psyche, all the while staying more sensorially than cognitively connected to distinction and union tendencies. Eigen (2004, 2011) asserts the two leanings are one and the same, but our sensing equipment is not yet evolved enough to perceive their relationship as such. It is in this sensing but not-knowing state of togetherness and separateness that a therapeutic possibility arises. Spotnitz's joining technique (2004; Margolis, 1983/1994) dwells in this transitional place of polar tensions. Joins work with opposition to resolve resistance to progressive communication in the session. The intervention fosters a feeling of oneness. Eigen speculates that the psyche may be limited by the nature of how it mentally represents two or more, and so conjures the binary of distinction and union. The join relieves the cognitive apparatus and intuitively operationalizes this dualistic function.

The distinction-union structure helps to organize the connections between all that is said by a patient in a given session and the individual items of speech. When a patient is cooperating with the fundamental rule of psychoanalysis and each next thing that comes to mind is verbalized, self-consciousness over self-other binaries tends to disappear. Spotnitz calls this *saying everything*. Eigen (2011) sees "distinction-union tendencies as branches of a single trunk" (p. 1). Spotnitz's image of everything-being-said visually construes as a composite act of speech

DOI: 10.4324/9781003322993-4

that includes all the possibilities of language. To further give meaning to Eigen's metaphor of the tree, we can conceptualize the psyche as growing and growing with speech and yet all the while remaining an essential structure of word flow. As simple as an acknowledging grunt to more subtle and nuanced agreements with the patient's unconscious attitudes, a join from the therapist propels and contains this flow.

The theory of resistance factors into the distinction-union structure as it is applied to the joining technique. Most importantly, resistance to progress in therapy and life are seen as one and the same, and an expression of the ego using its defenses to protect the psyche against damaging stimuli. Joins support these vital resistances through fostering a union and the associated insulation needed to naturally strengthen the ego. Considering the contemporary anxieties around the construct of resistance, I would like to make it clear that by resistance, I am not accusing the patient of willfully (albeit unconsciously) interfering with the progress of the treatment. Here, resistance is taken as a structure just as indigenous to the life of the psyche, as is distinction-union. We can even theorize that it is resistance that drives the distinction-union structure. Or vice versa. Psychic life is viewed as a state of ongoing adaptive changes that uses unions and distinctions to manage the ego's relationship to the object.

Joining and Being Born from Narcissus' Reflecting Pool

Joins reflect the patient's preverbal functioning and express an agreement with the manifest content of what he is talking about and/or his unconscious attitude about the subject matter (Spotnitz, 2004). A join seeks to modify the patient's ego on an emotional and symbolic basis as opposed to an intellectual one. By joining a patient, their ego is spared the intrusion of a new idea via an interpretation or explanation. Instead of going against or in some way mentally exceeding the patient's conscious state, the therapist goes with the flow of the patient's psyche and defenses, protecting them from foreign infringement. On the developmental level, as will be explored below, the join primarily addresses the patient at the symbiotic phase with its inferred next phase of separation. The distinction-union structure reframes this early relational bond both inside the traditional analogy of the therapist as mother and the patient as infant, and all the while conceptualizes that mode of therapeutic relation as rooted and flowing from a primordial psychic essence that is both ineffable and tangible to clinical work.

To illustrate how the distinction-union structure illuminates joining, I will turn to the metaphor of weather as it is commonly used to communicate emotion in everyday speech. Such a comparison to climate is apropos of my introductory statements that drew a parallel between sensing the grandness of a beach in the morning and how the baby perceives the primal object of the mother. Weather may allude to the early mother, but also a "primordial other" (Elkin, 1991, p. 125) who is both primitively human-related yet mysteriously beyond that and germane to wordless experiencing in therapy. The communication of rainy weather from the patient can be met with a variety of uniting responses. A simple acknowledgment that it is in fact physically raining rings much differently than any hint that the mention of rain is representing a given moment in a gloomy light. An unusually strong agreement with the patient's statement about rain may give him the feeling that his experience with the therapist and therapy is understood. In this case, a join promotes a union between patient and therapist, expressive of a deeper despair that runs to the core of the patient's feeling for life. Eigen (2004) emphasizes that work with the distinction-union structure can help the patient give up false distinctions of the self and enter more undifferentiated states so that "genuine distinctions" (p. 307) can be born. Seen this way, joins invite aspects of the patient's personality to both metabolize and gestate in the shared emotional experience between patient and therapist. Such oneness can transform false distinctions; parse them, break them down, and make them embryonic so that the raw elements of the personality are accessible to new growth.

Eigen (2004) puts forth that therapeutic work is primarily done by the therapist functioning as an "open-ended container," who conveys that in "psychic life almost anything is possible, and at the same time that a sense of limits deepens and sharpens the search" (p. 310). Joining views as a function of this analytic attitude. It conveys that the psyche is as open-ended as the patient needs it and experiences it to be. The analyst both nourishes this exploration by joining with its expansive perimeters and then delimits this raw territory with borders that arise from a feel of the distinction-union structure. Like the baby going from symbiosis to individuation, the patient stimulates the therapist to say, in essence, "Now that's enough of this infinite searching, you've gotten what you need from this particular moment of formlessness, and now it's time to put some form to it."

The framework of the narcissistic transference-countertransference (Spotnitz, 2004; Margolis, 1983/1994) houses a developmental continuum of the patient and therapist's object relations. This primitive range starts with total object-self undifferentiation and moves to the patient experiencing the therapist as a part of the self, to the feeling that the therapist is exactly like him, and on to the feeling that the therapist is like but different than the patient. While the patient-therapist relationship doesn't necessarily reflect such a linear sequence, the primitive link can be seen through these various object configurations of distinction and union. Spotnitz (2004) speaks of peak moments in the narcissistic bond as being typified by the patient's fantasy that it would be the most wonderful thing in the world to go everywhere with the therapist, be together all the time, and travel the world. The use of narcissistic here is close to Mahler's sense of the symbiotic phase, and the newborn's newly emergent being re-finding union with his mother in the outside world of her body. In this context, the union between patient and therapist is a chance to start again with early unmet needs.

It can be hard to pinpoint primitive transferences, precisely because they are from the time before words, and so definitions easily elude words. The distinction-union construct repositions this confusing preverbal quality of symbiosis so that it can be viewed as inherently conjoined with the subsequent separation-individuation phase. In fact, seen from the distinction-union perspective, the symbiotic and separation-individuation phases are parts of the same relational, developmental, and psychic structure. We can sense how this is true through the experienced theory of our internal objects as being an ongoing part of ourselves, both mergers and separations that never fully occur. Eigen brings this elusive idea into bold relief by visualizing the distinction-union construct through Michelangelo's sculptures, "'Slaves' or 'Prisoners' in Galleria dell'Accademia in Florence." He writes:

> We see figures emerging from the rock they are being carved out of. They are partly formed, partly semi-formed, partly emerging, partly embedded in the unformed stone, a birth or semi-birth in progress, permanently embryonic as well as in process of formation. (2011, p. 14)

Michelangelo's sculptures situate the *join* in a larger picture of ever-changing birth forms. We can view the join as simultaneously uniting/dividing the patient and therapist, so that as one resistance is resolved, another resistance is immediately created by virtue of the former's resolution. As discussed above, Spotnitz (2004) emphasizes that the narcissistic transference-countertransference is a variable oneness. The primary job of this clinical double is to create a space that allows for the patient's innermost impulses to come out in words. It's the loving and hating of the like-other that Spotnitz finds keenly expressed in the myth of Narcissus. For Spotnitz (1976), Narcissus' gaze into the reflective pool of water is not one that is motivated by the vanity of self-love. We are tipped off by the deleterious effect of Narcissus' gaze in that he remains transfixed by a watery mirror. We can speculate that an inner deprived self is being revealed through seeking such primitive attention from a substitute for the mother's early eyes. Narcissus is ultimately destroyed by so intensely losing himself in his reflection. He falls into the body of water and drowns.

Spotnitz (1976) derived his theory of the *narcissistic defense* from the above imagistic narrative, extrapolating a basic pattern of self-attack that runs the course of the human psyche. Instead of Narcissus expressing his murderous aggression toward the failed mother object, he unconsciously sacrifices himself to a substitute. This cruel turning inward begins with the birth of the psyche and emphasizes mental life as over-collecting frustration-aggression and bottling it into myriad forms of self-hatred. The psychotherapy session comes to be a transformative location for the murderous forces of the mother-inside as she is externalized onto the therapist.

Eigen writes, "[t]endencies to link together and hold apart permeate our psychic field with variable antagonisms and complementarities" (2004, p. 211). Extending the analogy of Michelangelo's sculptures to the session, we can conceptualize regression in the transferential field as softening the psyche's sculpting so that it becomes malleable enough to be worked with. By putting long, rigidified tensions into words in relation to a new trusted object, the psyche achieves a clay-like atmosphere in which seedling beginnings of the patient's personality start to recover and grow.

Falling Apart/Coming Together and the Catastrophe of the Distinction-Union Structure

Killick (2014) recapitulates Eigen's (1985) distillation of Bion's (1963) thoughts on the birth of the psyche, "locating the core of the individuation process in its earliest phase in a rhythm of falling apart/coming together" (p. 859). She uses Eigen's summary to explore the analytic frame for working with psychotic anxieties, providing us with a relational bridge for the joining technique and the distinction-union structure. "Falling apart/coming together" (Killick, 2014, p. 859) prioritizes the join as a maturational agent for helping the patient to survive and grow from reenactments of early catastrophic experience. Important to note, "falling apart/coming together" (Killick, 2014, p. 859) also constitutes a theoretically focused observing ego (Greenson, 1967; Ormont, 2001) through which the therapist can sense and organize the fragmenting/cohering movements of the session. He is granted a developmental paradigm for a challenging back-and-forth motion.

Killick (2014) underscores that the most important function of the analytic frame is for the analyst to bear the patient's unconscious pain until the patient can naturally allow their core anguish to unfold in the transference. Joins attend to this slow opening up, preserving the defensive needs of the ego. Joining in its syntonic form serves to neutrally build the support structure, though dystonic joins more directly address painful material tangled in the psyche's reversing capacities. Spotnitz (2004) states that ego-dystonic joining "is employed primarily to facilitate the discharge of negative affects" (p. 188). A sub-category of ego-dystonic joins that is of particular relevance is called "falling apart" (p. 188). This type of join is characterized by making fragmenting statements "whether faithfully or in a somewhat exaggerated manner" (p. 188) to a patient verbalizing an escalation of confused thoughts.

Killick (2014) highlights Bion's idea that during early psychical life, the unstructured instinctual pressures of the infant "emerge as 'signs of catastrophe'" (Killick, p. 860). The prime example of this sign is the scream of the infant. Such metaphorical screams in the patient are to be taken both literally and figuratively in the sense that the unanswered cry of the infant continues to communicate through the defensive formations of the patient's character structure. In the case of joining with fragmenting symptoms, Spotnitz (2004) writes that the therapist can say that "he feels unreal and confused too" (p. 188) in response to the patient's dissociative verbalizations. As the therapist "repetitively reflects the pattern blocking emotional release" (p. 188), the degree of confusion the therapist puts across may oscillate in variable proportion of more and less than the patient's splintering statements. The therapist is tasked to make use of the pre-symbolic pressures underlying the patient's communications as they arise in the countertransference. Killick also emphasizes the importance Bion (1963) places on the therapist's capacity to evolve the patient's pre-symbolic functioning. It is through the "falling apart/coming together" (Killick, 2014, p. 859) that the therapist and patient do together that lets the patient be heard and felt understood in a way that the original object ignored or could not bear.

Later in this paper, I identify a depressive expression of the original cry in a patient I call Jack. Echoing back an exaggerated version of his hopelessness constitutes an emotional reception of his early screams. Setting the conditions for the original aggression behind the cries to be experienced and put into words makes room for a new and genuine hope. Similar to a mother soothing the infant who fears dying from his unbound impulses, the therapist can show the infant-as-patient that the agony of his unstructured instinctual pressures is survivable. Creatively participating in the patient's encounters with catastrophe sets a resilient tone. Through falling apart and surviving together, what were once chaotic drives begin to metabolize into a new confidence for coping.

"Falling apart/coming together" (Killick, 2014, p. 859) mediates the distinction-union structure so that it can be used for the work of individuation. Joins help the patient to internalize the therapist under the transitional duress of overwhelming catastrophic feelings. By learning to fall apart and come together in therapy, flexibility toward the rigors of emotional life is increased. Life can be construed as a journey centered in the ongoing work of digesting and linking to the original distinction-union tendency. Viewed this way, the therapist stands in relation to Elkin's (1991) notion of the "primordial other" (p. 125). His theory locates an object preceding focalization in the mother's face and suggests a spiritual essence that the infant perceives in his earliest surroundings. Surviving the relational catastrophe of therapy shows the patient that a genuine connection to a developmental partner is possible, making a new opening for further nurturing figures. The distinction-union structure points to a principle underlying mental life that exceeds the mother as a resource for growth and yet is made available to the patient through the therapist functioning as a maternal container.

Phenomenology of Transference and Resistance

A join circumvents the intellectual smoke and mirrors of the psyche so that extremely painful material can be worked through in the transference. In other words, the intervention helps to make unthinkably awful feelings associated with an original way of relating into something tolerable via a new mode of connecting (Bion, 1963). An effective join links two disconnected elements in the psyche of the patient through a transitional oneness with the therapist. The outcome is a welcoming of the pre-symbolic level of early self and object into the maturational container of the therapy. The therapist identifies a nameless feeling sent through the projective pathways by the patient and then communicates back the underlying message of that feeling. The join fuses the unsaid emotion with its implied idea, and in so doing, resolves resistance to progressive feeling states. This refining of preverbal communication allows for more to be said, and so the join is like a complex probe that explores as it integrates. On the plane of symbol formation, the join structures preverbal cognitions in a new language so that the associated internal object representation transforms in resonance with the real person of the therapist.

The transference distills down the infinite forms of resistance into the finite container of the patient's relationship with his therapist. Yet, what appears small, controllable, and observable quickly becomes large, uncontrollable, and imperceptible. The unruly life force of the defenses inevitably pushes back on this therapeutic union. In the distinction-union context, resistance is defined as what is 'not infinite.' More specifically, consciousness itself is viewed as a rebellion against the infinity of unconsciousness, and the ego is seen as coming into existence via the need to discharge and reverse the tension of its non-being (Eigen, 2020). The transference welcomes these psychic birth tendencies to play out within its field, or rather, the therapist invites the resistance to pushback in relation to their person. Patient and therapist reenact the basic conflict between finite and infinite. The transference-countertransference functions as a resistance to the awareness that there is an unknown potential for change in the session. The aim is to say everything, and yet to do so is never entirely possible as the resistance of the transference-countertransference prohibits a purely conscious relation to the distinction-union structure.

Resistance protects the patient and therapist through the defensive function of the transference-countertransference. As the patient and therapist have a need to recreate what already was, they also work toward what has not yet been said nor occurred. In this way, they are unified in a joint ego struggle with time that pulls them back into the old as experienced as all there is and pushes them forward into the future as *all that can be*. At a given nodal point of the treatment, the therapist may want the patient to move forward, but the patient may feel he has to stay still. In another instance, the patient pushes forward, and the therapist worries it's too soon and resists. And at other times, they both want to advance, and in yet other moments, they trade off by enforcing varying quantities of stillness, forwardness, and backwardness.

On the interpersonal landscape of the transference-countertransference, patient and therapist speak within the delimiting range of their known biographical details. They only say to each other what they can comfortably say to themselves. The subtext of the communications will convey something like *I know this about him, and he knows that about me.* Such projected particulars provide uncanny proof that the past is true in the present. Still, the therapist and patient have not come to therapy to infinitely repeat their assumed trajectory, regardless of the repetitively compulsive truths in their universe. At a given opening in time and somewhere inside of themselves, they will begin to say, *well, this I do not know about him, and that he does not know about me.* As the aperture widens, they will begin to ascribe to Bion's (1970) analytic attitude of "faith in the unknown, unknowable, formless infinite" (p. 31). They will begin to feel that the session is more than just the sum of their current individualities. Their relationship will be permeated by an optimistic atmosphere, and they will sense that how they have known themselves as individuals up to that point is becoming more than what they have ever known. In this union, what is rigidly distinct about their past selves will begin to metabolize in new and unknowable ways and lead to novel distinctions.

Jack

Jack entered treatment with me under what could be called a distinction-union crisis. A shapeless upheaval had been permeating his being since he could remember. Jack's feeling for life was characterized by an infinite number of half-starts and returns to the blank sea of his depression. A thirty-year-old poet, his initial complaint centered on the obsessive anxiety that his poetry writing was going nowhere. After sitting down to do the actual work, Jack's poems soon disintegrated in meaningless distraction, regardless of the initial inspiration. To numb the pain, he drank too much. Not a determined, biologically entranced drinking, but a troubling parody of one. Jack had been in therapy a number of times before, but to no real effect. His prior therapists seemed to keep Jack at a distance that left him feeling judged and just as out of reach. Girlfriends came and went as if they were never there, leaving him to reiterate his 'elevator pitch' for why he is an essentially defective person. Bosses would take chances on him based on his exceptional intelligence and sensitivity, but the job would soon end for one reason or another without any real accomplishment. Petering out patterns characterized the ebb and flow of his life, adding a continual supply of negativity to his reservoir of self-hatred.

Although a writer steeped in the classics, Jack found nothing poetically heroic about his struggle in life. His start and stop failures only offered more evidence for why he was an inherently flawed person who would never live a 'real life.' The territory of these flawed self-feelings became the initial area of our work together. I saw what he called flaws as creative wounds from which to generate meaningful connections to writing and living. I logged this good feeling and entered his rhythm of "falling apart/coming together" (Killick, 2014, p. 159) that appeared to go nowhere. Pretty quickly, I found a place in this cycle of tormenting half-processes. The more he complained, the more I felt him burrowing into my psychic breast. Once he was solidly entrenched, I felt that I could listen to and slowly decode his cries, all the while wondering about his early devastations.

Jack was quite adept at verbally painting the misfortunes of his everyday life into the room. He conveyed an unending hopelessness by reporting strings of vivid details that transported the listener into the world of his humiliating failures. Despite his expressing extreme torment about not making progress in life, I felt a deep comfort generated by the overall gestalt of his stagnation. This comforting stillness created in me the same warm feeling of oneness one gets from holding a napping baby. Union and distinction tendencies tore at each other. As the flow of primitive unity began to embrace us in an amniotic-like affection, a nameless anxiety soon interrupted the good feeling. Before long, Jack would start helplessly shouting into the air that he was the worst sort of person there could be.

When Jack was a kid, his mother drank alcohol and self-righteously yelled. His father, a distinguished academic, intellectually diminished the family woes. As an adult, Jack struggled with finding the right words when faced with the object-audience of the blank page. He felt entirely unable to work with the displeasing mystery of himself. After years of wrestling with intellectualized idealizations of his parents and devaluations of himself, Jack and I have slowly made our way to basic psychodynamic causes and effects of how his mother's rage and alcoholism have had a burdening effect on him.

Jack came to the meaning of these realizations not by the deductive reasoning route. This reframing of relentless self-attack arose from addressing his deeper emotional attitude. Jack needed and needs a symbolic meeting with his depressive and anxious character at the place that it bogs him down in states of self-other confusion. One gets strong impressions of Jack's object pain being embedded at the deepest levels of psyche-soma. These preverbal forms show through the exaggerated state of Jack's muscle size, the rigidity of his speech, and the tattoos of violent imagery that cover his skin. One gets the sense that Jack is speaking at the level of soma in a most primitive way. How to speak back? It is not verbal. The distinct expression of his suffering grows from the whole of his origins, as though sea life from the dark and formless depths, emergent at the two-plane surface.

Bion (1963) throws a strong light of clarity on why psychoanalytic explanations aren't necessarily helpful. Jack's internalization of his mother's hatred is not accurately represented by how interpretations use conscious reasoning and language. The thought form of words that comprise an interpretation is like the language of elements that harmed him, but not emotionally enough like the original harming elements to be helpful. Bion likens this unhelpful aspect of psychoanalytic language to an ideogram that only signs a basic abstraction of what might have happened to Jack. All Jack knows is that he is lonely and wants more friends but can't stand to be around people. A person's slightest ethical inconsistency can throw Jack into a rage. The idea that he is still influenced by a mother who is overbearing and cannot tolerate him having much contact with others shines a mental light and emotionally inflames him at the same time. Jack is together and alone at the same time. Lucky for him and me, we have formed a progressive relationship along this proposed system of original family misery.

In the early phases of treatment, joining was particularly resonant with Jack. One sensed that he was enlivened by the simplicity and directness of joins and experienced a much-needed emotional truth. Concurrently, their nourishment opened up an old craving. When Jack entered my office, his life was a syncopated rhythm of painful and numbing moments. He held the daily causes of this pain at an intellectual distance and consequently suffered from an overpressurized foreground. Joins had a neutralizing effect on the ache and throb of this distancing-pressurizing rhythm. Having had to run from his raging alcoholic mother and be pacified by a remote and literary father, the double layering found in ego-dystonic joins landed finely with Jack. In fact, the line between syntonic and dystonic blurred—the agreeable and disagreeable harmonizing—allowing him to develop a taste for being accepted in his unacceptable state of being. Jack told me that the first time I agreed with his self-diagnosis of incurable despair and reiterated that he was in fact a hopeless case, he experienced an immense relief. He could be as he was in therapy.

I felt Jack's communication of hopelessness to be an aggressive act in and of itself. His clever use of language hid this fact. Still, one could hear the angry essence permeating his phrases as a variation of crying, "You're not helping me! You're not helping me!" The attitude of being hopeless functioned as what Bion (1957) calls a *bizarre object*. The negative feelings toward the object were distorted into a depressed sense of his future, blurring the unsupportive object representation with an impoverished self-concept. Spotnitz (2004) frames this as the egotization of the object field, and its de-egotization can take priority in the beginning stages of treatment. For the purposes of this paper and understanding how these defensive-developmental formations play out in the session, I will reify the underlying axis of reversal in order to show how the psyche blends ego and object. Eigen stresses this fusing tendency alongside its ripping apart counterpart as a function of the distinction-union structure. By virtue of the transference, the join has a paradoxical fission effect in that while it separates out the patient from the parent object, it brings the patient and therapist closer together in the original dynamic. The warded-off aggressive element and the associated early object spin apart, so that the ego emerges as though separated out in a centrifuge. Closer and closer to each other, disowned feelings of the ego come in clearer and in closer relation to the therapist. The obfuscating representation slowly transforms through a therapist who begins to hear what the ego cannot say. One soon hears, "Help me! Help me!" And spinning even faster, "You can't help me because I am attached to being un-helpable!" Cry! Cry! Underneath it all is the cacophonous cry symphony of the infant who was left alone far too long with his impulses. In the background is the original caregiver who just couldn't or wouldn't get it right. And like this first maternal figure, the therapist is experienced as an object who can handle distorted aggression only. One sees just how actual Jack's internal objects really are as they experience the passive aggressive complaints that leave him bottling up way too much.

In the session following my first join of Jack's hopelessness, I upped the ante when he made a similar declaration of despair and replied, "Indeed, one of the most hopeless cases ever." Spotnitz (2004) calls this style of ego-dystonic joining "echoing the ego" (p. 189). And to this cruel echo, Jack did not take it so kindly. As his tone changed, I wondered what would come of his dormant object anger as it quickly pushed out of his ego, widening and strengthening his stance toward my person. I shoved my defensive urge to the side and silently listened to his angry refutations of being the most hopeless case ever. One could almost taste a newly structured aggression blooming my way. *Was it me who was unable to help him? How come I hadn't been helpful yet? Did I have a plan? There wasn't time to waste. He wanted effective therapy right now.* Working with ego-dystonic joins calls upon the therapist to stay emotionally present to the preverbal field, yet only submerge into the emotion enough so as to be able to make use of the induced feeling. Detecting and working with the atmospheric fluctuations in the session environment likens to painting the motions of a tree reflected in moving water in order to glimpse concealed aspects of the actual tree (Bion, 1965). By learning to feel the variable intensities in a solidly receptive way, a working readiness emerges to join with the emotion that unconsciously moves the patient's psyche.

At the root of a syntonic join is the simple and easily digestible communication to the patient that the therapist agrees with him. The delicately textured agreement "informs the patient that it is acceptable to entertain both his resistant attitudes and the unneutralized aggressive and libidinal feelings which they defend against" (Margolis, 1983/1994, p. 214). In response to Jack's call for effective therapy, I asked how I could help. He paused and began to bitterly counter-argue that all was lost as too much time had passed. A feeling of intensive fragility shot through his words. After making a gentle concession, I joined him in a long, solemn quiet.

We entered a paradoxical period of the treatment that I privately framed as *mobile timelessness*. A current of progress had opened that led him to make positive concrete actions in his professional and romantic life, as well as a stagnating counterpoint of getting more in touch with his lack of confidence. Jack and I swirled from session to session in an entropic feeling of changelessness, tasting the omnipotent flavor of being trapped in the cozy depths of infantile depression. In his outside life, Jack began to push the boulder over the top of the hill and onward, while in the clinical realm, the Sisyphusian rock snowballed us backward into one hopeless being. This mythical place was echoed in his actual studio apartment, where he drank and mourned the perpetual gaining and losing of himself. The treatment proceeded to a syncopation of emotional impotence with agency, with the former decreasing and the latter growing stronger and stronger.

Eigen (2011) illustrates a variation of distinction-union through Winnicott's *primary aloneness* (1992). The paradox of separateness-togetherness is brought to life by the infant who begins to achieve a capacity to be alone from spending time with a mother who can indirectly support his sense of being. The world takes on a nourishing feel as the external perception of the object blends as environmentally present to the internal self. The outcome is a sense that one's surroundings are neutral and welcome the self to fill it. The patient wounded at this phase of relating to the world-as-self, develops a lack of psychic insulation around their personality's sensors. This primary wounding of the distinction-union structure manifests through the chronic and vague feeling that the world as a whole is hostile and will either push the ego away or suck it into oblivion. Unity and distinctness are both experienced as equally dangerous.

Jack's initial sessions were frequently punctuated with outbursts of self-hatred. The lack of an early nurturing presence reconstituted in the consulting room and infused my being with a chaotic aloneness. His loud blasts of loneliness painted an isolated foreground in our meetings, invoking the feeling that I was nothing more than an aloof and obstinate background. Still, the inherent waiting and quiet openness of therapy allow for a "blank horizon that encompasses and subtends all psychic figures" (Eigen, 2004, p. 308), suggesting a new possibility for the background object. With Jack, I found myself paying particularly close attention to a bi-planular experience, helping me to sense and formulate his volatile emotions as they emerged. And most importantly, I noted his need for basic support that quietly floated behind the scenes. Foreground-background can be viewed as perceptual fields that are a function of the distinction-union structure. At the intervening level, the relational dynamic of these two planes of self and object correspond to an optimism embedded in the therapy dyad.

A poignant lonesomeness seemed to invite me into a closer relationship with Jack's blank horizon. While Jack presented with the nebulous impression of being chaotically alone and hopeless, I did not experience him cemented as such. In fact, I felt great hope in his willingness to tolerate this solitude with me and trust that whatever the coldly-aloof-I represented for him was for a purpose and was in fact part of a transitional period. By announcing his hopelessness back to him from the cradle of my therapist position, the background presence of absence seemed to rush forward to meet him in the foreground of his aloneness as a newly articulated intimacy. The tone of Jack's response was one of feeling reached on an emotional level that was finally tangible. His preceding therapist would ply him with sweet tea as she gave him spiritual advice on his drinking, as if to actively fill in the hole of this primary absence. Instead, I fed Jack the despairing sustenance of his origins in a finely granulated form. I had to build up this state of emotional resonance by slowly getting to know and process down all that his morose aggression stimulated in me. By listening over a course of many months, I became familiar enough with my internal desolate responses so that I felt at home with Jack's unbearable isolation. The reciprocal value of this aloneness eventually swapped the distinct experience of being abandoned for one of being unified and together in that abandonment. The *join* had inaugurated a oneness-aloneness.

While I did not feel an ameliorating saccharine urge toward Jack, I could understand how his previous therapist had wanted to pacify his antagonistic despondency with sweetness. Jack sounded a jarring music of complex and contradictory feelings. I felt a troubling love for his emptiness in the face of his loud-voiced righteousness and an equally unsettling aggressiveness in response to his sadly weaponized muscles. I was particularly mystified by a carefree guilt that he assigned to my role as his helper. I felt that I could abruptly walk away from him and no one would care, and at the same time, a warm pulsation drew me into his maudlin neediness in such a way that I felt that there was no one more important than him. Regardless of these torrents of strong emotion, I knew that I had to contain any intense counter-reactions to fix his problems. Jack made it clear that advice was equivalent to a bulldozer and alcohol was the numbing agent he used to cover up his lack of self-confidence. What I could do was simply hold back any impulse to instantly repair and instead make a psychic clearing for him to just be. I gave Jack the room to talk endlessly about the terrifying stories that are the most twisted occurrences of human life and regularly made their way into his family's dinnertime discussions. It was as though he needed to vomit up the endless meals of poisoned horror that filled his childhood and that he continually fed himself on a nightly basis. He poured forth, and I listened.

The unutterable haunted Jack precisely for the reason that he was raised with such a large amount of talk about the horrible things in life. Exploration of his shouts soon led to miserable tales of the latest exploits of his acting-out family members. I found myself joining him in the unbearable feelings of these narratives and reflecting his morbid intellectual attitude, but in a slightly higher optimistic register. A Spotnitzian join delivers what Bion (1963) calls a "dynamic relationship between container and contained" (p. 3). The patient is invited to process the painful feelings that lie underneath the defense and do so within the comfort of knowing that the therapist is glimpsing what it is like to need to block a given painful feeling but make room for it anyway. As one joins the patient, one can feel the harsh force of the patient's defensive frustration almost soften and dissolve atop the therapist's willingness to simultaneously feel and psychically attend to a defense giving way to raw emotion.

Jack's initial complaint in therapy was that he was wasting his life and couldn't do a thing about it. When Jack initially complained of his immobilizing agonies, I would feel a hopelessly stuck silence scream up inside of me. Asking him why I should help a hopeless case would elicit an aggressive challenge from him that would spark both of us into related attunement. The emptiness as it existed between us would fill with an energizing anger—that just seconds before—drained vital feeling from our shared space. The outcome was a transmuting of the emotional deafness of the object, as it had been influencing us up to that point. The layered static of Jack's unheard feelings seemed to dissipate, and I could hear what he was actually wanting and needing.

As Jack's shouts shoved through miserable family tales and then on to endless complaints of drowning in a bottle of alcohol, one could keenly hear the depressive's self-criticisms as indirect (albeit unconscious and so unknown) criticisms of the object (Freud, 1917). He seemed to be literally drinking alcohol as a weapon against his inner mother. We can wonder how his mother psychologically restrained Jack as an infant from directly expressing his aggression. Was it simply by virtue of not being able to receive the force and contain it, or was it a more active form of pushing back on his frustration? Also, why was Jack's mother unable to receive and metabolize his instinctual cries in a manner that would have helped the pair grow? These questions entered the transference-countertransference as a touchstone of defensive and emotional transformation.

The join links patient and therapist at the most primitive level and invites the long-ignored aggression to speak out into the world. Consequently, the intervention allows for attachment to a feeding and genuinely helpful object. The aggression is not merely mechanically released but done so on terms sensitive to the patient's need to verbally bond with the therapist. Positive and negative aspects alternate from moment to moment. Spotnitz (2004) quotes Balint's (1959) feeling-image of a therapist "merging as completely as possible into the friendly expanses surrounding the patient" (p. 143). It is this type of object-audience that speaks to the patient's deepest craving for love and lets him "talk out his painful feelings with the least strain on his vulnerable ego" (Spotnitz, p. 143). Jack ranted and raved for hours, and I was there to link to it and help open up its flow. The fresh currents of language came across as an anti-alcohol of sorts. The narcissistic transference freed his rage and softened the drinking war against the void-mother inside.

A join is momentary, yet its effects can contribute to a lasting therapeutic relationship. The intervention has helped Jack and I come into a "falling apart/coming together" (Killick, 2014, p. 859) growth tapestry. New distinctions and productive unions have been woven along the way. At present, the feeling that Jack has for wasting his life comes and goes in intensity. Its sensation of draining vital energy for living has found a transformational home in our therapy. Five years into the work, Jack and I have learned to go through cycles of hope and hopelessness in progressively intimate ways. Rather than being an inarguable fact of reality, hopelessness is digested into a psychic experience that can be thought, felt, and talked about.

Jack and I have become active partners in exploring what he does to sabotage his professional, social, and romantic efforts. Mutually analyzing his behavior for efficacy currently fills our sessions. When I first met Jack, he was unable to speak about his feelings toward other people and would instead shout and endlessly complain. He is now learning to articulate his aggression toward me as he wrestles with his self-hatred in his more generalized transferences in work and love situations. We collaboratively sift through the distancing messages he sends to individuals and groups in question. More and more, he shares in the active roles of societal living. The distinction of his depressive isolation fades as a varied communal unity enlivens his weekdays and weekends. And still, there are further depths to probe, memories to drudge up, turn over, and process through. His depressive anger still rises, inducing counter-impatience in me. By patiently sensing these pulsations of irritation, I am able to utilize the induced tension as an awakening agent that slowly directs my attention to what is not being said. As I accompany Jack on the unfolding waves of his story, I have found it critical to honor the back-and-forth rhythm of his capacity for insight. Joins help to soften the returns to a needed baseline of self-dissonance.

In a recent session, the sound of Jack's speech came in louder than usual, making the non-meaning of his words unusually harsh to my ears. I wondered if a crucial opening was showing itself in the bitterness that came to him way too young. Had we reached the meeting point where hope and hopelessness split inside? Exploring the quality of his voice while steadying the reactive tension in mine helped him talk about his mother's early attitude of intolerance toward him. On the one hand, Jack wants more for himself, more of himself. He wants to do things that are effective and bring satisfaction. And he is doing so. His life is getting better and better. The freeing of old aggression is charging the life drive with a new passion for goal-directed tasks. And on the other hand, he is wedded to his internal mother who wants him to do nothing more than skirt by and be down on himself. The depressive aggression is plain. Still, an ever-emerging distinction struggles to be born in the wake of Jack's muted cries. Like Michelangelo's sculptures, we are constantly returning to the wombstone of our preverbal love and hate.

Joins have cycled in and out of the session picture. But now, when I join Jack's hopelessness, he may heartily laugh. This playful gush of life force is palpable and indicates a shifting at the depths of resistance. Jack and I are learning to breathe in and nourish from hope together, as though fresh air and food are co-produced from our relationship's ambiance. By letting hopelessness just be a given, it tends to resolve into a good feeling for what the session may bring. Jack has started to entertain mourning the absence of support that permeated his childhood years. By acknowledging this lack, he can further delve into the verbal art of clarifying his feelings with me and do more than just push others away. We are aroused to a disruptive oneness. Waiting at a darkened crossroads, we are full of an anticipation that highlights how we have learned to usefully fall apart and come together. One suffers the need to fall apart to move forward, to come together again and then alight in a new individuating form, and once more survive the hopeless fall.

Bibliography

Balint, M. (1959). Regression in the analytic situation. In *Thrills and regression* (pp. 91–100). International University Press.

Bion, W.F. (1957). Differentiation of the psychotic from the non-psychotic. *International Journal of Psychoanalysis, 38*, 206–275.

Bion, W.F. (1963). *The elements of psychoanalysis* (pp. 28–32). London: William Heinemann Medical Books Limited.

Bion, W.F. (1970). *Attention and interpretation*. Tavistock.

Eigen, M. (1985). Toward Bion's starting point: Between catastrophe and faith. *International Journal of Psycho-Analysis, 66* (3), 321–330.

Eigen, M. (2004). *The psychotic core*. Karnac Books.

Eigen, M. (2011). *Contact with the depths*. Karnac Books.

Eigen, M. (2020, Oct. 20). *Bion's A Memoir of the Future Seminar*. New York, Zoom.

Elkin, H. & Stern, M. (1991). Toward a Freud-Jung reconciliation. In K. Gibson, D. Lathrop, & E.M. Stern (Eds.), *Carl Jung and soul psychology* (pp. 116–130). Routledge.

Freud, S. (1917). Mourning and melancholia. In *The standard edition of the complete psychological works of Sigmund Freud, volume XIV (1914–1916): On the history of the psycho-analytic movement, papers on metapsychology and other works* (J. Strachey, Trans.) (pp. 243–258). London: The Hogarth Press and The Institute Of Psycho-Analysis.

Greenson, R. (1967). *The technique and practice of psychoanalysis*. International University Press.

Killick, K. (2014). Soundless screaming: Psychotic anxiety and analytic containment. In E. Kiehl (Ed.), *In 100 years on: Origins, innovations and controversies. Proceedings of the 19th congress of the international association for analytical psychology* (pp. 859–866). Daimon Verlag.

Margolis, B. (1994). Joining, mirroring, psychological reflection: Terminology, definitions, theoretical considerations. In Selected papers on modern psychoanalysis: Benjamin D. Margolis. *Modern Psychoanalysis, 19*(2), 211–225. (Original work published in 1983)

Ormont, L. (2001). Cultivating the observing ego in the group setting. (L.B. Furgeri Ed.) In *The technique of group treatment: The collected papers of Louis R. Ormont, Ph.D. Louis R. Ormont, Ph.D.* Create Space Publishing.

Spotnitz, H. (1976). *Psychotherapy of preoedipal conditions: Schizophrenia and other severe character disorders.* Jason Aronson Inc.

Spotnitz, H. (2004). *Modern psychoanalysis of the schizophrenic patient: Theory of the technique.* YBK Publishers.

Winnicott, D.W. (1992). *Psychoanalytic explorations.* Harvard University Press.

Chapter 5

Nomad to No-Mad – Welcoming the Psychotic Core

The Primary Process Psychoanalysis of Michael Eigen

Loray Daws

> *G-bless the Open Broken.*
>
> Eigen, personal correspondence, June 25, 2023.

Introduction

Growing into life from being unwanted, unwelcomed, and symbiotically trau-matized speaks to Eigen's *primary process psychoanalysis*.[1] Eigen's writing-as-connecting scaffolds the sensibilities needed to accompany the psyche in returning (an immersing-emerging dialectic) to its indestructible generative core (1973, 1993, 1995, 1996, 1998, 2006b), thereby engaging in articulating the primal lan-guage of union-distinction pressures in the area of the basic fault. In so doing, *primary process psychoanalysis* has as its aim the 'revivifying' of the union-distinction body-affect-thinking potentialities and storms within a *dyad* held by a unique *rhythm of faith*, while remaining steadfast in the importance of learning 'from' experience. Eigen's primary process writing as an emotional grid informs my understanding and approach to working with analysands in need of an organ-izing experience (Eigen, 1986, Hedges, 1994a&b), those souls brutalized by both lack (privation and deprivation) and exposure to Winnicott's Z-dimension, that is, by petrification, impingement, engulfment, and appropriation. The paper will aim to evoke Eigen's *welcoming primary process psychoanalysis*, the language of Virgil, in working with both psychotic and deeply schizoid patients through a close reading of '*A Basic Rhythm*' (2002) and '*Tears of Pain and Beauty: Mixed Voices*'[2] (2011) interspersed with three case vignettes as psychoanalytic *bricolage*.

The Bare-Life Environment of Moral Violence

A stanza from the Grande Chartreuse[3] (circa 1850), by Matthew Arnold, reverber-ates through the analytic echo chamber as I listen to Sam and Simon,

> Wandering between two worlds, one dead,
> The Other powerless to be born
> With nowhere to rest my head

DOI: 10.4324/9781003322993-5

Whereas Sam is unkept, disheveled, enraged, and haunted-looking, Simon seems unnaturally quiet, barely present in such a way that I, similar to a mother straining to hear if her firstborn is breathing and fearing a crib death (an initial psychic signifier indeed), remained concerned for his fragile aliveness. Two very different men barely surviving in the world: gentle souls "ravaged," "wrecked," "gutted," "deadened," and "murdered" by maternal absence, paternal violence, and cultural indifference. Epistemic and ontological insecurity meets D.W. Winnicott's *moral sin*, the unthinkable catastrophe when one seeps into another's core[4] and 'steals him from himself.' Such psychic experiences, '*acts of psyche intrusion and theft*,' wherein the autochthonous I is either robbed from developing its own idiom or unable to save/salvage the ego from maternal madness or lack, frequently culminate in unlived and unhoused lives (in Eigen, 1996, p. 81).

What kind of inner and outer psychological environments were Simon and Sam exposed to? Simon frequently reflects on his *Gehenna experience*, being bound (Akedah) by immense hatred and misunderstanding of both his earthly *and* heavenly family. Sam reflects on his continual need to flee from the world after internalizing the continuous, rather brutalizing sadomasochistic enactment between his parents – parents felt to "lose their minds." Mothers and fathers of mindlessness are instinctually driven reactors able to dissolve and (seemingly) reconstitute their ego capacities at will. Periods of quiet, functional togetherness *suddenly* turned upside down, something to be escaped. Whereas Sam "fell out of the world" at the tender age of six,

> I saw the Tundra, and I wish I could just walk there and disappear, but I suddenly knew they would also get me there too ... I fell out of the world and spent my whole life trying to fall back into it.

Simon looked up at the heavens and gave his soul to G-d, hoping to be transformed into his bride – both desert children and adults – true *Orphans of the Real*[5] (Grotstein, in Allen & Collins, 1996).

The Return of Ferenczi's and Eigen's *Unwelcome Child* and His *Death Instinct* – The House of Nauseating Recurrence

It is an unimaginable catastrophe to live in or between two worlds, one characterized by *deadness* and the other unable to *support rebirth*. Children named but not seen, mirrored, or heard. Children handled but never tenderly held. As mentioned, both Simon and Sam describe family life limed by sadomasochistic tragedies – unthinkable and unmitigated hatred, rage, immense fright, and shock traumas – Eigen's *disaster anxieties* (1996) abound. Simon, the youngest of four children, struggles to recall childhood memories as psychological survival necessitates pre-oedipal mental-spiritual T-ego inflation (Perry's *compensatory overblown self-image, 1974)* – a psyche exposed to a devaluing mother and a menacing, mocking, dangerous, violent, and intoxicated earth father. Solace was initially sought in drug use, and after an initial close-to break-down moment, Simon turned[6] to the Christian faith after hearing Jesus whispering salvation. Tragically and frighteningly similar to the case of the great Judge Schreber, it was not long before symbiotic trauma and chronic alcoholism exposed his "little person" to an archetypally destructive homicidal flood-sending mother-father G-d during a significant break-down. Barely surviving three suicide attempts that spanned over nearly a decade after being harassed by the spirits, Satan, Jesus, and God, "They tried to kill me, murder me, they stoned my soul (soul murder)," Simon settled on a very constricted and isolated life and worked with his "faith-grief and disappointment-trauma" in analysis, his splendid isolation.

In contrast, after living on the streets for nearly a decade, following an acrimonious divorce where he was "dismissed from being a husband and father," Sam entered analysis as a last-ditch effort, as euthanasia was unavailable to him.[7] Neglected, profoundly lonely, isolated, and enraged by societal injustices, Sam flooded his initial sessions (twice weekly for the first four years) with rage and immense resentment, reminiscent of Eigen's beautiful concept of *injury rage*. Rage as protection, as psychic skin, and as a talisman to re-injury permeated all human contact, and silent moments were only possible through obsessive smoking, Sam's "living in a cloud of smoke," a particular psychic envelope negotiating both claustro-agoraphobic stresses and strains.

Both analysands remind of the complex relationship between *disaster anxiety* and *chronic broken-down-ness*, "Still, there is more chronic broken-down-ness or areas of break-down, which *never seem to heal*, which simmer and seep in *insidiously stifling ways*" (Eigen, 2001, p. 24–) (italics added). *Welcoming* such chronic areas of broken-down-ness remains central to Eigen's *primary process* psychoanalytic work, especially the *rhythm of faith* conceptualization. In spite of "psychoanalytic faith," Eigen writes,

> It is unclear to what extent the psyche can regenerate itself or what that might mean. Psychoanalysts, like prophets, refer to another chance at new beginnings. *In the present paper this does not mean leaving trauma behind. The latter is one term in a larger rhythm.* Psychoanalytic writers have made important contributions to the sense of this rhythm, the movement between *blockage and flow, trauma and new beginnings.* (2002, p. 722) (italics added)

Such work is especially evident in *Coming Through the Whirlwind* (1992), the *Psychotic Core* (1986), *Damaged Bonds*[8] (2001), *Toxic Nourishment* (1999), and *Madness and Murder* (2010), to name but a few. Eigen's writing furnishes an immensely helpful and contextual understanding of being unwanted and the impact disaster anxiety can have on our being-alive-feeling dead rhythms, as well as the impacts as found in *living between worlds*, i.e., damaged dreamwork, psychic deadness, mindlessness [Eigen's triad], self-nulling tendencies, agony X, and suicide. Disaster anxiety, frequently referred to as annihilation anxiety, impacts the individual's psychological birth and his growing ability (if not autochthonous right) to transcend the vagaries of object-relating fallout beyond its initial organizing necessity and usefulness. Simon and Sam, characterized by a symbiotic-psychotic and schizoid core, respectively, reflect the psyche's valiant efforts to ward off Eigen's disaster anxiety and exposure to immense fright. More specifically, Eigen's work maps a shock (or shocks) that infinitizes in the negative (negative valence, anti-meaning, and anti-apparatus), finding a psyche desperately working on further fright and fragmentation, even preventing *synthesis* of various kinds, most notably of the *frightening super-ego*,[9] as the synthesis[10] may destroy the psyche's going-on-being. As previously written and based on the work of *Damaged Bonds* and *Toxic Nourishment* (Daws, 2023, p. 97),

> Similar to the work on the psychotic self (Eigen, 1986), the deadened self (1996), as well as Shengold's *Soul Murder* (1999, 2011), the personality may have to contend with a most sudden kind of mind-body fright. The sudden fright (terror, shock, panic) may also, unthinkably so, be subject to repetition. The person born into a frightened or frightening world is primarily subject to a world characterized by the absence of *alpha functioning* and subject to the *Omega function.* (Williams, 1999; Daws, 2006)

Being exposed to an *Omega nucleus and process* finds a personality either collapsed or congealed around the experience of fright and attack, profoundly impacting the psyche's ability to 'alpha' betize experience. Given the lack of background support[11] and following not only the logic of the unconscious as infinite sets (i.e., Matte-Blanco), Eigen's deep Jungian felt[12] sense serves as a link to the collective unconscious in his work on the *Psychotic Core* (1986). That is, given the Omega nucleus, the *Idea of the Father and Mother* may become infinitized in the negative: "Personality is stifled by this terror. Abrupt, alarming moments become an *Eternal Idea, Eternal Reality*, although the face on everyone's fright is different" (Eigen, 2001, p. 25). In the language of Elkin (1958, 1966, 1972), the individual may fall back, or be unable to move from, an inner experience characterized by the mental-spiritual torment (snuff-out primordial conscious, primordial doubt, primordial anxiety) as found in the Diabolical Mother-Father and Frightened Child Complex desperately in search of the Divine Mother and Child constellation (Elkin, 1958, 1972; Eigen, 1986, 1999, 2001, 2011).

From Bion's perspective, a malignant, tyrannical, ego-destructive super-ego (intolerant object terrifying super-ego) (2002, p. 40) becomes throughout time and space, in the conscious-unconscious, the personal and collective unconscious, a force that keeps on destroying long after it has destroyed. Ontological and epistemic violence meets archetypal anti-life figures, i.e., destroyers of form, time, and life as we experience it.[13] Although conceptualized from another theory of mind, the work of Neville Symington (2019) may also support the thinking here; the lack of a *life-giver* may be reflected in the presence of the obstructive object in its various forms and functions, i.e., as a petrifier, intensifier, and liquefier. In archetypal language and logic, the latter may be found in conscious representations, i.e., in the form of mythical figures and sagas such as Medusa, the Great Flood, and much more. How to survive being exposed to such psychic brutality, or, as Simon put it, "To be stoned to my soul"? Parental stonings (β-element flooding), similar to Medusa, function as signifiers of petrification, ushering in the language of hardening-liquefying of psyche, the gnashing of teeth, and unknown fright, damaging alpha functioning. Petrification and the stoning of the soul are also indicative of exposure to the impervious object overflowing with projection – the domain of disorganized attachments or, in Grotstein's[14] rich conceptualizations (2000), the world of chimerical monsters and rogue subjective objects. There is no acting in good faith or in good spirit: "Why are people so *mean*-spirited – where is the love?" frequently articulated by Sam in despairing moments.

Given the lack of parental and societal containers (limited ego-coverage), the psyche may also come to be overexposed to the deep spiritual and archetypal unconscious, an unconscious filled with uncanny affects able to destroy the novitiate. Eigen teaches in volumes such as *The Psychotic Core* (1986), *Flames from the Unconscious: Trauma, Madness, and Faith* (2009), and *Contact with the Depths* (2011) that contact with the G-d depths may be too great for a psyche. Unprotected contact, if not fusion with the depths, may not only induce T-ego inflation but may eclipse the autochthonous I, i.e., similar to Freud's notion of the shadow of the object that falls on the ego, the energies contained in archetypal patterns may fall on the personal unconscious, the body ego and T-ego,[15] threatening the individual with various forms of *traumatic non-existence*. The pre-psychotic ego faces twin threats – from within and without – and primordial anxiety will mount in multiple ways; Freudian anxiety finds the ego being either flooded by Id pressure or colonized and shackled by a primitive super-ego. Jungian psychology adds by finding the ego either inflated by archetypal energy (manic like the savior, King, or God) or swamped/subsumed by an archetype. Differently stated, the symbiotically traumatized self can fall under the spell of being *possessed and cursed*[16] (the demonic), i.e., ego possession, super-ego possession, id possession, archetypal possession, and more. Eigen adds conceptual clarity to the current thinking when he writes,

[Eigen reflecting on the undue burden on the ego for psychosis] If psychosis occurred, it must have *befallen unconscious and conscious processes*. The very ground through which the ego emerges and must look to for support also undergoes deformations in psychosis. Jung's insight that deep unconscious processes appear destructive in response to an overly narrow conscious ego is an important truth. But the ego is restrictive, also because of the *warped foundation of which it is part*. In other words, *conscious and unconscious functions are part of the same fabric, and in psychosis, deformations spread through both, reciprocally or in a vicious circle. To place the burden of blame (causality) on either consciousness or the deep unconscious is too simple*. (1986, p. 60) (italics added)

Ontological Anxiety and the Existence-Non-Existence Dialectic: Disaster Anxiety Fallout and the Presence of Disaster Affects

Eigen's disaster anxiety and R.D. Laing's various forms of ontological anxiety serve as a glimpse into symbiotic and ontological trauma. Both Eigen and Laing, if not Bion (1958, 1959), Winnicott (1945, 1953, 1955, 1958, 1965, 1967, 1969, 1971, 1974, 1975, 1984, 1988), Perry (1974), Rogers (2006), Scheshye (1951a&b), and Little (1981), to name a few, write on the sense of non-existence that could "metastasize" into psychosis and its many variations. Struggling to exist and come into being can indirectly be found in psychological phenomena such as engulfment, implosion, petrification, or depersonalization. It should be mentioned that although the individuals discussed here have been exposed to either unimaginable psychological brutalities and/or physicochemical vagaries of which a sense of self is struggling *to be*, I am not referring to *a weak ego per se*, ala Sullivan's critique of the concept of a so-called weak ego in psychoanalytic terminology (1953), but rather that the analysands speak from a region that, in Elkin's logic (1958, 1972), belongs to the area of the mental-spiritual,[17] the *world before cause and effect* (the world of natural values) took hold or could be used in ways most conducive to neurotic adaptation (*being-able-to-be*[18] *before being-allowed-to-be, or existence precedes essence*). The psyche may be exposed to various mental-spiritual dramas attempting to articulate the fundamental experience of being impinged, attacked, and flooded if not exposed to mental-spiritual-body ego extinction. It is not that further development also did not occur; that would be an unreasonable assumption and is skillfully articulated by Eigen's *psychotic self* (1986), Vamik Volkan's concept of *the infantile psychotic self* (1995), and Peter L. Giovacchini's *Schizophrenia and primitive mental states-structural collapse and creativity* (1997). It can instead be held that deformations in the *mystical pre-Oedipal phase* of development may have unique psychological and developmental fallout and creative use of the natural order of pre-Oedipal, Oedipal, and post-Oedipal developmental demands.[19] Even for many able to move through the developmental realities to be discussed and found in Elkin's 1958 and 1972 work, Eigen rightly argues that none of our primordial experience is ever lost[20] and may become part of our overall psyche-tapestry in various forms with varying degrees of psychic familiarity, danger, and creative use.

To return to both Eigen, Elkin, and Laing, and as will be related to the *ideal mothering qualities* of Elkin in a later section, a person exposed to ontological trauma finds an inner world characterized by engulfment fears, having to cope with implosion-explosion dramas, injury rage, petrification, and Eigen's *deadening triad* (i.e., stupor-hallucinosis-megalomania). Concerning engulfment fears, the ontologically traumatized individual may feel under siege even in a mundane conversation to the extent that simply losing an argument represents the extinction of their identity (imploding of identity),

(Sam) I argue, fight, to keep alive- its not that the opinion of the other is not important, its more I have to protect mine as I have been thinking on it for years.

My arrogance goes so far as to say they are stupid and non-thinking ... I actually remember now my father punching his fists and saying that is it, the end, no discussion, it was just his thoughts, always overriding me!

Engulfment could also imply the horrifying fusion, the "complete *loss of being* by absorption *into the other person*" (Laing, in Ruitenbeek, 1962, p. 48) (italics mine), reminiscent of Melanie Klein's understanding of claustrophobia and the claustrum.[21] Contact per se *is* frightening. Given the symbiotic-psychotic trauma, the psychoanalytic gaze itself can evoke engulfment fears; engulfment is felt as a risk that being understood (thus grasped and comprehended), being loved, and being seen will imply appropriation and the loss of selfhood. To preserve a sense of self or identity, the ontologically traumatized may prefer splendid isolation, a desperate safeguard against absorption (symbiotic-psychotic) or appropriation (schizoid). There remains no safe third, no safe transitional relatedness able to support the development and needed experience of the object objectively perceived. The expectant need to be understood, so important in psychoanalysis, may prove paradoxically fatal,

> To be understood correctly is to be engulfed, to be enclosed, swallowed up, drowned, eaten up, smother, stifled in or by another person's supposed all-embracing comprehension. It is lonely and painful to be always misunderstood, but there is at least from this point of view a measure of safety in isolation. (Laing, in Ruitenbeek, 1962, p. 48)

Combined with petrification,[22]

> one has the feeling of having been transformed *into an object*, literally *turned to stone*.[23] Conversely, in this state, one also harbors the irrational belief that they can turn others into objects, thus symbolically eliminating those by whom they feel depersonalized. (Laing, in Ruitenbeek, 1962, p. 50)

It is not only staring at Medusa but suddenly becoming her and stoning the world! The world is dangerous – I am dangerous.

Concerning 'implosion,' Laing relies on the Winnicottian notion of the *impingement of reality* – reality as a persecutor, gutting and hollowing out the person. "Impingement does not convey, however, the full terror of the experience of the world as liable at any moment to *crash in an obliterate all identity, as a gas will rush in and obliterate a vacuum*" (Laing, in Ruitenbeek, 1962, p. 49). These experiences can be represented by various images, articulating the terror of contact, impingement, and appropriation;

> There are many images used to describe related ways in which identity is threatened which may be mentioned here, as closely related to the dread of engulfment, e.g. being buried, being drowned, being caught and dragged down into quicksand. The image *of fire recurs repeatedly*. Fire[24] may be the uncertain

flickering of the individual's own inner aliveness. It may be a destructive alien power which will devastate him.[25] Some psychotics say in the acute phase that they are on fire, that their bodies are being burned up.[26] A patient describes himself as cold and dry. Yet he dreads any warmth or wet. He will be engulfed by the fire or the water, and, either way be destroyed. (Laing, in Ruitenbeek, 1962, p. 49)

According to Simon,

The Holies took over, threaten me with fire, the pit, with Gehenna[27] – *You will be burned! You will be bombed*! ... This kind of attack served as the reason for my suicides.... You know it's frightening ... God can override my thinking, override my tongue, a puppet.... a horror ... a horror with people too, I deteriorate quickly with people too!

Desecration, Thingifying, and Resurrection – Surviving Areas of Extreme Destruction of Mind

Eigen's works on *Psychic Deadness* (1996), *Toxic Nourishment* (1999), *Damaged Bonds* (2001), *Feeling Matters* (2007), *Emotional Storm* (2005), and *The Birth of Experience* (2014a) map the various ways moral violence may attack both meaning and the very equipment needed to support meaning. *Moral violence* may contain violence to the gathering of experience needed for growth, attack time and space, rely on the overuse of causality (both parataxic and syntaxic), and nourish restrictive definitions,[28] all culminating in Eigen's *deadening triad* (stupor-hallucinosis-megalomania). The deadening triad can be viewed as attempts to undo meaning, thereby ridding the self of the no-thing, a reflection of being subject to intrapsychic and interpersonal *thingification*, in turn, *thingifying* self and other (Laing's description of the fear of being controlled and fear of controlling, the negative transference). Written previously (Daws, 2023), for Eigen, in stupor, the analysand rids himself of the no-thing, filling it with numbness, versus cultivating a state of creative emptiness, a creative waiting.[29] In hallucinosis (the lie, gaslighting, and psychic forms of interrogation),[30,31] there is an evacuation of self and object representations that could have stood for thinking and reverie. In megalomania, "one does not find a transformative high, the high of moment of revelation, revealment or releasement, but of arrogance, a closing of learning from experience, the use of self and Other as a thing in themselves" (Daws, 2023, p. 85).

In essence, for both Eigen and Bion, cultivating a psychoanalytic attitude of 'no-thing'[32] serves as a foundation to protect the injured psyche from the impact of the *negative grid functioning* – Bion's *Catastrophe Machine* (in Eigen, 1998, p. 199). Omega function fallout permeates ontological trauma, hardening the psychic arteries in Eigen's language, finding the propensity to concretize, literalize, and objectify (*thingifying*[33] or stone 'ing') the self-other-psyche-body.[34] Mental and bodily life cannot remain immaterial, creative, and intangible if thingified.

Thingifying the inner world and the psyche needs to be slowed down. Unfortunately, the no-thing is frequently eradicated both intrapsychically and interpersonally in ontological trauma, suspending transitional relatedness and the development of an object objectively perceived, nourishing psychic deadness, psychic murder, and death narcissism:

> Bion characterizes psychic murder as *moral* violence. The conviction that the object is no-thing itself can act as a coercive demand that the object be more and less than what is possible. The psyche becomes entangled in the reductionistic misuse of basic categories and functions, e.g., space, time, causality, and definition. (Eigen, 1996, p. 49)

Inner and outer life becomes subject to the concrete, the literal, a word of commands. Most frighteningly, the complex interplay is a desperate attempt to ward off, is the product of, and is a further conduit for petrification, implosion, and impingement. An unfortunate dark epistemology based on ontological trauma.

To illustrate the psychic processes evident in the psychotic core, I turn to Eigen's psychoanalytic pen, especially his psychoanalytic treatment of Kurt, as a further primary process example (see Eigen, 2011, pp. 86–87);

Kurt: [meeting Eigen for possible therapy] The simplest kind of proposition, an elementary proposition, asserts the existence of a state of affairs.

Eigen: You are here [I was thinking *perhaps* this was an elementary proposition asserting the existence of a state of affairs, *although I was not sure*. I *recognized* his words as a quote from Wittgenstein's Tractatus and something *in me translated it into a probe* of existence, his existence. My mind conjured that he was seeking and feared some kind of elemental contact, dread and hunger for elementary contact with himself and that I was here to help mediate that contact. I was also aware of *my thoughts as a psychoanalytic phantasy*]

Eigen goes on to write that he learned later that his words "You are here" were both relieving as well as threatening. To be *here* was where he was not and preferred to be outside, reflecting the fear of being suffocated. "There is no question that he pictures therapy as a *violation, robbing him of himself*" (2011, p. 86) (italics added).

Kurt: (a month later) I was impressed that you knew the Wittgenstein quote and said nothing about it. You pointed out I was here, proposition in action, beyond proposition. You let me off the hook. You didn't rub my nose in anything, not those first moments. *You let me escape. That enabled me to come in.* I felt I could get out and felt that you felt I could. How *here* I can be remains to be seen. I suppose you feel the way about yourself too.[35] (2011, p. 86)

Eigen: It's a challenge to stay in the same room together and a challenge to stay in the same room with oneself as well.

Kurt: I didn't know it was like this everywhere. On the street it's not there. You
walk and walk and walk and look and look. You don't have to be anywhere
with anyone. You don't have to be anything at all. Just walk and look ...
Being somewhere with someone is too hard for me. There is Hell in me and
walking is like pouring water on a fire. The fire doesn't go out but the water
feels good while it's there.

Eigen: [quiet contemplation] You walk yourself out, walk out of yourself, into
yourself, through yourself. An area of freedom. But stuck comes again.

With Kurt, one immediately senses Eigen's primary process of presencing psychoanalysis, his ability to take the other into his psychological bloodstream and
think ahead of the difficulties to be dreamt and met in psychoanalytic phantasy
and reveries,

> What paralyzed Kurt was not so much another voice, but fear. Blind fear for sur-
> vival ... My mind perceived vast tangles, too early to mention aloud. *Perhaps* we
> would never talk about them.[36] *Maybe* they are intellectual exercises and reality
> is something else. My mind quickly ran ahead, tying, untying knots, switching
> switches, a kind of manic assault on psychosis. *One madness pursuing another*.
>
> Here is what I saw. To leap into the True Path to his death might be a kind
> of psychological-spiritual 'death,' part of a transformational process, a 'rebirth'
> process. A problem in psychosis is that commands are taken 'literally'. You
> must do this, must not do that. They could not be taken as invitations to change,
> messages, or announcements: more exists, more is on the way ... The com-
> mands stick with unimpeachable authority. One is judged by them ... There
> are no shades, no continuum, no variation through which one mutates. One is
> stuck with the judgment and paralyzed by the need to survive. One is rendered
> profoundly immobile, no matter how fast the flight of ideas. (Eigen, 2011, p. 88)

Eigen continuously reflects on various threads in Kurt's tangles, reminiscent of
Laing and Bion, that is, being caught *between* the catastrophe if one follows the
'commands' and if one does not follow the 'commands' of the other (imaginal or
otherwise),

> Psychosis is a catastrophic process. And the sensed catastrophe is given expres-
> sion in thought and image (delusions, hallucinations). Catastrophic roots are
> unknown, whether physical, emotional, environmental, or all combined. But
> the result is an emotional catastrophe of grand proportions. An upheaval of the
> I, the sense of self, the ground one stands on. The ground opens and swallows
> one, but one returns. Over and over. How to make the return fruitful, a growth
> experience, a creative happening. Is it possible? Not for everyone, perhaps. But
> some come back and testify, there is life after psychosis. It is possible to return
> from decimation and enter larger areas of life. Part of the process is, little by
> little, over time, making room for catastrophic processes. (Eigen, 2011, p. 89)

Making room will find, as in Kurt's case, further tangles such as the 'Tyranny of Truth,' supported by a "mix-up of voices" (Eigen, 2011, p. 89), the primordial God-Devil fusion. On both sides of the God-Devil fusion, there is a risk of condemnation if an authority is not followed. Even more catastrophically, "What is most sane about one- the urge to survive- gets condemned." Despite the latter, Eigen's primary process ear also hears and finds areas of freedom, although knowing such areas will also be subject to the tyranny of "Truth,"

> In Kurt's case, his walking, sensing. For in his walking he saw colours, smelled scents, felt breezes through his skin, felt the inside good feelings of body movements in cells, tissues, pores, felt alive. And it was this very goodness of feeling alive that was assaulted by the demonic, godly commands, masquerading as 'The Truth'. The tyranny of 'truth'. (2011, p. 89)

Given such a need to survive, Eigen describes in Kurt's case a fourth ominous tangle: "To be caught between the urge to survive and following The Truth. Either one can be tyrannous, murderous" (2011, p. 89). The psyche may go to extremes in self-other murder (in all its forms) to survive. Despite the various musings, Eigen remains committed to the 'no-thing' when he states,

> It is unclear what my meditations on 'tangles' contributes, since my thinking-envisioning does not 'solve' anything, does not make problems or torment go away. Still, whether right or wrong, whether used explicitly or not, psychic cud chewing forms part of the background feel of what I bring to the room. I may or may not have the details right. But such reveries carry emotional weight in that they embody concern for a catastrophic impasse that Kurt lives, a tragic impasse. They contribute to an empathetic background appreciation of difficulty, a modicum of a shared sense of pain and quandary, ongoing wonder about what it is we are caught in. (Eigen 2011, p. 90)

Eigen's *rhythm of faith, a process of 're' awakening and revivifying* the traumatized ontological self, welcomes the *nomadic parts of self and other with the analysand,* holding the potential to rework disaster anxieties, the Omega nucleus, and chronically broken downness.[37]

Rhythm (s) of Faith

Eigen's 'rhythm of faith' concept (2004, p. 33) remains an essential organizing principle, a background to the analytic pair as the Omega nucleus and tyrannical super-ego are held and dreamt, liming mental-spiritual trauma and possible healing,

> Here I suggest that part of the rhythm Freud intuits has to do with a kind of psychic pulse, an opening–closing linked with death–rebirth (Elkin), break-down–recovery (Winnicott), coming alive–being murdered–feeling all right (Bion)

[...] For Elkin, one is born through a merciful Other after suffering boundless horror. For Winnicott trauma breaks personality as it forms, dread of break-down persisting as an undercurrent associated with new beginnings [...] For Bion it is as if one is murdered every time one tries to come alive. (2004, pp. 33–34)

In analysis the patient *experiences the analyst variously as a traumatic force or wounding object, supportive background presence, vehicle of wisdom and stupidity, auxiliary dream-worker, agent of faith.* The experiential arc described here constitutes a *rhythm of faith. For Elkin faith evolves and is sustained as the primordial self is nursed through despair and stupor, quickening into life with the Other's help.* (Eigen, 2004, p. 34)(Italics added)

As evident in the case of Kurt, functioning as an agent of faith as held by Elkin, as for Winnicott, is the consequence of good enough midwifery of the *primordial self in mental-spiritual despair.* A good enough psychic midwife is tasked to both *initiate* and *sustain* a *mental-spiritual break-down–recovery rhythm.* Within such a rhythm, *faith* is born not only in the primordial trust in the Other's goodness but also in one's psychic ability "to come through the trauma–recovery sequence, and experience one's own *generative capacity.* Gradually one's experiential reach is able to encompass blends of intrusiveness/obtrusiveness/abandonment/support that is part of all 'inter'-'subject'ivity" (Eigen, 2004, p. 34) (italics added).

During such coming through and relying on the thinking of Bion, the *rhythm of Faith* finds and depends on the growing capacity to tolerate, contain, and symbolize primary process damage, "*going through* the murderous object that psychic birth evolves – as process of opening the worst and coming through" (2004, p. 34). Eigen's psychoanalytically informed meditative untangling of Kurt allows Eigen to dream Kurt's mental-spiritual catastrophes actively and, in doing so, 're-'vision Kurt's deadening states of mind (also see Eigen's corrupt bodily and mental self, 1986), not through thingifying the psyche (concretizing and literalizing approaches), but by remaining present, attentive, and open within Kurt's psychic catastrophes. Given the presence of the earliest trauma of Simon and Sam's despair and desuetude, being available as a primary process processor for such entropy remains central,

> (Simon) We have done good work here, here we seek understanding. I wish G-d could see I am injured in love. My little person trauma. Too much damage ... (Sam) I was gutted, totally gutted. Mother madness, father rage, wife abandonment ... how could I ever trust again.

As evident in Eigen's holding, the primary process approach is based on being present in such a way that primordial consciousness and the primordial self can be 're'- born or revivified in a type of communication within the *psychoid field* (Ulanov, 2017) that aims to *not* prematurely structure and command, invade, facilitate implosion, or further the experience of petrification[38] but allow the very slow unfolding of a deracinated subjectivity, respecting the complex and age-old psychological katabasis-anabasis dialectic. Furthermore, for the symbiotically traumatized individual, the inner world is already filled with fright, and the outer world is, for many, a tragic facsimile of being purloined. Sam reflects,

> Its taken me over 9 years … closing my ears to it, to you, hearing about fear, I am fearful, still difficult to say it, to know it … fearful, frightened … memory floods- angry father, psychotic mother. Feeling I don't fit in anywhere. I fit here with you. Simon: I have no home.…

Reading Eigen, *primary process holding* serves as incubation, initiating the slow process of recovering- slowly freeing encapsulated ego structures as found in autistic-like ego adaptions given mental-spiritual trauma. Again, an example of the analytic practice of Bryce Boyer,[39]

> During one session, after I silently called her a liar, I became sleepy. While dozing, I pictured myself as a young child whose contradictory wishes to be good and bad controlled me without my will. With a start I became alert and thought that it must have been necessary for her to subject me to her emotional experience and that my own needs were being satisfied by an empathic response. I briefly recalled Searles oft-repeated statement that work with severely regressed patients requires *mutual emotional growth*. I then consciously put myself in her place and supposed that she was experiencing similar helplessness in the face of contradictory wishes. (1983, p. 205)

After sharing his observations, various behaviors and experiences became more accessible to the analysand and for the analysis. Periods of calm and turbulence permeated this analysis, and Boyer frequently 'returned' to fantasizing, a creative form of participation,

> Over the years, I have come to the conclusion that the fantasies I have during sessions are often my empathic responses to what patients are trying to tell me or have me experience. Accordingly, I thought that I had forgotten my fantasy because I had needed to defend myself from internal conflicts that our relationship had re-awakened. That night, I had a dream that reminded me of my own past.… (1983, p. 208)

For Eigen's Elkin (1972), it is essential to also note the *psychological*, if not physical, link between the mysterious, the mystical, and *mystical participation* (primordial mental-spiritual union), as it speaks to the earliest primal collective-erotic co-mingling with the needed maternal environment. Essential qualities of being 'in' and 'with' such a state of experience remain inexpressible in general relational terms, as seen in the case of Kurt as well as Eigen's description of serving as background presence for another analysand called Abe (see 2011, chapter 1),

Total mystical relations, to an immaterial *non-self* or *other* – as we know by examples from dream life, religion, and psychopathology – involve the total or absolute feelings, the consummate passions, that are symbolized by the mythological-religious conceptions of heaven and Hell. Such feelings as ghastly dread, dire agony, tremendous awe and sublime bliss, import the *unitary, undivided awareness* of *numinous* power absolute, infinite, "sacred" power, whether *divine or demonic. Total mystical experience,* at least in later life, is thus the most intense-though ineffable of human experiences. On the one hand, it is most *dread-full,* and may result in the shattering of the self as in psychosis. On the other hand, it is a most sublime experience of profound conversion, or spiritual rebirth.[40] In any case, the fact that total *mystical experience involves the disruption or the regeneration of the self, or soul,* indicates that it is, essentially, a re-experience of the original process of spiritual birth and creation: *the emergence of the self and of the primordial cosmos out of the chaos of sensation-feeling in the earliest, collective-erotic phase of infancy.* (Elkin, 1958, pp. 66–67) (Italics added)

Even Winnicott added to Elkin's thinking in his work on *Communicating and Not Communicating Leading to a Study of Certain Opposites* by stating,

In thinking of the psychology of mysticism, it is usual to concentrate on the understanding of the mystic's withdrawal into a personal inner world of sophisticated introjects. *Perhaps not enough attention has been paid to the mystic's retreat to a position in which he can communicate secretly with subjective objects and phenomena, the loss of contact with the world of shared reality being counterbalanced by a gain in terms of feeling real.* (Winnicott, 1963, in Caldwell et al., 2016, p. 439)

Lack of maternal protection, for whatever reason, fails to insulate the infant from the various primitive agonies soon to be faced, i.e., nameless dread and the Z-dimension. Both Eigen and Elkin describe the lack of such communion as 'disruption,' as being exposed to 'shocked awareness,' evoking, if not falling into, *primordial anxiety, being exposed to* "ineffable, *awe-full* or *holy* terror," re-livable in psychotic states of mind,

For whatever the actual time span of the child's frustration, he passes through a *subjective eternity* of agonized *primordial doubt* about the existence of both himself and the Other. Excruciatingly aware only of his unrequited need amidst nothingness, he may then, as in the conversion of psychotic excitement into stupor, pass into a state of numb insensibility and *spiritual darkness*, that of *primordial despair.* (Elkin, 1958, p. 68)

Spiritual darkness, the dark night of the soul as many would describe it to me in their analysis, reflects a primordial sense of betrayal and despair, evoking *primordial injury rage-fear* dialectics, and infinitely *binding* mental-spiritual progress, a dark mental-spiritual Akedah,

> (Simon) This is the story of the undeniable man after God lied and all was lost. I am enraged at the injustice to my little person ... (Sam) I cannot trust, not my gut, not other people, nothing. My compass is permanently broken ... when I fear, there is anger ... rage, rage-fear, fear-rage. Not certain which one comes first. But I am bipolar [laugh]!

Eigen's *rhythm of faith*, as mentioned, directly holds to the possibility that the infant-adult may be 'saved,' 'resurrected,' from such tormenting anxiety and despair through the (m)other's "merciful intervention" (Elkin, 1958, p. 68), akin to a "*spiritual resurrection*" (Elkin, 1958, p. 69), *awakening an even greater awareness that the self's psychic existence depends* on the merciful love of the *Other.* Both a hope and a further fear for the psychotic self. With a merciful Other as background support, the primordially injured self remains hopeful and faithful to the 'spiritual' realm, and the merciful love within a primordial union over time,

> In Abe's case, inherent permeability and unconscious background emotional support were wounded. He was wounded as personality began to form: beginnings met with damage. A pattern of damaged beginnings characterized important aspects of his life. *When something good started, disaster followed, a devastating pattern beginning in infancy/ childhood continuing into adulthood* ... Therapy supported a situation- *blindly, mutely-* in which Abe's psyche, in conjunction with mine, created *a sequence wherein begins were sustained and led to something creative* (sustaining is itself creative). One of the most creative moments of all was apperception of a radiant I-point that lifts existence. This experience occurred unexpectedly in a situation of extreme abstinence and contraction. Although it happened spontaneously, it seems likely that an *excruciating birth process of many months paved the way*; *a process in which neither Abe nor I knew what we were doing or where we were going* ... It was hair-raising, and I was filled with self-doubt, and if I had inklings that we were involved in something as significant as a personal revolution, I did not connect with them in any reassuring way. (Eigen, 2011, pp. 9–10) (italics added)

As with Kurt, despite doubt and analytic uncertainty, Eigen remained an analytic environment to be trusted – boundless background support. This stands in contrast to the very real experience of reaching out to another due to painful physical-affective needs, where failure to reach and to be reached finds the analysand suffering "an eternity of dire need in the presence of a cruelly indifferent Other" (Elkin, 1966, p. 169). Sam reflected on it as follows:

> I was married for all time, all time and eternity. I allowed myself to trust to the point of oneness. ... Time has always confused me, even more so after my divorce – if I take the life of a fruit fly- they do all in one day- that is how we

are maybe in the world of God … but a few seconds … trying to figure it out … what was I saying, going off track? A few seconds to figure something out, only to die. My time slippage did not help me at all. My situation until analysis felt forever lost. Now I am thinking of a chrysalis, me as the worm, hopefully, can metamorphize into something more, a different phase of living.

Moving forward stands in contrast with Simon, who introduced a dark katabasis when he stated,

> They send me to the pit, a darkness I cannot explain, a terrible pit, terror and there was no one to help me … this lead to a suicide attempt, soul murder, they murdered my soul, I did not think I would survive, a voice *You will be burned….*

reminiscent of Elkin's description: "This brings on a panic terror which, beyond a certain span, fades into an unconscious stupor that, subjectively, is an experience of death" (Elkin, 1966, p. 169). Specifically, and closer to Christian *annihilationism,* the coming of God will not see people sent to Hell but rather be *exposed to extinction.* The most primordial fear of the psyche is not being imprisoned or attacked per se but being exposed or returned to a psychic state of nothingness, that is, mental-spiritual extinction!

Meeting the other to facilitate an experience of "resurrection into a blissful communion *(co-union)* with the Primordial Other" remains a desperate psychoanalytic imperative in treating the psychotic self, supporting the possibility of resurrecting remnants of a Divine Mother-Child union rather than the diabolical (Elkin, 1966, p. 169). The Divine Union, even exposed to unavoidable break-downs may, with subsequent 're'-'unions,' serve as psychic building blocks expected to bridge the *mental-spiritual dilemmas and the natural world.* Mental-spiritual death and resurrection experiences will sustain the possibility to survive the coming threat of a *"new order of values* which the child perceives through his handling and mouthing of objects, and his being handled by others: the *natural values,* relating to physical power and weakness, which apply to the objective, phenomenal world" (Elkin, 1958, p. 69) (italics added). Mental-spiritual awareness in time becomes an embodied self with added fears,

> Tormented by such fears and depressed by his helpless inferiority, his insignificance in terms of natural values, the child falls into the pattern of all later human anxiety: *doubt as to his personal identity and the validity of the primordial experience on which it rests.* (Elkin, 1958, p. 69)

It is here paradoxically that the analyst must pay careful attention to mental ego and body ego collapse – heart attacks, psychosomatic eruptions, and unexplained physical deterioration. Many of the analysands may feel frighteningly vulnerable to the world and others,

> (Simon) I get ill with people, with the world. Too much, but I blame it on God and Satan- their work through people … (Sam) I want to relate, but then my

megalomania works against me when I run into people – they are stupid and don't think. But I have come to see here it is my way of distancing from them.

As with the needed holding of the most primordial mental-spiritual fears of extinction, the "merciful love" of a mothering Other/analyst supports the child/analysand to take 'in' the "mediating function"[41] of her ministrations, bridging the inner and outer worlds. "(Sam) Here I have learned to mediate between myself and the world- to live between rather than outside of the world … (Simon) Therapy is the mediatrix for me- G-d and you also witness it all."

For Elkin, it is also evident that primordial contact with the numinous, powerful Other serves as the basis for the "divine-good mother" as well as the "evil-bad mother." The 'good' results from merciful love, whereas "Evil is numinous power without love that may destroy him like an object" (Elkin, 1958, pp. 69–70). Simon stated it as follows:

> Why would they do that to my little person, God, the Holies, Jesus all got it wrong about my being- misjudging my being, saying that I am a failure, mocking me, destroying me- the first great obscenity. Shouting in my face for seven days and seven nights, not allowing me to sleep.

Laing's petrification personified. Elkin also includes, for reflection, various biblical narratives, mythology, and fairy-tale characters wherein children are maimed, eaten, and dismembered. The Divine Mother-Child archetype meets the catastrophic anxieties and fears evident in the *Diabolic Mother – Frightened Child archetype*,

> In contrast to the Divine Mother image, that of the Diabolic Mother marks a sharper break in the infant's continuity of experience from the primordial to the fully human world. For by evoking panic terror, the Diabolic Mother revives feeling-memories of a satanic aspect of the primordial Other, prior to its virtual disappearance following 'the primordial drama of spiritual regeneration.' The present terror, however, unlike primordial dread of an *irretrievable loss of consciousness*, or the *loss of Self and Other in an abyss of nothingness*, is linked to imaginings of *physical destructiveness drawn partly from the infant's own experience of tearing, biting, and swallowing*. Projected onto the actively frightening aspect of the mother which he experiences as the Diabolic Mother, they evoke ghastly fear of her dismembering and devouring propensities. This is reflected in cultural history by such mythological figures as the Medusa's head which petrifies with fright, man-eating lamias, goddesses conceived as lionesses, pantheresses, or attended by such feline beasts (which are associated with distinctly feminine, and hence originally maternal, erotic grace of movement), and by witches in fairy tales who dismember, cook, and eat little children, or otherwise handle them like physical objects.
>
> The infant is thus *critically* involved, with regard to the Divine and Diabolic Mother images, in a cosmic struggle between omnipotent powers of Good and

Evil. He offsets his "holy terror" by "holy wrath" (this may be repeated in later life in an acute out-break of psychosis or in going berserk), thereby participating with the full energy of rage on the side of the Divine Mother, the embodiment of primordial and cosmic Goodness. In this terrible opposition to the Diabolic Mother, however, as well as in his joyful communion with the Divine Mother, the infant remains an integral mind-body unity or, in Winnicott's term, a *psyche-soma*. (Elkin, 1972, pp. 402–403)

Holding the Diabolical at bay rests on various forms of *affirming maternal virtues*[42] (Elkin 1966) that include *receptivity* (empathic responsiveness) to the child's physical and mental-spiritual gestures and feelings, supporting the validation of an inner mental-spiritual reality. Receptivity could also be combined with the *experience and expression of delight* and joy in both her child's *uniqueness and unique way of being in the world*. This, in turn, gives the infant and later adult an experience of not only being part of a joyful union but also the earliest Oedipal experience – a mother who can experience and express delight for life itself! A mother of joy, a joyous mother – a life-affirming and life-enhancing mother, if not Andre Greens' life narcissism? This reads opposite to Andre Green's *Dead Mother Complex* and should be integrated into psychoanalysis as an initial joyful-based pre-Oedipal mother.

Elkin added a second pair of values that, although seemingly polar to the affirming maternal values, aim to preserve the *integrity of the union*. They are *maternal self-assurance and humility*. Herein is a beautiful description of Elkin's logic,

The mother's self-assurance, quite simply, preserves the tranquility of the utterly dependent and easily frightened child. Maternal humility, on the other hand, is a most subtle quality that enters into, and is reflected by, the genuine, uncompensatory nature of the mother's responsiveness, joy, and self-assurance. It depends on her realization of the fact that she cannot be the *perfect mother which, ideally, the child should have; and that he can be deeply hurt by her failings which are more or less inevitable*. The mother's humility itself, however, resides in, just as her self-assurance is truly grounded on, her *profound inner acceptance of this fact*. When this humility is conveyed to the child through her spontaneous expressions of feeling, especially when he tends to feel hurt or rejected, it transposes incipient pathological tendencies into the psychological foundation of healthy growth: the child learns to forgive the mother, just as the mother forgives the child.[43] (Elkin, 1966, pp. 172–173) (Italics added)

Since no mothering can ever be perfect, *mutual disturbance* between mother and child, analyst and analysand, is to be expected, necessitating, as stated, "*mutual forgiveness*," as it is expected to serve as the basis for "*whole-some* human love," i.e., reciprocal tenderness, communion, grace, solicitude, felt concern, and reverence. "Through mutual forgiveness there is spiritual love, experienced in feelings of tenderness and esteem, or inherently, a reverence ("pity" and "piety" in their original unity of *pietas)*[44] that ultimately derives from the experience of communion between mother and child" (Elkin, 1966, p. 173). These virtues are ever-present in Eigen's primary process psychoanalysis and are found in the case material of Kurt and Abe, as described above.

When these virtues are *absent*, various adaptations are to be expected, and it is primarily the lack of humility that fosters an awareness that the primordial Other acts as an omnipotent, omniscient Great Mother-Goddess[45] unaware of her maternal impact. The child remains aware, although psychically split, as he is dependent (swamped, engulfed) by her way of being and "on her ministrations and must suffer her *terror-provoking* stupidities, caprices, and vagaries" (Elkin, 1966, p. 173). If the child/analysand fears the mother/analyst, he may literally and figuratively close his eyes and ears to her, yet still suffer dependency. Neither virtue serves autochthonous articulation and fails to adequately support the need for background support. Eigen's primary process psychoanalysis rests on affirming and welcoming values: receptivity, sagacity, percipience, humility, and faith. This contrasts with values based on omnipotence, omniscience, and megalomania, stimulating in the ontologically traumatized self further encapsulated states of mind.

Epilogue – Keating's Secret Embrace

Eigen's voluminous work limes a unique primary process psychoanalysis able to dream unwanted, unwelcomed, and symbiotically traumatized analysands. Similar to Ann Ulanov's transformational Jungian work, *The Psychoid, Soul, and Psyche* (2017), Eigen's being with another personifies the *psychoid archetype*, a rare psychoanalytic sensibility informed by a mysterious revivifying undercurrent. An example given by Ulanov exemplifies, to me, Eigen's most *welcoming* way of being *with* the world,

> Is the psychoid known only in clinical relationships? No, of course not. After lecturing on the psychoid in Australia, a man told me he used to keep beehives. He described standing in their midst without protective clothing with the bees all over his body and around him. I perceived he *received* in his bodily way deep connectedness to the real. He said, 'I loved my bees'. (2017, p. 41)

A love able to sustain the *Secret Embrace*, enlivening the 'wandering between the two worlds,' (one dead, the other powerless to be born), with somewhere to rest my head,

> The transition from eternity to time
> Is full of suffering, fears, and little deaths.
> But, in the transition from death
> To eternal life,
> The silence of pre-existence
> Bursts into boundless joy.
>
> – Thomas Keating

Notes

1 My aim is also to, over time, differentiate between primary and secondary process psychoanalysis and analysts.

2 I am deeply indebted to my analyst, Janet Oakes, FIPA, for making me aware of Eigen's way of holding the *psychotic core and self* (see 1986, especially chapter, 8, pp. 313–364) in his article 'Tears of pain and beauty: mixed voices' (2011, chapter 6, pp. 85–102) as related to how she heard my current musings on Eigen's *primary process psychoanalysis*. It served for me as an organizing experience on many levels.

3 Stanzas from the Grande Chartreuse by Matthew Arnold, by www.poetryfoundation.org.

4 Winnicott (1963, in Caldwell et al., 2016, p. 441): "At the centre of each person is an incommunicado element, and this is sacred and most worthy of preservation. Ignoring for the moment the still earlier and shattering experiences of failure of the environment-mother, I would say that the traumatic experiences that lead to the organization of primitive defences belong to the threat to the isolated core, the threat of its being found, altered, communicated with. The defence consists in a further hiding of the secret self, even in the extreme to its projection and to its endless dissemination. Rape, and being eaten by cannibals, these are mere bagatelles as compared with the violation of the self's core, the alteration of the self's central elements by communication seeping through the defences. For me this would be the sin against the self. We can understand the hatred people have of psycho-analysis which has penetrated a long way into the human personality, and which provides a threat to the human individual in his need to be secretly isolated. The question is: how to be isolated without having to be insulated?"

5 Grotstein differentiates between two types of "ontological orphans" and can be read on pages 13–15, in Allen and Collins (1996), in greater detail.

6 Given the understanding provided by Jungian's such as Perry and the deep phenomenologically informed work of Eigen (1986, 1992), it could also be written that Simon did not necessarily turn to the Christian faith *per se*, but that crisis necessitated archetypal approaches to a psyche exposed to catastrophic events and transformations. Perry's classical work arranged various categories and started with the observation that a negative self-image "at the ego level presents itself, along with a *compensatory overblown self-image* at the fantasy level, in mythological and delusional form." (p. 29). The latter may contain both negative and positive forms. In the negative, one could see the clown, ghost, or witch, and in the positive, the hero, saint, or chosen leader. Furthermore, in a creative way as a form of a thematic archetypal Grid or archetypal rhythm, Perry describes the ideational imagery following a pattern consisting of ten areas of psychic processing;

A. Center: A location is established at a world center or cosmic axis (the point where sky world, regular world, and underworld meet; between opposing halves of the world, center of attention).

B. Death: Themes such as being crucified, being dismembered, to delusional themes of being dead or died – still either in a state of death or having returned.

C. Return to beginnings.

D. Cosmic Conflict.

E. The threat of the opposite.

F. Apotheosis.

G. Sacred marriage.

H. New birth/new beginnings.

I. New society.

J. Quadrated world.

Also see the work of Giovachinni (1997, chapter 3, pp. 76–81), *Primitive Rituals, Autonomy, Regression, and Progression.*

7 A frequent request in my work with ontologically traumatized individuals. Although an area in need of further research and much contemplation given our culture's movement to MAID for the mentally ill, the immense despair and desuetude evident in ontological trauma and grief, may predispose the ontologically traumatized to ask another to initiate death rituals. This stands in contrast to my experience with the ontically traumatized individual who frequently relies on suicide as a desperate communication to others to ward off abandonment anxieties. Variation will, of course, exist – although the felt sense of the ontologically traumatized individual's request for MAID may reflect a hidden unconscious hope that one can be reborn through the other [the other bringing one into life].

8 The case of Lena, chapter 1, pp. 9–28, serves as an artistic rendering of our need for an organizing experience and the impact a self-destructive superego can have on bonding, i.e., self-other-God bonding.

9 Also see 2001, pp. 24–28 in greater detail.

10 In contrast to the needed states of unintegration for further psychic development, James Grotstein in his usual synthetizing brilliance, reminds psychoanalysts that "The term devil, which is derived from the Greek word *Dia-bolos*, literally means 'scattered asunder.' Thus, the devil became the incarnation of chaos, whereas God became the incarnation of the coherence that mediated chaos" (footnote 2, p. 146, 2000).

11 Please refer to Eigen's *Contact with the Depths*, 2011, chapters 1 and 2, *Distinction-Union structure* and *Spirituality and Addiction,* for a felt sense of *background support*. The case of Abe is of importance as a clinical example (also see Eigen, 1973).

12 In Eigen (1986, pp. 52–65).

13 One can now come to appreciate the psychotic's *reorganization of the self*, chapter 3, pp. 25–36; the *ritual drama of Renewal*, chapter 5, pp. 53–61; *and Mysticism and Madness*, chapter 8, pp. 95–105, in John Weir Perry's *The Far side of Madness*, 1974, as attempts at reconstitution of the time-space continuity of a viable self wherein emphasis is given to Binswanger's ontic conceptualizations of man- "These ontic characteristics apply to the total being of man as rated and described by Binswanger (a) as *being-able-to-be, being-allowed-to-be* and *having-to -be-in-this-world* (thrown-ness)" (Hora, in Ruitenbeek, 1962, pp. 70–71).

14 Grotstein's (2000) chapter 6, *Internal Objects*, remains a transformational read.

15 For an in-depth discussion of Freud and Jung, see Eigen (1986, pp. 52–65) under the headings *Jung: Mythic Journeys*, and *Problems with Jung's Basic Terms*.

16 Grotstein (2000) describes the experience of being cursed in his chapter on *Internal Objects* in his work *Who is the dreamer who dreams the dream? A study of psychic presences.*

17 "Primordial consciousness, on the other hand, is a momentous ontogenetic break-through from the vital into the mental-spiritual life (or in terms which Teilhard de Chardin applied to phylogency, from the biosphere into the noösphere). Thereby man, lacking the animal's instinctive endowment of early postnatal motility, *acquires mental-spiritual autonomy before acquiring physical autonomy.*" (Elkin, 1972, p. 394). As previously written, Daws (2017), I would note it *mystical pre-Oedipal, natural order pre-Oedipal,* Oedipal, and post Oedipal. Each stage brings into being a unique participation, self-other reality, affects, ideation, and lived world demands.

18 For Eigen (1986), "The failure of the self to have *come into existence adequately is scarcely distinguishable from a collapse to a null point. The self hovers over zero.* In Freud's energetic terms, decathexis presupposes cathexis. But what if cathexis of other and self is extremely weak or partial? The individual who bitterly complains about losing his I-feeling and who is pained by a sense of numbness is not the same as the individual whose I-feeling and affective density were never strong enough to be missed. In the latter instance, one hopes to stimulate a sufficient self-feeling the individual will

find worth struggling for. We may need to trace either a subject's lack or loss of self, the moment out of or lapse into nothingness" (p.113) (italics added).

19 Space prohibits a more detailed exposition on the Jungian concept referred to as "psychoid," which articulates many thoughts similar to my thinking here. The volume written by Jungian analyst Ann Belford Ulanov's *The Psychoid, Soul and Psyche- Piercing space-time barriers* (2017), is of immense importance.

20 "No primordial experience is lost, so that initial radiant self-other identification, intermediate dread, rage and stupor vis-à-vis a menacing Other, and culminating faith in the divine Other's merciful love embrace each other, fuse, ebb and flow, interpenetrate, threaten, support and feed emotional life. 'For the Self has realized,' as Elkin concludes, 'that its very existence depends on the merciful love of the often inscrutable, seemingly cruel or indifferent, yet eternal, omniscient, and omnipotent Other. Only when the child learns to rely trustfully, when beset by instinctive fears, on the divine *Loving-Cognition*, does his mind-spirit remain fixed in the light of primordial consciousness.' Elkin tends to see the initial moment as more Hindu ("I and God are one," "Atman Brahman"), the culminating moment as more Judeo-Christian (rebirth through the Other: "Yea, though you slay me, yet will I trust you."). *Various threads of mystical and psychotic experience draw on oscillating combinations of these and intermediate phases*" (Eigen, 2004, p. 21) (Italics added).

21 "Then in 'On identification' (1955b), Klein, whilst discussing Julian Green's novel *If I Were You*, develops her argument significantly. She suggests that:

…projective identification may result in the fear that the lost part of the self will never be recovered because it is buried in the object. In the story Fabian feels— after both his transformation into Poujars and into Fruges—that he is entombed and will never escape again. This implies that he will die inside his objects. There is another point I wish to mention here: besides the fear of being imprisoned inside the mother, I have found that another contributory factor to claustrophobia is the fear relating to the inside of one's own body and the dangers threatening there. To quote Milton's lines, 'Thou art become (O worst imprisonment) the dungeon of thyself'. (1955b, p. 166)

The twin danger sources described, of entrapment in one's object or one's own body, are connected by Klein in her final paper, 'On the sense of loneliness,' wherein she writes that claustrophobia 'derives from two main sources: projective identification into the mother leading to an anxiety of imprisonment inside her; and reintrojection resulting in a feeling that inside oneself one is hemmed in by resentful internal objects' (1963, p. 308) (in Willoughby, 2001, p. 920).

22 Furthermore, according to Laing:
In using the term petrification, one can exploit a number of meanings embedded in this word;

1. A particular form *of terror*, whereby one is petrified, i.e., turned into stone.
2. The dread of this happening: the dread, that is, of the possibility of turning, of being turned, from a live person into a dead thing, into a stone, into a robot, an automaton, without personal autonomy of action, an *it without subjectivity*.
3. The 'magical' act whereby one may attempt to turn someone else into stone, by 'petrifying' him; and by extension, the act whereby one negates the other person's autonomy, ignores his feelings, regards him as a thing, kills the life in him. In this sense one may perhaps better say that one depersonalizes him, or reifies him. One treats him not as a person, as a free agent, but as an *it*. (Laing, in Ruitenbeek, 1962, p. 50).

23 1 Peter 2:1–25

So put away all malice and all deceit and hypocrisy and envy and all slander. Like newborn infants, long for the *pure spiritual milk*, that by it you may grow up into salvation— if indeed you have tasted that the Lord is good. As you come to him, a *living stone* rejected by men but in the sight of God chosen and precious, you yourselves *like living stones are being built up as a spiritual house*, to be a holy priesthood, to offer spiritual sacrifices acceptable to God through Jesus Christ....

24 Sam would in a session, 12 years into his analysis, spontaneously talk about his traumatized but vital self coming alive as follows: "I read that in Africa those that are nomadic peoples that carry ambers in a leather sort of bag, ambers that can light a fire quickly if they need to." Primordial self as ambers....

25 Simon, "I dreamt of the pit, going doing, being burnt alive, excruciating pain.... The worst fear... hell is real".

26 See the dream of Lawrence Hedges in Chapter 7, *I dreamed of being scared to death*, pp. 44–49, 2012.

27 Please see the Valley of Hinnom (Gehenna) – Wikipedia:
   In the King James Version of the Bible, the term appears 13 times in 11 different verses. *Gehenna* is frequently used to describe the opposite of life, guilt, punishment, and death. Furthermore, "In certain usage, the Christian Bible refers to it as a place where both soul (Greek: ψυχή, psyche) and body could be destroyed (Matthew 10:28) in 'unquenchable fire' (Mark 9:43)"

   • Matthew 5:29: "...it is better for you that one of the parts of your body perish, than for your whole body to be thrown into Gehenna."
   • Matthew 5:30: "...better for you that one of the parts of your body perish, than for your whole body to go into Gehenna."
   • Matthew 10:28: "...rather fear Him who is able to destroy both soul [Greek: ψυχή] and body in Gehenna."
   • Mark 9:43: "It is better for you to enter life crippled, than having your two hands, to go into Gehenna into the unquenchable fire."
   • Mark 9:45: "It is better for you to enter life lame, than having your two feet, to be cast into Gehenna."
   • Mark 9:47: "It is better for you to enter the Kingdom of God with one eye, than having two eyes, to be cast into Gehenna."
   • Luke 12:5: "...fear the One who, after He has killed has authority to cast into Gehenna; yes, I tell you, fear Him."

   Another book to use the word *Gehenna* in the New Testament is James 3:6: "And the tongue is a fire, ... and sets on fire the course of our life, and is set on fire by Gehenna."

28 Higher-level thinking may work overtime to cover defects in affective processing. The individual, for example, may use naming and definition to bind or contain persecutory feelings rather than explore them ... In such an instance, the individual has all he can do to keep up with his self-attacks or nameless dreads and imitations of catastrophe. He has all he can do to try to cauterize his sense of fragmentation or put a verbal tourniquet around disintegration. Here the aim of naming is to stop the horrible movement. *The result is the proliferation of elements meant to tie the psyche up rather than to enable it to evolve* (Eigen, 1996, p. 54) (italics added).

29 See the work of Eigen with his analysand named Abe, in both Eigen's (1973 and 2011) publications.

30 Simon would frequently externalize an inner dialogue reminiscent of a jury; "Did he or did he not" positioning me as witness/ juror/ judge/ opposing counsel.

31 Eigen; "Hallucinations may not simply express distorted messages about the self and others, coded pleas for help or clues to an aborted inner journey, but they may also be mis- and anti-communications. Their aim may be to ward off the possibility of genuine communication of any sort, a smoke screen to throw self and others off the scent..." (1986, p. 77).

32 Also review Eigen's "I don't know," in 2011a, 2011b.
33 Eigen writes,

According to Ehrenzweig, psychotic individuals are in extreme horror of giving them-selves over to the ebb and flow of more and less differentiated modes of perception. They fight ego loss or more "undifferentiated" functioning. The ego is caught in the grip of a relentless rigidity and is bent on sealing itself off. It neither trusts itself nor the psyche as a whole. Ehrenzweig thus felt that it was a mistake to intensify psychic rigidity further by simply or mainly trying to help the psychotic individual strengthen his defenses. What is necessary is the discovery of an entirely new way of relating to deeper modes of perception. The unconscious life of the ego or self needs nourishment and growth. By degrees, the individual has to be helped to let go and trust the rhythms of deeper processes. At the same time, one's work must facilitate the incessant reorgani-zation of these deeper processes. More important than supporting the superficial ego defenses is a kind of wholesale replenishment and redirection of psychic life, so that the subject can become more receptive to the mystery of experiencing. The unconscious ego matrix must come to act more as fertile womb or a container capable of sustaining the play of opposites, particularly the plasticity and determination of psychic work. (Eigen, 1986, p. 347)

34 Eigen (2021) notes:

Our minds are partly magnifying-minifying machines we use the term "to blow up" to characterize certain "exaggerated" states. On the other side, I remember a patient who said she had a disappearing machine that made thoughts and feelings vanish ... Our mind can maximize states and move towards zero at the same time, as well as develop maximizing-minimizing rhythms, a little akin to crescendo-decrescendo in music. Our mind can act like a plus-and-minus infinitizing machine blowing oneself up in both directions, intense and overflow and null. Maximum emotion and minimum emotion. Emotion moving towards infinity and emotion moving towards zero. (p. 36)

35 A beautiful moment, similar to Little's idea that she was allowed to know Winnicott, about him and later to be ringed up by him and told her perceptions about his heart con-dition were accurate. Similarly, Eigen reflects on his own bolting tendencies, see pages 86 onwards in 2011, chapter 6.
36 Eigen's chapter on primary process and shock (Psychic Deadness, 1996, chapter 12) accentuates the need often to not only allow the impact of the other, but to protect the client from a too early return of it- *if it is returned at all*. Even in earlier work (1992), Eigen writes under a section *Growing the psyche*,

It is often unnecessary to analyze explicitly what is going on between patient and thera-pist. Much work goes on in the covert interplay of affective attitudes without being expressed in words. Often the expression is in new dream images, perhaps new ways that parents appear in dreams, or new figures all together, or new possibilities in living. Many of my *interventions are not directed to the details of transference or to the 'real relationship' in therapy, but to the emergence of new capacities and to the tone or spirit of communications*. Sensitivity to tone or spirit or affective attitudes is akin to what use to be called 'discrimination of spirits,' although the form of discrimination evoked here involves sensing more than judgment and is anything but judgemental.

37 Also see the transformational writing of Ofra Eshel's *The Emergence of Analytic One-ness: Into the Heart of Psychoanalysis* (2019).
38 Harry Stack Sullivan writes, "Per contra, if you have to deal with schizophrenia, then this formulation of mine implies the importance of carefully putting almost a scaffold-ing under the patient's self-system in its relation to you- that is, establishing a 'me-you'

pattern, if you please, between yourself and the patient which is of an utterly previously *unexperienced solidity and dependability*. Only then can you get to the point where you can deal with disturbing material without causing this sudden disturbance of the self-function of suppressing more primitive types of mental process, with, as a result, the abolition of communication and God knows what results in the patient, in the sense of what finally comes out as a result of your efforts" (1953, p. 363). Also, in a section entitled *Postcript*, Margaret Little writes that "Trust in the analyst has had to be built up through experience of his reliability and general predictability. A good deal of repetition is often needed in the working through... the original damage cannot be undone, but providing other experience to put alongside the earlier ones enables the patient to bring his more mature, non-delusional self into action" (1981, p.106).

39 See chapter 9, pp. 187–213.

40 Various chapters in the book entitled 'The Living Moments: on the work of Michael Eigen' (2015) opens such realities. See especially Chapter 1 entitled *Bion, Eigen, and the dreaming of Kali* by Stephen Bloch, and Chapter 6, *Psychic aliveness: on "being murdered into life"* by Marian Campbell, both senior Jungian analysts in South Africa.

41 Elkin's reference to the *Mediatrix* remains of importance here, i.e., Mary as adjutrix and mediatrix.

42 Space prohibits a comparison between Elkin and M.A. Sechehaye's work *Symbolic Realization: a new method of psychotherapy applied to a case of schizophrenia* (1951), although great overlap exists. In her volume, Chapter 9, *Re-education*, Sechehaye wrote, "I want to make some remarks concerning the procedure which was adopted from the educative viewpoint. Each time that contact was established through symbolic satisfaction, I strove to take advantage of it in the attempt to rebuild Renee's personality. This of course was only possible after the patient had received the necessary satisfaction through the symbol. Here are the different means which I employed according to the need;

1. Developing the patient's confidence in the analyst.
2. Reassuring her.
3. Guessing her needs.
4. Satisfying them successively so that they became appeased, thus permitting the expression of new needs.
5. Awakening new desires according to their stage.
6. Developing attention.
7. Establishing a plan for our patient (that is to say, regulating her actual life, placing limits upon time employed).
8. Upholding an activity which was adapted to the stage reached.
9. Exclusion of inadequate methods.
10. Assistance by a capable helper. (pp. 109–110)

43 James Grotstein's *Memory of Justice*: "Transcendental Bion seems to be clearly stating that the infant must project in order to survive and that mother must absorb, contain, translate, transform, and communicate in order to establish the model for thinking which the infant is then able to undergo only because of mother's observed capacity. Further, the infant must project into reality, and herein lies an extraordinarily intuitive point that Bion has lit upon. Projective identification never occurs in a vacuum. There must always be an external realization, which *justifies* the projection so that the projection can take place. Mother must frustrate, err, disappoint, etc. – seemingly purposely so as to justify the projective identifications into reality – and mother must acknowledge these "goofs," as must analysts, so that the *Memory of Justice* can be restored [...]" (Grotstein, 1987,pp.69–70).

44 For more on these psychoanalytic observations, the reader is referred to two articles by Grotstein in his 2000 work, Why Oedipus and not Christ, Parts I and II, Chapters 8 and 9, respectively.

45 Given various modern institutional treatments of the ontologically traumatized self, forced secondary and structuring processes may inadvertently subsume the infantile psychotic self, relegating it to institutional fawning and compliance. At worst, the therapeutic pair becomes part of Ferenczi's "professional hypocrisy" (1933).

References

Balint, M. (1968). *The Basic Fault: Therapeutic Aspects of Regression*. London: Tavistock.

Bion, W. R. (1957). Differentiation of the Psychotic from the Non-psychotic Personalities. *International Journal of Psychoanalysis*, 38, 266–275.

Bion, W. R. (1958). On hallucination. *International Journal of Psychoanalysis*, 39, 341–349.

Bion, W. R. (1959). Attacks on Linking. *International Journal of Psychoanalysis*, 40, 308–315.

Bloch, S., & Daws, L. (2015)(Ed.). *The Living Moments: On the work of Michael Eigen*. Karnac: Routledge.

Boyer, L. B. (1983). *The Regressed Patient*. New York: Jason Aronson, Inc.

Daws, L. (2016)(Ed.). *On the Origins of the Self: The Collected Papers of Henry Elkin, Ph.D.* Missoula, MO: EPIS Press.

Daws, L. (2023). *Michael Eigen: A Contemporary Introduction*. New York, NY: Routledge.

Drewermann, E. (2006). *A Violent God-Image. An Introduction to the Work of Eugen Drewermann* (Trans. By M. Beier). New York and London: Continuum International Publishing Group, Inc.

Edinger, E. F. (1986). *The Bible and the Psyche. Individuation Symbolism in the Old Testament*. Toronto: Inner City Books.

Edinger, E. F. (2000). *Ego and Self. The Old Testament Prophets, from Isaiah to Malachi*. Toronto: University of Toronto Press Inc.

Edinger, E. F. (2004). *The Sacred Psyche: A Psychological Approach to the Psalms*. Toronto: University of Toronto Press Inc.

Ehrenzweig, A. (1967/1995). *The Hidden Order of Art*. Berkeley: University of California Press.

Eigen, M. (1973). Abstinence and the Schizoid Ego. *International Journal of Psychoanalysis*, 54, 493–498.

Eigen, M. (1986). *The Psychotic Core*. Northvale, NJ: Jason Aronson, Inc.

Eigen, M. (1992). *Coming Through the Whirlwind*. Wilmette, IL: Chiron Publications.

Eigen, M. (1993). *The Electrified Tightrope* (A. Phillips, Ed.). Northvale, NJ: Jason Aronson, Inc.

Eigen, M. (1995). *Reshaping the Self: Reflections on Renewal in Psychotherapy*. Madison, CT: Psychosocial Press.

Eigen, M. (1996). *Psychic Deadness*. London: Karnac.

Eigen, M. (1998). *The Psychoanalytic Mystic*. London, UK: Free Association Books.

Eigen, M. (1999). *Toxic Nourishment*. London: Karnac.

Eigen, M. (2001a). *Damaged Bonds*. London: Karnac.

Eigen, M. (2001b). *Ecstasy*. Middletown, CT: Wesleyan University Press.

Eigen, M. (2002). *Rage*. Middletown, CT: Wesleyan University Press.

Eigen, M. (2004). *The Sensitive Self*. Middletown, CT: Wesleyan University Press.

Eigen, M. (2005). *Emotional Storm*. Middletown, CT: Wesleyan University Press.

Eigen, M. (2006a). *Lust*. Middletown, CT: Wesleyan University Press.

Eigen, M. (2006b). The Annihilated Self. *Psychoanalytic Review*, 93: 25–38.

Eigen, M. (2006c). *Age of Psychopathy*. (http://www.psychoanalysis-and-therapy.com/human_nature/eigen/pref.html).

Eigen, M. (2007). *Feeling Matters*. London: Karnac Books.

Eigen, M. (2009). *Flames from the Unconscious*. London: Karnac Books.

Eigen, M. (2010). *Eigen in Seoul: Madness and Murder (Vol. 1)*. London: Karnac Books.

Eigen, M. (2011). *Eigen in Seoul: Faith and Transformation (Vol. 2)*. London: Karnac Books.

Eigen, M. (2012). *Kabbalah and Psychoanalysis*. London: Karnac Books.

Eigen, M. (2013). *Contact with the Depths*. London: Karnac Books.

Eigen, M. (2014a). *The Birth of Experience*. London: Karnac Books.

Eigen, M. (2014b). *Faith*. London: Karnac Books.

Eigen, M. (2014c). *A Felt Sense: More Explorations of Psychoanalysis and Kabbalah*. London: Karnac Books.

Eigen, M. (2016). *Image, Sense, Infinities, and Everyday Life*. London: Karnac Books.

Eigen, M. (2018). *The Challenge of Being Human*. Abington: Routledge.

Eigen, M. (2020). *Dialogues with Michael Eigen* (L. Daws, Ed.). London & New York: Routledge.

Eigen, M. (2021). *Eigen in Seoul Volume Three: Pain and Beauty, Terror and Wonder*. London: Routledge.

Eigen, M., & Govrin, A. (2007). *Conversations with Michael Eigen*. London: Karnac Books.

Elkin, H. (1958). On the Origin of the Self. *The Psychoanalytic Review*, 45, 57–76.

Elkin, H. (1966). Love and Violence. *Humanitas*, 2, 165–182.

Elkin, H. (1972). On selfhood and the Development of Ego Structures in Infancy. *The Psychoanalytic Review*, 59, 389–416.

Eshel, O. (2019). *The Emergence of Analytic Oneness: Into the Heart of Psychoanalysis*. New York, NY: Routledge.

Ferenczi, S. (1933). Confusion of Tongues between Adults and the Child- The Language of Tenderness and of Passion. *Contemporary Psychoanalysis*, 24, 196–206.

Fuchsman, K., & Cohen, K. S. (2021) (Ed.). *Healing, Rebirth, and the Work of Michael Eigen*. London & New York: Routledge.

Giovacchini, P. L. (1997). *Schizophrenia and Primitive Mental States – Structural Collapse and Creativity*. Northvale, NJ: Jason Aronson, Inc.

Grotstein, J. S. (1981). *Do I Dare Disturb the Universe? A Memorial to W.R. Bion*. London: Karnac.

Grotstein, J. S. (1996a). *Orphans of the 'Real': I. Some Modern and Post-modern Perspectives on the Neurobiological and Psychosocial Dimensions of Psychosis and Other Primitive Mental Disorders*. In J. G. Allen and D. T. Collins (Eds.). *Contemporary Treatment of Psychosis. Healing Relationships in the "Decade of the Brain."* (pp. 1–26) Northvale, NJ: Jason Aronson Inc.

Grotstein, J. S. (1996b). Orphans of the 'Real': II. The Future of Object Relations Theory in the Treatment of the Psychosis and Other Primitive Mental States. In J. G. Allen and D. T. Collins (Eds.). *Contemporary Treatment of Psychosis. Healing Relationships in the "Decade of the Brain."* (pp. 27–48). Northvale, NJ: Jason Aronson Inc.

Grotstein, J. S. (1997). Integrating One-Person and Two-Person Psychologies: Autochthony and Alterity in Counterpoint. *Psychoanal Q.*, 66, 403–430.

Grotstein, J. S. (2000). *Who Is the Dreamer that Dreams the Dream? A Study of Psychic Presences*. Hillsdale, NJ: The Analytic Press.

Hedges, L. E. (1994a). *In Search of the Lost Mother of Infancy*. Northvale, NJ: Jason Aronson.

Hedges, L. E. (1994b). *Working the Organizing Experience: Transforming Psychotic, Schizoid, and Autistic States*. Northvale, NJ: Jason Aronson.

Kalsched, D. (2013). *Trauma and the Soul: A Psycho-Spiritual Approach to Human Development and Its Interruption*. London: Routledge.

Laing, R. D. (1962). Ontological Insecurity. In H. M. Ruitenbeek (Ed). *Psychoanalysis and Existential Philosophy* (pp. 41–69). New York: E.P. Dutton & Co., Inc.

Little, M. I. (1990). *Psychotic Anxieties and Containment. A Personal Record of an Analysis with Winnicott*. Northvale, NJ: Jason Aronson, Inc.

Perry, J. W. (1974). *The Far Side of Madness*. Dallas, TX: Spring Publications, Inc.

Rogers, A. G. (2006). *The Unsayable. The Hidden Language of Trauma*. New York, NY: Random House.

Rogers, A. G. (2016 [2018]). *Incandescent Alphabets. Psychosis and the Enigma of Language*. London: Karnac. (Routledge, 2018).

Schreber, D. P. (1955/2000). *Memoirs of My Nervous Illness*. New York: New York Review Books.

Sechehaye, M. (1951a). *Symbolic Realization*. New York: International Universities Press.

Sechehaye, M. (1951b). *Autobiography of a Schizophrenic Girl*. New York: Grune & Stratton.

Shengold, L. (1999). *Soul Murder. Thoughts about Therapy, Hate, Love and Memory*. New Haven, CT: Yale University Press.

Sullivan, H. S. (1948).The Meaning of Anxiety in Psychiatry and in Life. *Psychiatry*, 11, 1–13.

Sullivan, H. S. (1953). *The Collected Works*. New York: W.W. Norton & Co.

Sullivan, H. S. (1966). *Schizophrenia as a Human Process*. New York: W.W. Norton & Co.

Symington, N. (2019). *A Pattern of Madness*. New York, NY: Routledge.

Tustin, F. (1990). *The Protective Shell in Children*. London: Karnac.

Ulanov, A. B. (2007). *The Unshuttered Heart. Opening Aliveness/Deadness in the Self*. Nashville, TN: Abingdon Press.

Ulanov, A. B. (2017). *The Psychoid, Soul and Psyche- Piercing Space-Time Barriers*. Einsiedeln: Daimon Verlag.

Van Buuren, J., & Alhanati, S. (2010). *Primitive Mental States. A Psychoanalytic Exploration on the Origins of Meaning*. London and New York: Routledge.

Van Kaam, A. (1970). *On Being Involved. The Rhythm of Involvement and Detachment in Human Life*. Deville, N.J: Dimension Books.

Volkan, V. (1976). *Primitive Internalized Object Relations*. New York: International Universities Press, Inc.

Volkan, V. (1995). *The Infantile Psychotic Self and its Fates. Understanding and Treating Schizophrenics and Other Difficult Patients*. Northvale, NJ: Jason Aronson, Inc.

Williams, G. (1999). On Different Introjective Processes and the Hypothesis of an "Omega Function." *Psychoanalytic Inquiry*, 19(2), 243–253.

Willoughby, R. (2001). The Dungeon of Thyself: The Claustrum as Pathological Container. *International Journal of Psychoanalysis*, 82, 917–931.

Winnicott, D. (1953). Transitional Objects and Transitional Phenomena—Studies in the First Not-me Possession. *International Journal of Psychoanalysis*, 34, 86–97.

Winnicott, D. (1955). The Metapsychological and Clinical Aspects of Regression within the Psychoanalytic Set-up. *International Journal of Psychoanalysis*, 36, 16–26.

Winnicott, D. (1958). The Capacity to be Alone. *International Journal of Psychoanalysis*, 39, 416–420.

Winnicott, D. (1963). Communicating and Not Communicating Leading to a Study of Certain Opposites. In Lesley Caldwell (ed.), Helen Taylor Robinson (ed.) (2016). *The Collected Works of D. W. Winnicott*, Volume 6, 1960–1963, chapter 8 (pp. 433–446). Oxford, England: Oxford University Press.

Winnicott, D. (1965). *The Maturational Processes and the Facilitating Environment*. London: Hogarth.

Winnicott, D. (1967). The Location of Cultural Experience. *International Journal of Psychoanalysis*, 48, 368–372.

Winnicott, D. (1971). *Playing and Reality*. London: Routledge.

Winnicott, D. (1975). *Through Pediatrics to Psychoanalysis*. London: Hogarth.

Winnicott, D. W. (1945). Primitive Emotional Development. *International Journal of Psychoanalysis*, 26, 137–143.

Winnicott, D. W. (1969). The Use of an Object. *International Journal of Psychoanalysis*, 50, 711–716.

Winnicott, D. W. (1974). Fear of Break-down. *International Review of Psychoanalysis*, 1, 103–107.

Winnicott, D. W. (1988). *Human Nature*. London: Free Association Books.

Winnicott, D. W. (1984/1990). *Deprivation and Delinquency*. (C. Winnicott, R. Shepperd, & M. Davis, Ed). London & New York: Routledge.

Chapter 6

The Welcomed Object

Alitta Kullman

In December of 2020, at the height of the COVID-19 epidemic, I unexpectedly learned that I would need to undergo major surgery. Having been fairly healthy to that point—give or take the inevitable creaks and caveats that go along with aging—I was terrified. After several days in shock, I decided to reach out to Michael Eigen—whom I had "known" for more than a decade online in various iterations—in the hopes that he could help me figure out how to *think* the unthinkable. Mike was amazing. He made me laugh and let me cry. He listened and opined on my rational fears and walked me through the irrational ones. He helped divide and dissect terror, and was so sure I would survive that I suspect even God Himself would not have dared crossing him. Mike was *with* me—the partner, the witness—I needed to contain the terror. If there was an upside to such a traumatic event, it was to have been blessed with "meeting" Michael Eigen from the inside out.

In Mike's care, I felt myself becoming a "welcomed object." But this was far from unique to me. Putting out the welcome mat for the human soul and psyche infuses all of Michael Eigen's contributions—recognizable both in and between the lines of his vast body of work. The warmth, support, and validation in his freely offered personal and professional communications indelibly partner with his astonishingly meandering and creative mind, irrespective of what he might otherwise be exploring.

But there is more to the story: In yet another unexpected and fortuitous gift of the pandemic, earlier in 2020, it had become necessary for Mike to move his 50+ year-old weekly seminars from his Manhattan office to the surprisingly intimate environs of a Zoom meeting. This made it possible for those of us who did not reside in New York City to experience Mike's mind at work first hand. The seminars were wide-ranging and endlessly fascinating. But what I often found myself most intrigued by was not so much the topic at hand—nor even Mike's extraordinary insights into Freud or Bion or the myriad of psychoanalytic, mythical, spiritual, political, scientific, biblical, and literary (and so on) figures that peppered his discussions. Rather it was the tiny nuggets embedded in the discourse, the rich gems of wisdom, kindness, and compassion for those of us sentient beings caught up in the crosshairs of life—"whatever it is," as Mike would say—that captured my imagination and remained with me throughout the week. When Mike made recordings

DOI: 10.4324/9781003322993-6

of the seminars available to us, I spontaneously began transcribing them—perhaps in an effort at holding on to the "moonbeam" in my hand—the mysterious kernel of Michael Eigen's wisdom that so nourished me.

For Eigen, therapy—including his own—has neither a beginning nor an end; analysis and its inevitable companion, self-analysis, is a forever thing. In fact, he doesn't believe in therapy, he tells us, and dislikes the concept of "treatment." He does not view struggle as only affecting others, hold himself out as the "authority," or insist on a theory or model to define himself. Rather, he searches relentlessly for meaning in his own actions, reactions, thoughts, and feelings—and those of others. He shares his own vulnerabilities right along with his patients' challenges, not seeking credit for an outstanding interpretation or holding himself out as "knowing" better or best. We are all "in the soup" together, he reminds us, trying our darndest to survive ourselves and make sense of the other. Some people look at a screaming baby and see rage; others see terror. Eigen sees both and *more*, ever vigilant to those aspects of Self that have been missed, forgotten, or rejected.

In the collection of quotes that follows—though representing the tiniest sliver of thoughts, ideas, and brilliance put forth in his works and seminars—I hope to offer a taste of the "psyche/soul" experience that is Michael Eigen. How does he do what he does? How does he manage to be so profound and down-to-earth, so erudite and yet so welcoming to the souls and psyches of his patients, students, and readers—to just plain "us?" We are all in need of support and validation, of someone to witness, welcome, believe in, and connect with us—to be *with* us. For those of us practicing psychotherapy or psychoanalysis, the dual or "multi-variant" nature of our psyches is particularly vulnerable. We learn from our patients as they learn from us. We are nourished or wounded by their responses and affected by their moods, as they are by ours. How do we all manage to be in the soup together, learn from our experiences, and keep on growing in the process?

Though I ache for all I have had to leave out, it is nevertheless my hope that I may succeed in awakening your "psychic tastebuds," as Mike would put it. I hope that the following quotes may entice you to further sample his work, to explore with him "the challenge of being human" while simultaneously "making contact with [his] depths."

I welcome you to cozy up and share some nuggets.

Moments

This is life. This is my life. This is your life. 'Kafka called his life an incomplete moment'…No moment is *the* complete moment…there's no 'The End'. It's all moments. Even if they say this is the *W-H-O-L-E*. But it still has the *H-O-L-E* in it. There's still more to go. *(Eigen, 2021c)*

We're different ways at different moments. And sometimes we're tough-skinned when we should be thin-skinned and thin-skinned when we should be tough skinned…Start with the weakest spot and everything opens. And you get the fruit; you get the whole fruit. *(Eigen, 2021c)*

So much goes on moment to moment once we tune into it. How much of ourselves and each other can we endure or enjoy? How much and in what ways dare we let ourselves and each other in? *(Eigen, 2001, p. 5)*

A lot of therapy is to make self-love accessible so it does not get drowned out by self-hate. Self-hate doesn't go away. Make room for it. It's got a spot; it's got a role to play…it's moments. *(Eigen, 2020d)*

What will we give birth to in this moment? *(Eigen, 2021c)*

On Tolerating the Self

We have these two systems working in lots of ways. We have the feeling itself, or the feeling we think we should have, or the feeling we do have and think we shouldn't have, and something above it. Something that Freud called the 'observing ego'. People call it 'the witness'. *(Eigen, 2021k)*

Liberation from oneself… How does one get freer from oneself…Fighting myself! God, enough of that! How do you get free of yourself, get some freedom? Breathe! *(Eigen, 2021b)*

You have to get rid of yourself to find yourself. You have to tolerate both functions, towards and away… *(Eigen, 2021e)*

No one else is with me 24/7 all my life. How am I flooding myself? How am I suffocating myself? How am I abandoning myself? It's part of the pull; it can't be left out. *(Eigen, 2021c)*

The inner critic, the inner put-down, the inner 'You're no good', whatever it is. The way you torment yourself: 'I'm not good enough'. So tell me someone who's good enough. You know someone who is good enough? OK. *(Eigen, 2021a)*

Whoever you are, whatever you've done, no matter what you feel, you have not exhausted yourself. You may not know that; you may not feel that, but it's true. You're still embryonic [as Bion would say]. You have an embryonic germ. *(Eigen, 2021e)*

Eating oneself alive is a kind of destructive cannibalism, psychic cannibalism. Hurting oneself with one's own psyche, with one's own qualities, one's own capacities, one's own abilities. *(Eigen, 2021l)*

How to approach the 'unsolvable' problem of affective life? What to do with our emotions and feelings? My way at the moment is simply to try and stay with 'it'. Stay with it as best you can, even intermittently. Experientially feel what you are feeling.…it is an important avenue of growth for individuals. *(Eigen, 2021a, p. 45)*

You can't just make problems go away. They are part of what define you. We have to build capacity to work with ourselves and the problematic nature of our beings. We are this enormously complex, overwhelming package, and we are very much embryonic in learning how to work with it. One main thing about this challenge is to keep learning from experience about experience—its makeup, qualities, structures, impacts; our own impact on ourselves, our self-impact. Keep on finding what works for you, although what works for you now may not work for you in ten or twenty years from now…Building and making room for the human condition doesn't stop. *(Eigen, 2020a, pp. 127–128)*

How do you leave room for yourself? That's one of the great functions of meditation, trying to leave room for yourself; not crowded out by all your thoughts, all your worries, your anxieties, your feelings, whatever it is. *(Eigen, 2021e)*

Winnicott was the first analyst I read who validated rest…Rest is very important…the body needs rest. The body needs to sleep. The body needs a vacation from itself. We need a vacation from ourselves. *(Eigen, 2021h)*

Don't apologize for your feelings, for your sensations, for your thoughts, for your hunches, for your hints, for your clues, for your little bits of 'uh-oh'! Don't apologize. This very special capacity, this receptor, this sensitive receptor that no machine can replace [Bion]—it is you. No one can replace that, not even yourself. Because you are going to keep growing. You are going to keep opening and there will be more. *(Eigen, 2021b)*

On Therapy

Actually, I don't believe in therapy. Therapy is a path, a dedication, a search… The word 'treatment' is not right as well. Inappropriate. There are other words I like: 'to foster', to 'encourage'. It's like taking a child for a walk, giving him a hand, bringing him candy; to hold her, take care of her. Not only like a therapist but also like a parent. *(Eigen, 2020a, p. 174)*

In this way', in this function, the therapist is always doing what Freud describes as the mother to soothe the baby's pain, disquiet, discomfort; to bring some sort of peace to the pain. 'Life is an infection that keeps throbbing'…that keeps on struggling. 'Is there a physician for life? I'm not doing too well. Are you?' *(Eigen, 2021e)*

I suspect deprecating supportive work was a madness psychoanalysis went through, a phase I hope is over. Good supportive therapy can be a blessing. If a psychoanalyst does good supportive work, psychoanalysis is automatically happening. *(Eigen, 2020a, p. 39)*

I don't feel myself as a gratifier or frustrater. I do different things in different situations, depending on what my feeling is, what my sense is. Sometimes this sensing is right, sometimes wrong. An important element as time goes on is the patient senses me sensing. She feels I'm in the soup with her, yet still myself. Over time this can make a difference. *(Eigen, 2020a, p. 43)*

Some people can't be rushed. It takes years, sometimes a lifetime. Some of the work involves taking the edge off destructive feelings towards oneself. A lot involves working with unconscious self-hate, modulating it, allowing something else to build. *(Eigen, 2020a, pp. 47–48)*

I don't like to use the word 'enactment' because what is happening is *life*. It's not something outside us. It's my life affecting your life, your life affecting mine. Our personalities impact each other now. *(Eigen, 2020a, p. 51)*

I think one of the main things in therapy is dosage, not doing too much, too fast. Not doing more than a person can bear. It's so easy to shame, to flood, increase despair…. We are challenged to build resources to work with our capacities, to partner our capacities. *(Eigen, 2020a, pp. 122–123)*

It is often unnecessary to analyze explicitly what is going on between patient and therapist. Much work goes on in the covert interplay of affective attitudes without being expressed in words…Many of my interventions are not directed to the details of transference or to the 'real relationship' in therapy, but to emergence of new capacities and to the tone or spirit of communications. *(Eigen, 1992, pp. xi–xii)*

How do we respect each other's defenses?… You don't push someone's face in: 'Why are you doing this'? You explore. What are you doing? And how? Maybe after thirty years, you can say why. *(Eigen, 2021e)*

We came through—unplanned, by staying with what we felt. I call this coming through a rhythm of faith (Eigen, 2004, Chapter 4)….The experience of coming through shifts the psychic economy from something worse to something better in the long run. One learns in therapy better quality ways of coming through. This doesn't do away with bad. Bad will happen. You don't get rid of bad in life, but something happens. *(Eigen, 2020a, pp. 51–52)*

In therapy we have a chance to slow things down, to chew on moments of injury/regeneration, and to taste and partly digest what ordinarily sweeps us along. We get a chance to test out, absorb, and work with what we fear (often rightly so) may be annihilating about life-giving bonds. *(Eigen, 2001, p. xi)*

Much of what happens in therapy, often what is most important, is non-verbal—permanently outside the reach of words…Words do lead to new aspects of reality. But in therapeutic work, there is a tone or atmosphere or 'feel' in the room that is more important. *(Eigen, 2001, p. 4)*

A therapist is a kind of specialist in letting the other in, feeling the impact of the other, staying with images and thoughts to which the feel of the other gives rise. *(Eigen, 2001, p. 5)*

A patient not only senses the therapist, but senses how he affects the therapist… The patient, in a way, reads himself in the therapist's being and vice versa. *(Eigen, 2001, p. 5)*

I take myself with a grain of salt. Take ourselves with a grain of salt and contribute what you can, do what you can, be what you can—with a grain of salt. *(Eigen, 2021f)*

We have to alter our consciousness because we can't take too much of ourselves. *Shatter, return, shatter, return.* Therapy helps build resources to work with our breakdowns. *(Eigen, 2020a, p. 13)*

We use psychoanalysis in part to pump out our psychic stomach aches and restore ability to digest experience. *(Eigen, 2021i)*

You don't have to have one model for therapy. You can have many. Bion used to think one theory, many models—though I can't claim to have one theory either. I am patchwork. I am open to the model of the moment, the realities of the moment. *(Eigen, 2020a, p. 38)*

Trying to communicate an unsolvable emotional predicament; trying to communicate and have someone *hear* an unsolvable emotional predicament. It happens a lot in therapy. It's an amazing happening to have that happen, to be able to communicate the uncommunicable and have someone hear it at that level without trying to make it into something else, something nicer. To actually hear the incommunicable at that level is a salve. Oh my God, someone heard it." *(Eigen, 2020d)*

[Therapy is]…someone you can talk to; someone you can say *anything* to. You don't even know what you're going to say what's going to come out of you. You can share all your deathly secrets; you can share all your bad feelings about yourself. Whatever it is, you can share your grandiosity, your megalomania, your narcissism, your despair. Maybe things that come out that you had no idea of. And there's someone there who will say, 'Tell me more. I'm interested'. Just wait on it and see what's there… This is one of the great functions of therapy: Having someone to talk to. *(Eigen, 2022)*

Let's see what this little germ of truth is that you want me to understand about yourself… We do that with our patients. We don't confront them with all the ugliness that's there. We try to pare out what's usable, what they can grow with. *(Eigen, 2021f)*

We had to find ways of being together. The unknown and unfamiliar was part of the basis of our relationship. *(Eigen, 2011, p. 8)*

Don't understand your patients too well; they'll be trapped. They'll be trapped by your understanding. They're going to fight your understanding. Everyone wants to be free…the mind wants to be free! So be free together. *(Eigen, 2021i)*

Building up a tolerance for the experiencing of the pain of experiencing, the pain of thought. To be thought-*less* is easier. It's good to be thought-*less*, too. There's nothing wrong with being thought-less. But can one also tolerate the pain of thinking about who one is, what one is doing, who the other person is, what they are doing…Both are true. *(Eigen, 2021b)*

I think there's a kind of therapy intimacy that is part of the deep bond of therapy, especially when it's working well. And if something carries over into real life, I think it's at least part of that feeling of intimacy with oneself. Because one now knows that that's in the world, that it's possible. *(Eigen, 2020a, p. 132)*

Therapy is imbued with an ethics of waiting, an ethics of the unknown. There is always more that can happen. Infinities keep opening in the here and now, between you and me and within oneself. In a life of mystery, one unknown meets another, unknown to unknown. Humor dances on the edge of tears…your deeper self and being is waiting for you. *(Eigen, 2020a, p. 194)*

On Going Deeper

Any of the emotions, depending on the context and how they're used and how you approach them, what you do with them, can stimulate growth, even the most pathological emotions. You catch on, you look at it, you see it, you taste it, you feel it, you work with it. Turn it around kaleidoscopically, walk around. What's it doing…It can stimulate growth because you are seeing it. You are saying, "What is this?" "This is me?" I'm more than this; I'm other than this…Let's take a look, go deeper, go deeper. *(Eigen, 2021f)*

Wherever you go, wherever you are, wherever you find yourself, there's something deeper, inexpressible. There's something deeper. It's a blessing, if one can allow it, if one can allow this grace. Wherever you are stuck, there is something deeper. *(Eigen, 2021f)*

You can always go deeper than your current state. Enjoy the current state, or whatever—be tortured by the current state. Go deeper. You can go deeper and become other, more, fuller, whatever you want to call it. You don't have to be imprisoned by any particular state. *(Eigen, 2021k)*

On Being

Feel what you can feel. It's alright. Whatever you can manage to do and to have, do that. *(Eigen, 2021g)*

The fact that we can't do everything doesn't mean that we cannot do anything. *(Eigen, 2021i)*

Let the mind itself reverie; don't worry about it being too rational. Don't worry about it. See what comes up. Give it room. Give it breathing room. *(Eigen, 2021i)*

Give psyche a space to be…whatever you want to call the thing you're struggling with. It's real. And grace, moments of grace. *(Eigen, 2021i)*

Tolerating an experience, experiencing an experience…what does it do? Where does it open? What dimensions open? You don't have to act on it…the action is just sitting, feeling the feeling, sensing the sensing, thinking the thinking. Wait; don't count it out. Don't count out what's unknowable about us. Wait on the unknowable. *(Eigen, 2021j)*

Feelings can cripple your life and make you all tied up: *I can't do, I can't, I'm too ashamed, I'm too guilty, I'm too afraid.* [Negative feelings are] "an invitation to say let's see what positive use can be made of these feelings…They're all useful. What use can we make of them now? *(Eigen, 2021k)*

We are all midwives and mediums. We are transmitting something that is speaking through us, through our vehicles, in this life form. But it is speaking through us, whatever you want to call it—the spirit, this creative "x," creative force, whatever it is… Breathing can be creative; sensing can be creative. That's what Winnicott was trying to give expression to by 'primary creativity', just by being. Wow! *(Eigen, 2020c)*

We're more than we think we are. We're more than we know we are. We're more than we feel we are. Don't give up on yourself… 'You're going to be a surprise to yourself; You're not done surprising yourself. You've just begun surprising yourself!'…Whatever it is, you don't stop surprising yourself. *(Eigen, 2021d)*

On Birth and Re-birth

Life is all a learning experience. Learning how to live life, learning how to live *your* life and what works for *you*. Learning to live your life in a way that works for you and others. Learning to undergo further births because birth never stops. Being born doesn't stop, and learning to undergo it, learning to be there, to be your own midwife, your own doula. And everyone is part of this. We're all midwives for each other…we're all involved in helping this birth process go on and on…. *(Eigen and Daws,* 2020a, *pp. 47–48)*

The birth of the human spirit. It doesn't stop getting born. Don't worry, don't worry, if you think you're stuck this way or stuck that way. OK, so you're stuck this way. That's not ALL you are. There's going to be more—more births of your spirit. It doesn't stop. Can you keep up with it? No, you can't keep up with it. But you can taste it; you can get some of it. You can get a breath of it. You can make use of it. It can use you. *(Eigen, 2020c)*

You are a creative spirit. *Your* DNA; *your* feeling for life, *your* life feel. Difficulties, the toxic elements, the uplifting aspects—whatever it is: Your *life* feel. We all share that. We all know what it's like to be alive. We all share it. But it's absolutely unique, absolutely yours—no one else's. *(Eigen, 2020c)*

Our mixed capacities can stymie us, cause confusion, a kind of centipede not knowing how to use its legs. But they also are a source of plasticity, ability to survive and survive well—if only we keep learning how to use our evolving makeup, do not give up on it, or it on us. *(Eigen, 2011, pp. xii–xiv)*

The area, the space of the unknown makes more possible, further growth possible, something else possible. You don't have to stay tied up in the knot of your known self. *(Eigen, 2021k)*

Accepting your life and working with it and seeing what it wants. What is it aiming at? What can it do? Take a walk, look around, feel, do nothing. Just accepting who you are. It sounds so simple, and it's a relief. Such moments bring a relief. *(Eigen, 2021l)*

So, let's be like a friend, a partner, a partnership, protect each other from ourselves; from each other and from ourselves. Can you help me protect myself from myself? That's what psychoanalysis is, one of its functions. Come to a therapist and let the therapist help you protect you from yourself. *(Eigen, 2021d)*

Partnering

Psychoanalysis has made a real contribution in talking about ways we run away from [ourselves, and how can we tolerate a little more support of being with, or towards, ourselves. And that's a different model for culture, a partner model: With, being with, being with oneself, being with another, being with life, partnering with life. Not a simple matter. *(Eigen, 2020b)*

Therapy helps to improve psychic digestion. At a minimum, we suspect that it will help us learn something about our relationship to emotional processes, so that we become better partners to ourselves and others. *(Eigen, 2001, p. xi)*

The internal *Covid*: Can my feelings breathe? How? In what way? And what use are they? With what do they partner? How can my feelings be of value, of use in this world, to myself, to enhance my life rather than destroy it? So you and I can help others. It goes on and on. To let our feelings breathe. We kind of have emotional *Covid*. We're working on it. It's ongoing; it's not a done deal. *(Eigen, 2020d)*

We are made of both peace and turbulence, both elements of our paradoxical being. We're not one thing. We're many things. An over-arching psycho-spiritual question: how do we relate to any of our capacities? What kind of quality of partnership can we evolve with our capacities? ...We're in the business, in a sense, of working on ourselves, on society, on our thought processes, on our feeling processes, to try to become partners with our beings and the amazing capacities we've been given and develop a better quality of relationship to our own capacities. *(Eigen, 2020a, p. 146)*

We stand on the shoulders of many giants in helping us learn how to partner with ourselves and not be done-in by ourselves. To work with it in some useful way, in some healthier way. *(Eigen, 2020d)*

Do away with the binaries, successes and failures. Don't persecute yourself with that. Do what you *can* do, keep on doing what you can do. Be a partner to yourself, a friend. Learn how to work with the enemy. *(Eigen, 2020d)*

The struggle is never over. From that war there is no end, says Bion: The struggle with oneself and life and learning how to partner. But moments of grace, moments of peace. Wow! It gives an affirmation, an affirmation of life. It gives a faith that is deeper than all this. *(Eigen, 2020d)*

In the Talmud it says every dream is an unopened letter from God. Whether you can understand it or not isn't the point. Treat it with respect. Treat it with care. It is a baby asking for your partnership. And it is a basic model: A basic model of treating yourself and treating others. But treating your own self with care; the dream of yourself, whatever it is, all the dreams. *(Eigen, 2021b)*

There is a Kabbalah myth that we bring [all the ruptured pieces] together and search for them. If you find your little piece, it's a little piece for you, a special spark, a special piece. It's a creative piece. You unite. Love that creative piece of you that you happen to find. God knows where you'll find it, in another person, underneath the carpet, in the sunlight. Who knows where you'll find a broken piece. And God bless it: It's a spark of life, a creative spark. *(Eigen, 2021b)*

Conclusion

I have chosen passages that have stirred me, moved me, welcomed me, enriched my capacities as a therapist—and as a human being. They are undoubtedly not the same passages that might be chosen by others; they may not even capture what

Eigen himself would consider the "essence" of his message. But therein lies the beauty and potency of Michael Eigen's work: He speaks to the individual soul; he offers food to those with their own hungers for meaning and connection. He makes it safe to open old wounds and consider the possibility of filling them with the salve of acceptance. He invites each of us to glean what we can, to take what we need, and, along the way, to welcome and treat ourselves with dignity.

It is awesome to be a living being who feels, cries, laughs, sings, dies. Who hurts others and is hurt, who goes mad, becomes inspired, or is just happy to be alive to each day, to the extent one can. Life never ceases being an unpredictable sea, raising up, dashing down, pressing us through ranges of emotions, more alive, threatened, empty, deadened, eager.... Our contact with life, ourselves, each other is challenged. And through it all we have a need for deep contact, contact with the depths, fulfilling and suspenseful. Contact we never stop growing into, a challenge daily growing in importance. *(Eigen, 2011, p. xiii)*

References

Eigen, M. (1992). *Coming Through the Whirlwind.* Chiron.

Eigen, M. (2001). *Damaged Bonds.* Karnac.

Eigen, M. (2004). *The Sensitive Self.* Wesleyan University Press.

Eigen, M. (2011). *Contact with the Depths.* Karnac.

Eigen, M. (2020a) (L Daws, Ed.). *Dialogues with Michael Eigen.* Routledge.

Eigen, M. (2020b, June 30). *Shame Seminar.* Zoom.

Eigen, M. (2020c, July 7). *Bion Seminar.* Zoom.

Eigen, M. (2020d, October 13). *Shame Seminar.* Zoom.

Eigen, M. (2021a, March 9). *Shame Seminar.* Zoom.

Eigen, M. (2021b, March 30). *Bion Seminar.* Zoom.

Eigen, M. (2021c, April 13). *Shame Seminar.* Zoom.

Eigen, M. (2021d, April 20). *Bion Seminar.* Zoom.

Eigen, M. (2021e, May 11). *Shame Seminar.* Zoom.

Eigen, M. (2021f, May 19). *Shame Seminar.* Zoom.

Eigen, M. (2021g, May 25). *Shame Seminar.* Zoom.

Eigen, M. (2021h, June 1). *Bion Seminar.* Zoom.

Eigen, M. (2021i, June 8). *Bion Seminar.* Zoom.

Eigen, M. (2021j, June 15). *Bion Seminar.* Zoom.

Eigen, M. (2021k, June 29). *Shame Seminar.* Zoom.

Eigen, M. (2021l, July 6). *Shame Seminar.* Zoom.

Eigen, M. (2022, September 13). *Bion Seminar.* Zoom.

Chapter 7

Welcoming Dreams

Willow Pearson Trimbach

Two Dreams and Opening Resistance

Last night, on the eve of my birthday, I was immersed in two dreams. Upon waking, both were difficult to be with. I immediately judged them as "not great birthday dreams!" But I didn't stop with that impulsive judgment. I stayed with a deeper curiosity about the two dreams. While a part of me, on automatic, had immediately closed to them, another part remained open. What's more, I was able to expand the part of me that remained open to the dreams with the internalized encouragement of the spiritual psyche (Pearson & Marlo, 2021) and her champions, including author and psychoanalyst Dr. Michael Eigen, whom I regard as a mentor.

More than the content of any particular dream, more than any interpretations we may bring to our dreams or even the messages our dreams convey, it is our openness to the dreams themselves—*our welcoming of them*—that is the most essential aspect of our relationship with dreaming. Why is this? The welcoming of dreams is the welcoming of the spiritual psyche in all its dimensions (Pearson & Marlo, 2021). Welcoming our dreams is a profound expression of welcoming ourselves in all our complexity. This welcoming is a never-ending and ever-renewing lifework. For this lifework, we need ambassadors—those who have welcomed us in all our shadow and light—emanating from and continuing with the pregnant void. And this is the welcoming generosity that Michael Eigen extends in his being through his writing and his teaching.[1]

First, I will explore the two dreams that visited me on the eve of my birthday as an illustration of welcoming the spiritual psyche and the self in all their dimensions. And then, I focus on the welcoming spirit that participates in opening such difficult dreams. I will also share an ecstatic dream that came to me on the last night of my honeymoon to offer a different sense of what the welcoming can also usher in. Finally, I reflect on the welcoming spirit itself and on Michael Eigen's particular flavor of welcoming as I experience it and extend it by example. For, as Loray Daws and Keri Cohen's companion volumes (this volume and its companion volume *Toxic Nourishment and Damaged Bonds in the Work of Michael Eigen: Working with the Obstructive Object and Primary Process Impacts*) on Eigen's work bring forth, it is the twin relationship between Eigen's reverence for both the

DOI: 10.4324/9781003322993-7

welcoming and the obstructing object that, in tandem, create such an expansive and all-encompassing opening. The practice of holding that expanse in view is, in turn, helped by my engagement with the work of Michael Eigen.

Difficult Dreams and Ecstatic Dreams

So allow me to share these two difficult dreams. They are both about being on the other side of death and also about dying. And they are about bodily harm/dismemberment, and psychic pain.

The first dream is as follows:

I am in a war zone and, at the same time, on the other side of that war zone in a kind of afterlife that witnesses the war. My eyes have been cut out and placed in a container in my pocket. The belief is that my eyes will soon be put back in their sockets. But they are not. The forces of fate do not put my eyes back in. And I see now from this post vision state.

The second dream followed:

A woman, who is both me and other than me, is lying down in a war zone and communicating that her feet have been burned off. What's more, she is also communicating that her children's feet have been burned off. She lies on the ground like a living mandala.

On a conscious level, when I wake up, I automatically judge these dreams as torturous. Why on earth would I dream about such horrific events on the eve of my birthday, no less? Instantly, I reject these dream images on a visceral level, as they are ambassadors of thinking about and feeling excruciating physical pain—a symbol for hellish psychic pain. But I keep going. Just a little further.

I open just a bit to the images. What else, I wonder, do they carry? My curiosity leads me to appreciate that not only are these two dream images about physical harm and the psychological harm they symbolize, but they are also about seeing and communicating on the other side of death, not as an escape from the world but as an expansion of it to include further dimensions of being. And for this vision, I begin to feel an emergent sense of gratitude for the dream images. The twin dimensions of the dream images are inseparable—the pain of the images and the beauty of opening to multiple dimensions of being that they also convey. Each points to the other—the pain points to the beauty, and, similarly, the beauty points to the pain—and the regard for each dimension, pain or beauty, expands the capacity to be with the other dimension as well. And this, I am reminded, is also a theme of Eigen's (2018): this doubleness of pain and beauty. I discover, as I tend the dream (a beautiful term introduced by Stephen Aizenstat's work [2011]), that Eigen's twin regard for the pain and beauty of life accompanies me at the edges of my awareness.

This is how it is: the pain and the beauty are co-emergent. Although this is not my wish, it appears as a dreamtime expression of life itself. As I open to it, it seems that the dream has a teaching of its own.

The third dream I wish to relate—an ecstatic dream—called for the same openness to receive it. I am a singer and songwriter, as well as a psychologist, therapist, and professor. And this dream brought me a song. The dream took place on the final night of my honeymoon. I awoke in the middle of the night on the heels of receiving the song. At first, I felt compelled to return to the sweetness of sleep. Part of me was beginning to let the song slip away back into the cosmic night from which it arose. But another part was receiving the beauty of the dream, and my intent to usher it to the other side of the waking mind quickly grew. I sat up. And I started to write down the song. The lyrics I could trace were not precisely as they had been given in the dream, but they were close and kindred and resonated with the feelings and expressions of the dream song. So I kept going. I wrote the lyrics and stayed with the melody that was given in the dream. My husband was sleeping, and I did not want to wake him, so I crept into the bathroom to record the melody on my phone. Sleep kept pulling at me, but true to the welcoming, I stayed with the dream long enough to write it down.

This is the song that the dream ushered in, which I later titled "Shown": copyright, Willow Pearson Trimbach, Lionessroars Productions, 1/10/23 used with permission of the songwriter

Well show me your face
From the inside of time
I'll reach back from the seam
And now inhabit mine

Well just show me the place
Where you circle the stars
And I'll cast you a spell
That does pray into ours

We'll find where we join
And I'll sing you from there
Then the treasure of love
Will cascade through your hair

Just lend me your hand
As it comes from above
So that I can feel
The heart of this true love

Just lend me your eyes
And do let me see through
So that I can see
Something calling, brand new

And this is the dream from which the song emerged:

It is the last night/morning of our honeymoon. I dream that a fellow-academic calls on me, among all the participants present at the academy, to perform. He addresses me as "Melody." It isn't a mistake. And I affirm, "You're asking me, Willow, who is sometimes confused as melody." And then, a male professor starts to sing a song. And rather than defer to him completely, I join in and collaborate and continue the melody and then lead the song myself. And the man I like who sits at the computer next to me takes notice. And a former professor of mine watches from the audience. And the song invitation comes out of my thesis/dissertation, which is being signed off on, as I had been working on submitting it. There are several hard copy files of my thesis/dissertation, and one of them is a plastic pouch that is akin to my makeup bag, with some change in it, but it is unclear if the change is mine or some other thesis student's.

I experience the song as a wedding gift. I have written elsewhere about dreaming as a form of original artistry (Pearson, 2021a), and this dream, with its song offering, is a particularly vivid example of dreaming as original artistry. It is a testament to my love for my husband and to the love we share. It is also a song about beginning our life together. It is about communion of love from and with the spirit world. Had I not followed the impulse to awaken and to write the song down from the dream, it would have been lost. Had I followed the impulse to return to sleep, the song would have disappeared back into the ethers from which it arose. It took extending a spirit of welcomeness to the ecstatic song, a willingness to bring such beauty into the world, to sing the song. It required bypassing any immediate judgment about the worth of the song or the dream that might have cast it aside, to instead extend a spirit of implicit value of the song and the dream in order to catch it.

I experience the dream in which the song arose as a complex drama involving healthy narcissism and my connection not only to music but also to my husband and to the academic world and to scholarship and the links among all those dream elements. What's more, I experience the dream song as an expression and conduit of spirit that embraces and yet also transcends the body.

Welcoming

Certainly, I could write a different paper that explores the ecstatic dream itself, which is rich and multifaceted. Instead, what I wish to do here is to attend to the welcoming required to be in relationship to the dream and to the song it contains. That moment of reckoning in which I could have fallen back to bed or gotten up was a moment of greeting the spiritual psyche in all her mystery. I did not know where the song would lead, if I would wish to stay with it, or what it would convey. But a welcoming spirit in me, aided by and joining with the welcoming spirit of several psychoanalytic mentors, of whom Michael Eigen is a key figure,[2] moved me toward creating a bridge between dreamtime and wakefulness.

And the welcoming didn't stop there. It went further: "A little bit at a time," an echo of Eigen in my introjection of his teaching (Pearson, 2019). I got up. I wrote the lyrics. I recorded the melody. And before I went back to sleep, I wrote down the dream. In the morning, I told my husband that I had the dream. Then, later in the day, I invited him to read the song and the dream. Then I returned to it again later, inviting a dear friend, Eva Tuschman Leonard, to receive the dream as I told it to her. Then, I returned to the song and the dream to share it in this chapter. My husband and I decided to record the song, entitled "Shown," and to share it on my music website, Lionessroars (visit https://www.lionessroars.org/music/weddingsong to listen to the song [Pearson Trimbach, 2022]). My husband accompanied my vocals with his electric guitar arrangement—a wedding gift that trails our wedding day and our honeymoon, bringing the dream song into the everyday life of our marriage.

Singing and recording this dream song is a way to keep *dreaming the dream*, to keep feeling the dream, to be open to the dream continually, to welcome the dream repeatedly, and to be in an ongoing relationship with the dream. Every time I sing or play the song, there is a quality of original artistry's further emergence. As dreaming is a kind of original artistry (Pearson, 2021a), singing the dream is to carry that artistry into Psyche's living room and into Psyche's expanse.

Opening to Unbounded Psyche

The work is in turning toward the unknown, meeting the mystery of the unknown—whether that unknown entity is rendered benevolent or malevolent or constituted by an admixture of both beneficence and malignance—with faith that whatever one greets can be faced with spiritual strength. This is faith in the truth drive.[3] This is faith in opening to unbounded Psyche and her dreams. A truth drive for O—Bion's symbolic designation for the unknowable unknown, the vast infinite, and emotional truth—for freedom, for a genuine glimpse of realization, is even greater than the nonetheless formidable ego drive toward positive self-reflection/self-image and comfortability within the self.

In dreams, as in life, there is a more profound satisfaction, beyond comfort, in companioning truth, however difficult that truth may be. And that truth drive in each of us is drawn on by a desire to transcend (and, yes, to transgress) the sociocultural bounds of knowing and to court Psyche in all her complexity and multidimensionality. Drawn on by the truth drive, we are compelled by a desire to know Psyche in her true home and to come home to ourselves in the process of courting Psyche. This truth drive compelled me to hold all three of my dreams—the two difficult birthday dreams and the ecstatic honeymoon dream—in the light of awareness.

Psyche is like a wild cat who can be immensely loving, loyal, bonded, independent, fierce, and courageous. She is equally capable of softly curling up in a treetop and purring the morning away as she is off quietly stalking her prey for survival. She is equally affectionate and ferocious, sweet and ruthless.

Psyche, however social, is not a domestic animal. Her wild nature must never be forgotten. Her true home is in the wilderness, where mystery is ever her cloud companion, even as truth, as bright sunlight, is her distinct gift. She commands respect for the places she, as Psyche, ventures. There, the unconscious teems like a wild forest, and although it beckons, it does not yield its secrets. Psyche, ever agile, can slip through this dense and otherwise impenetrable wilderness, but we cannot always follow her. Although her terrain within remains hidden from complete view, the essence of these wild places casts a presence at its discernible edge. And there are clearings where all that cannot be traveled can be sensed. In courting Psyche, I have an ever-deeper respect for all that she can and cannot show me directly. I have learned to become her apprentice, courting both difficult and ecstatic dreams, days and nights alike.

My view of and relationship to Psyche, as presented in my analogy of Psyche as a wild cat, has been deeply influenced by my reading and study of the work of Michael Eigen. As I have written in a previous review of his book *The Challenge of Being Human*, "With [Eigen] … as analytic guide and companion, the psychotherapeutic journey becomes one of an opening that is without end and that can begin again, and again" (Pearson, 2019, p. 69). This is no minor influence. To continue going further on the lifelong psychotherapeutic journey, gifted with the grace of beginning again and again, despite everything and anything that has gone before, is an immense gift. Eigen (2020) invokes, as he simultaneously observes, "Beginning never stops."

It is partly a testament to Eigen's (2016) longstanding teaching on shame—how to partner with it and be curious about it—that such an immense gift opens. Where shame can be a painful and obstructing roadblock to navigating Psyche's terrain, Eigen's partnership attitude toward shame (and toward all aspects of Psyche) invites us to welcome the otherwise off-limits parts of ourselves. Eigen invites us to welcome and partner with the parts of ourselves that become closed off in the frightening basement of the self or kept out of reach in the exalted heavens of the self. Whether abased or exalted, Eigen encourages us to bring Psyche into the living room, where we can sit with her and get to know her a little bit better, moment by moment.

Tethered to the Dream

This reflection on Eigen's welcoming attitude toward Psyche brings me back to my dreams. Eigen helps me to start again, approach anew, keep going … His teaching, as I experience it and as I receive it, is that opening to Psyche is the work itself, even beyond any particular disclosure that such opening may allow for. In the case of dreaming, it is the living partnership with the dream that fosters a relationship with the spiritual psyche.

I find myself opening further in exploring the second dream in which a woman and her children's feet have been burned off. I associate *burning feet* with walking across hot coals and not being immune to them. I associate it to the wisdom of respecting the destructive capacity of fire. I share this dream image with a dear friend, Max Regan, and he reminds me that the title of my first album is *Burning*

(Pearson, 2003). I am reminded of the horror of the wildfires that have ravaged so much of my home state of California and other parts of the world over the past three years. What is now called "wildfire season" is approaching. New pathways in the thicket of Psyche appear.

And yet another association visits me in reverie: I think of the rings of fire depicted in tantric Vajrayana Buddhist iconography and their symbolic burning of ignorance. What ignorance is being burned through this dream image? What lotus of further opening may yet appear here?

And the other birthday dream image, *eyes in my pocket*, I associate with the freedom of not being wedded to one point of view. New ways of playing with the meaning of "wedding" are disclosed. And the ghostly sense of disembodiment, as a being with *eyes in her pocket*, is another strong association that opens up....

It is not about having the dream images pinned down, explained away, or definitively determined. As I write about them here, they keep opening, according to my invitation, aided by Eigen. What's more, there is always a further opening to explore. The opening is without end. Eigen also teaches respect for and partnership with this welcoming of the infinite.

Welcoming the infinite is a portal to welcoming the endless possibility for change. Eigen (2016, 2018) accomplishes this in his writing and in his teaching by conveying a twin reverence for the difficult, even the unbearable, together with a reverence for that which is pleasing to us, even longed or ached for. Whether it be a dimension of Psyche that we reject or a dimension of Psyche that we desire, Eigen welcomes them equally into the living room of the self in relationship with the spiritual psyche.

Reverence for the Unseen

I take another look at the dream image of *eyes in my pocket*. This image is one of seeing that I cannot see. As I stay with the image, the beauty of the doubleness (Bagai, 2021) of the dream opens.

Infinities are by no means purely theoretical for Eigen. Infinities, according to Eigen's sensibility, are a testament to the mystery that we are at once embedded in and a living expression of. I am deeply moved by Eigen's mantric exhortation that life keeps opening (Fuchsman & Cohen, 2021), that there is no end to Psyche's reach, that there is always more to experience, that we can go further than we thought, and that there are places even dreaming cannot touch that affect us.

Under Eigen's (2011, 2014, 2020) influence, the infinite is a source of faith.

In this spirit of Eigen's faithful testament to the infinite, I am less rejecting of *eyes in my pocket* than I was when I first woke up and more accepting of the double truth of the dream image of seeing that I cannot see. I become more accepting of and even reverent of the depth of the unconscious, of which this dream image becomes an ambassador in this new light.

I become reverent of the unseen and the unknown. The rhythms of endarkenment and enlightenment (Pearson & Marlo, 2021) are complementary and revelatory in their incubation of the mystery rather than oppositional in nature, a negation of one another, or at cross purposes.

There is surrender here, an ability to meet the mystery with wonderment. There is a little less fear and a little more faith. There is an upward gaze, the edges of a half-smile, and the slight lift of a tilted brow. The feeling is one of asking, with curiosity, what's next?

In this light, those *eyes in my pocket* are the grace of not seeing, self-preservation in the defense of turning away, the benevolence of dissociation and compartmentalization and confusion, and the resource and restoration of sleep. And here I am grateful for and pay homage to all that is beyond me. With my *eyes in my pocket*, I can simply be human (Pearson, 2021b). I can have limits and boundaries. I can turn off, shut down, and go within. The *eyes in my pocket* imagine that I will see when I am able and, until then, I will be protected.

My zealous, revolutionary self scoffs at all this humanness; however, the lessons of the dream image allow for humility. I am hearing both dimensions in the second half of my life, yet now learning more from humility. From this vantage point, there is a growing faith in the rhythm of sleeping with conscious awareness and of the unconscious with waking. There is now a balm for the seeming split between sleeping and waking. Sleeping and waking become the nature of a caesura.[4] The parallel caesura of birth and death hovers at the edges of the un/conscious.

In the months since I began writing this chapter, tending to these dream images, hundreds of other dream images have visited me throughout the day and night. Most have faded from consciousness. Or so it seems. But have they? Perhaps, as I have written elsewhere (Pearson, 2021a), there is a place outside the light of self-awareness where Psyche is conversant with this constant stream of dream thought and the pregnant void that dreaming incubates, issues from, and is continuous with. This leads me back to an attitude of reverence and humility. I am comforted by the notion that the dreamtime is working on behalf of the mystery of the cosmic evolution of all. With that thought, I can go gently back to sleep, allowing dreamtime to do its necessary work (Civitarese, 2014). There is trust in the sustained gesture of dreaming, which is a medium of conversation between the realms of the seen and the unseen.

This reverence for the unseen takes me beyond the image, underneath the words; it allows for other dimensions of experience to open for a mysterious ongoing conversation.

In the Presence of the Dream

I return to the image of Psyche as a wild cat. I find myself writing in bed at night, on my iPhone, next to my beloved tom cat. He nudges the phone with his insistent chin, inviting me to play with the words and not be too tied to them, even as I tend to their crafting. My cat reminds me in a direct and visceral way that what we can say is not the thing itself. With that remembrance, I venture upstairs to the computer to open into the world of constructing words to imply and even transcend meaning. I wish to convey something of the unseen world itself—that which animates all and with which all is infused. My dreams, revealed in or sealed from self-awareness, are a portal to presence itself. And it is the dream song that creates a bridge between the feeling of words and a wordless feeling.

Often, my cat hides when I have visitors. Yet I know he is attuned to their every motion and inflection as he accesses his prospects for safety and his implicit knowledge of where and how long he must hide out or risk contact. My awareness of him assessing the visitors waxes and wanes with my attention to the interactive field of being with my visitors. This is, I now reflect, how consciousness is. It is a rhythm of attention and forgetting, a rhythm of being careful and carefree, a rhythm of being called out and called back in.

These, too, are Eigen's themes that I find surfacing in my awareness: the unseen rhythms of life and faith (Eigen, 2020), the presence of background support (Eigen, 2004).

Psyche Dreaming, Psyche Singing, and Psyche Being

To close, another theme that is linked to these themes, which also supports me, is Eigen's (2020) invocation of "psyche singing." This sense of psyche singing partners with my sense of psyche dreaming, allowing for a field of presence that emerges intermittently from and submerges intermittently back into a larger expanse of "psyche being." On both a metaphoric and literal level, Eigen's being as a musician and psychoanalyst/psychologist/psychotherapist invites me to creatively combine my lifelong twin kindred passions for music and healing, for music and psychology, and for music and therapy (see Pearson, 2021c). In a direct way, Eigen's example of writing about his love of music is a further welcoming of my bringing writing, singing, and dreaming into a conversation. This call to create across these spheres, to bring them into a direct relationship here through sharing the dream song "Shown" in its recorded and written forms, is an illustration and a manifestation of Eigen's background support, welcoming me, welcoming us, and welcoming Psyche. May "Shown," emanating from the dreamtime, be a lullaby to welcoming and opening into love, seen and unseen.[5]

Notes

1 Michael Eigen is the author of more than 30 books. He leads a seminar on Wilfred Bion's work as well as on his own scholarship; this seminar, which Eigen has been leading for more than 50 years in New York City, historically rotating among the work of Lacan, Winnicott, and Bion, opened to an international audience on Zoom at the advent of the COVID-19 pandemic, allowing me and many other students of Eigen's work to participate. Eigen is associate clinical professor of psychology (adjunct) in the Postdoctoral Program in Psychotherapy and Psychoanalysis at New York University and a senior member of the National Psychological Association for Psychoanalysis.

2 Another key welcoming figure in my life is the late James S. Grotstein. When I was engaged in doctoral study, he said to me during theoretical consultation, "You know, nobody

owns psychoanalysis. Everyone makes their own contribution to it. It keeps evolving" (personal communication, June 22, 2013).

3 See Pearson (2021a) for commentary on James Grotstein's usage of the concept of the truth drive.

4 See Grotstein and Pearson (2016) and Pearson (2021a, 2022) for a discussion of caesura.

5 For a presentation of integral dreaming, rooted in study with my principal meditation teachers, Lama Palden Drolma and Khenpo Tsultrim Gyamtso Rinpoche, see Pearson (2022).

References

Aizenstat, S. (2011). *Dream tending: Awakening to the healing power of dreams*. New Orleans: Spring Journal Books.

Bagai, R. (2021). Thoughts on mystery, paradox and doubleness. In W. Pearson & H. Marlo (Eds.), *The spiritual psyche in psychotherapy: Mysticism, intersubjectivity, and psychoanalysis* (pp. 44–68). Routledge.

Civitarese, G. (2014). *The necessary dream: New theories and techniques of interpretation in psychoanalysis*. Routledge.

Eigen, M. (2004). *The electrified tightrope*. (A. Phillips, Ed.). Karnac.

Eigen, M. (2011). *Eigen in Seoul: Vol. 2. Faith and transformation*. Karnac.

Eigen, M. (2014). *Faith*. Karnac.

Eigen, M. (2016). *Image, sense, infinities, and everyday life*. Karnac.

Eigen, M. (2018). *The challenge of being human*. Routledge.

Eigen, M. (2020). *Dialogues with Michael Eigen: Psyche singing* (L. Daws, Ed.). Routledge.

Fuchsman, K., & Cohen, K.S. (Eds.). (2021). *Healing, rebirth, and the work of Michael Eigen: Collected essays on a pioneer in psychoanalysis*. Routledge.

Grotstein, J.S., & Pearson, W. (2016). In conversation on caesura and reversible perspective. *Fort Da: The Journal of the Northern California Society for Psychoanalytic Psychology, 22*(1), 51–60.

Pearson, W. (2003). *Burning* [CD]. Lionessroars Productions. Retrieved from https://www.lionessroars.org/music/burning

Pearson, W. (2019). Opening to the challenge. *Fort Da: The Journal of the Northern California Society for Psychoanalytic Psychology, 25*(1), 68–71.

Pearson, W. (2021a). Caesuras of dreaming: Being and becoming, thinking and imagining. In W. Pearson & H. Marlo (Eds.), *The spiritual psyche in psychotherapy: Mysticism, intersubjectivity, and psychoanalysis* (pp. 180–201). Routledge.

Pearson, W. (2021b). Reckoning with the spiritual truth of aversive emotions: Evolving unconditional positive regard and discovering the good enough clinician. In W. Pearson & H. Marlo (Eds.), *The spiritual psyche in psychotherapy: Mysticism, intersubjectivity, and psychoanalysis* (pp. 118–137). Routledge.

Pearson, W. (2021c). Elemental contact: from madness to mysticism in celebrating the work of Michael Eigen. In K. Fuchsman & K.S. Cohen (Eds.), *Healing, rebirth, and the work of Michael Eigen: Collected essays on a pioneer in psychoanalysis* (pp. 227–236). Routledge.

Pearson, W., & Marlo, H. (Eds.). (2021). *The spiritual psyche in psychotherapy: Mysticism, intersubjectivity, and psychoanalysis*. London and New York: Routledge.

Chapter 8

Ah, Strawberries!

Shalini Masih

...Some momentary awareness comes
As an unexpected visitor.
Welcome and entertain them all!
Even if they're a crowd of sorrows,
Who violently sweep your house
Empty of its furniture,
Still, treat each guest honorably.
He may be clearing you out
For some new delight...

The Guest House, Rumi (2004)

This chapter is about falling. The title of this chapter came to my memory in a session. It is from an excerpt from Eigen's (2021) writing on 'Rebirth.' Eigen or Mike as he is lovingly addressed by his students, wrote,

> Falling is part of learning to walk, just as biting one's own mouth accidentally is part of learning to use teeth, self-injury part of the limits of our equipment. We liken tripping over our own feet or an unseen external obstacle to falling unexpectedly off a cliff. Or a moment's gap of loss of control as falling into an abyss or chaos. We swim in everythingness-nothingness. We swim in seas of pain. Even so, we may with the Zen master who falls off a cliff, spy a bunch of strawberries on the way down and murmur within our beings, "Ah, strawberries."

Here the author writes the story of her falling as a therapist who failed in her work. The author suffered multiple losses during the pandemic. Taken over by grief, she failed to allow for any aliveness in herself or in her clients. She kept falling and failed to 'spy upon any strawberries' or any beauty in life. She developed an impermeable shell around her that kept her from using her supervisions with Mike. This chapter is about how Mike cracked through that hardened shell. This story is written in an associative and exploratory style with a hope that the glimmers of psychoanalytic wisdom will shine through in some moments.

DOI: 10.4324/9781003322993-8

The summer of Delhi in 2021, felt hotter than in past years as thousands of bodies were cremated. As the second wave of COVID hit, the city ran out of wood for pyres and flowers for graves. The mass annihilation caused by the pandemic surrounded me, mirroring, perhaps, the familiar-yet-unknown internal annihilation I had somehow managed to avoid confronting. Each time my phone rang, I felt my heartbeat quickening. I wondered –Who has passed on, now? We lost family members and friends we once sat and laughed with, and created memories with. Some children of friends were orphaned, some elderly parents were left behind and some pets never saw their masters return. Words failed to console grieving family members, friends and patients. The image and sounds of my dying cousin brother's death rattle remained etched in my mind for a very long time.

My clients grieved their losses and shared their dread. With my all, I sat through the hours, trying to bear witness to our painpsychic permeability comes with a price. Sessions left me with an unbearable chest ache, thinking suspended.

Distraught, I saw Mike for our weekly online Zoom supervision. After many minutes of silence, Mike mentioned the news he saw about COVID deaths in India. He welcomed my pain along with the pain of all my patients. The pain burst out. Before I knew it, these words came out of me.

Me: *There are just too many deaths, Mike! Make it stop! Make it stop! Please!*

   I was sobbing. Mike heard and he too, wept, silently.

Mike: *We have to live through this.*

   Then, almost like an instruction, he said, *'Live through it!'*

I moved to a new country partly wishing that it would transform how I had been experiencing life. With immigration came other personal crises. Life demanded that I turn into a caretaker for the family. I shut out my pain and with it every other emotional experience. Surviving replaced living as I became stoic. Unbeknownst to myself, I was hardening into a different kind of psychotherapist. Like life, clinical work continued, but, today in hindsight I can recognize that something went missing. Meaning was missing. I was not alive as a person or as a psychotherapist.

As a student of psychic reality, I could sense I was failing and falling. But I let myself fall freely. In my clinical work, my responses became theoretical, intellectual, escaping the aliveness of emotional experience. In an interesting, even embarrassing, turn of events my patients made me confront my deadness. And I shall remain grateful to them.

My clients began to bring their palpable frustrations and complaints about an impasse in our work. But there were two clients in particular who shared this sense, in a rather hard-hitting way. A young man I was working with complained that he sometimes felt pressured by me to 'get better.' He went on to tell me that he had often seen me 'rolling my eyes' when he repeatedly brought the same concerns session after session. Another client on Zoom clicked a screenshot of her screen and sent it to me. She told me that she did this by 'accident.' After that session, I looked at the image she sent. It was my own face as it appeared on my client's screen. It was me, yet, I could not recognise myself.

I looked exasperated, utterly bored and even arrogant! My face in the image was saying to the client: *"How can you be so stupid?! We have been working for so long! And you still don't get it? How dumb is that?! Why aren't you getting better, yielding results!"*

Today I am reminded of the time when exactly these words were told to me by my mathematics teacher in school. His roaring voice made me freeze, I stopped breathing during my mathematics lessons. I deposited 'that which escaped my thinking' into my teacher, and my curiosity was not welcomed. I felt shamed by my teacher just as perhaps my patients were now feeling shamed by me.

Years later I met another teacher of mine, Mike Eigen. Mike has been a teacher who welcomes all experiences. I fondly remember Mike giving me his book, "The Sensitive Self" when I first met him in his Manhattan office years ago. But now I questioned – What happened to my sensitive self? Invoking Bion's (1985) reflections on hatred of pain, Eaton (2015) wrote, 'Bion seems to be warning that rather than finding relief when we go dead to pain, we open a door to even deeper forms of pain, like cruelty inflicted upon innocent others.' There was cruelty in the way I was using psychic truth with my clients. This use of psychic truth felt close to blasphemy to my psychoanalytic self. This discovery caused me pain but only momentarily. After some time it failed to evoke a guilt that could drive some sort of reparation. Poetry disappeared from my practice. I was closed to feeling, to sensing and to any beauty around me.

I felt incomplete in many ways and unable to conjure a desire in myself to do something about it. I saw Mike in supervision sessions but remained impervious to his impact on me. However, sometime later I was saved by something deeper in me. Mike appeared in a dream that recurred for many days. I dreamed that:

I visit a guest house. Many people of different ages are living here. No one is related to anyone else. In my individual interactions with each of them I am left feeling incomplete. There is a four-year-old girl who shares that she goes into the bathroom on the first floor of the guest house and speaks to her twin brother. She speaks into the commode using it as a telephone. Her twin brother responds. She worries that others in the house would think she is crazy, so she keeps this secret to herself. Another young woman laments about her lover who is trapped in another land. But she tells me that it is best if they are kept apart. Together they may die. Affected by the pain of these people I step outside the guest house into the garden. There, in the lawn I find Mike. The Mike in my dream has long flowing silver hair and a long silver beard. Like a wise sage he sits smoking a hookah, looking up at the night sky. Mike is studying the stars! I approach him and share my sense of the incompleteness (attacks on linking?) that plague the members of this guesthouse. In his characteristic blend of a composed yet animated tone, he tells me about another guest house in another realm where I must travel. Like a wizard, he equips me to travel between the two realms. He says that there is only one condition–I should tread stealthily and make sure that I do not catch the eye of the house owner, a Giant tyrant toddler. For this giant toddler, the guest house is like a doll house and its inhabitants are his puppets, prisoners of his playfield. If he sees me, he will hold me hostage like others. I am sent into a whirlpool and arrive at this other guest house. The inhabitants of this house are bizarre – part cat and part dog or part elephant and part mouse or part animal and part human. I enter the house, careful not to be noticed by the giant toddler. I meet the twin boy here who speaks to his twin sister via a commode, a young man who misses his love, and many other incomplete people. The dream ended as I woke up feeling anxious.

I recognise that my dream was an attempt at making sense of how, threatened by pain so unbearable, my mind was relying on splitting and projective identification. It would be dreadful and disorienting, to come together as a person. Unlike Rumi's (2004) welcoming guest house, the dream depicted the image of my mind as a guest house where guests were not only un-welcomed but also held hostage. I recall wondering how I could undo the incompleteness, the lack of links, I dreamed about. This question created an itch in my mind. Little did I know I was to be saved by this itch.

I saw Mike for our supervision. Yet again, I spoke about stuckness in clinical work. My own associations in these supervisions had become repetitive. Nothing Mike invited me to think about was taken in, however, this time was different. I brought stuckness to Mike but I also brought him a dream. I asked him in a complaining way:

Me: *Why are you studying the stars in this dream?*
Mike: *I don't know! It's your dream!*

In hindsight I think I pushed my own experience of not-knowing into Mike perhaps secretly hoping that he would offer some theoretical knowledge, thus taking on the role of an all-knowing teacher juxtaposed against an ignorant student. But, unlike my shaming mathematics teacher, Mike conveyed that he was very comfortable swimming in the sea of not-knowing. He, in turn, welcomed collaboration to think through the equations in the dream. He welcomed an emotional experience of dreaming the dream together.

I chuckled. Then Mike asked -

Mike: *Why do you think I am studying stars?*
Me: *You are studying constellations, perhaps...Psychic constellations?*

        After some silence, I asked him...

Me: *How can I bring the incomplete parts together with this giant tyrant of a baby always watching?*

Mike: *What does this tyrant baby want?*

Me: *(Mike's question made me anxious. I felt my heart racing with an inexplicable fear) I don't know.*

> Something in me was not ready to think.
> Mike persisted without shaming me.

Mike: *Well, can you welcome the tyrant?*

> WELCOME THE TYRANT! How preposterous! I thought to myself. I stopped speaking, Mike did not.

Mike: *Ask this tyrant baby what it wants…*

> Mike's tone became commanding and playful at the same time as he said,

Mike: *What do you want!?*

> *Some part of me responded: to hold all these people hostage…*
> I was surprised by what came out of me. I did not protest.
> Mike was now in direct conversation with the tyrant.

Mike: *Why? What will you do with these hostages?*

> *The tyrant part in* Me: *Play with them!*
> *Mike giggled like a toddler: Play with them? What else?*
> *The tyrant part in* Me: *keep them close*

Mike: *Why do you need hostages?*

> *The tyrant part in* Me: *I need them close…I am lonely.*

Mike: *Well, there you go…*

> Now, Mike allowed some silence.

Mike might say that the dream I had was a 'successful' dream because he believes that,

> To have a successful dream is not just to feel better, to succeed in wish-fulfilment, but to nibble on what is bothering one a little more. Nibbling on what is bothering one sooner or later brings one to a nameless irritant built into life, an agony that remains invisible no matter how one names it. Exploding dream bubbles challenges us to become artists of the invisible. (Eigen, 2018, p.28)

Mike, as 'an artist of the invisible' (Masih, 2021) was inviting me to also become one, to look at the ache that I wished to keep invisible. Like in the dream, in this dream-like supervision, Mike sent my mind into a dizzying whirlpool. He persevered and made sure I was impacted by him and this opened me up to feel my own impact upon myself. While I brought psychic tyranny, Mike, like Rumi (2004), introduced the concept of imagining welcoming the tyrant. By doing so he introduced a model for psychic democracy. The tyrant sought some companionship. The moment, Mike welcomed the tyrant, my own established stoic psyche-verse was disturbed. Experience felt welcomed now and I felt the too muchness of it in my mind and body. A war inside was unleashed. Awake, I experienced a persistent state of being on the edge, but not falling off the cliff. While asleep, images of mass destruction through wars were unleashed in my dreams, uncannily mirroring the state of the external world as one tyrant leader was waging war against another nation. The war in the external world had managed to make people sensitive to the pain of others. Gradually an alpha image came to my waking and dreaming mind unbridled – a tiny toddler squatted in front of a giant tyrant toddler, both looking at each other. The giant looked intimidating with his flared up nostrils, hunched shoulders and hands clenched in fists. The smaller toddler looked curious, relaxed yet alert and waiting. Did Mike welcome himself in my mind as this playful curious toddler? I had to allow this image to expand in my mind in all its myriad nuances.

In his talks and writings, Mike often hints at the tension between good and bad that marks all spiritual and mythic dramas. It is the oldest, perhaps even most primitive, of psychological wars known to the human mind. Mike invites his readers to imagine multiple permutations, various qualities, dimensions and ever-shifting combinations of our mind's capacities.

Something inside of me began to reconfigure. I did not realise that I was beginning again, all the while enduring the building blocks of this reconfiguration. I felt an unthinking dread, alongside the return of my sensing, feeling self states. This resurgence of feeling-sensing was the collateral beauty of Mike's intervention.

I was changing in ways that felt catastrophic. It would not be an exaggeration to say that after some weeks of being in this state, I felt new. When spiritual traditions talk about being born again, but being born of the spirit, is this what it feels like? Welcoming the tyrant meant extending an empathic hand to the stoic part of me. Unbeknownst to me, I began to crack up, allowing myself to feel the pain of those I had loved, lost along with the dread of losing the sick loved ones I was caring for. The giant tyrant baby began to shrink, occupying less and less space. It now felt like a scared, lonely baby.

A Way to Be(come) with Eigen

"When both hands are clapped a sound is produced; listen to the sound of one hand clapping."

In Zen Buddhism, the teacher presents the student with a *koan;* a riddle or a paradox. The student is not expected to resolve it but to sit with it meditating. Koan's are tools designed to help the student learn to abandon a dependence on reason and sharpen the intuition instead, to experience holding the tension that comes with the paradox rather than to explain it away.

Being in supervision with Mike is a lot like this. I experience his utterances as koans. For instance, I would share with him about my inability to contain a patient's intense feelings and Mike would respond with – 'Time is important!' I receive these koans and allow them to brew in my mind and inform my experience of being with my clients. Unlike the mathematics teacher from my childhood, Mike gently nudges the mind towards the cultivation of thinking. Therefore, this section is not about recounting reflections around *being* with Mike but reflecting on the experience of always *becoming* with him. Mike's koan-like responses have helped me appreciate that I am never a finished product, always a work-in-progress. He works like a midwife for thoughts that struggle to be born. He invites his students for creative waiting and a chance to expand the thinking apparatus by delaying succumbing to intensities. He balances his steadfast exploration of psychic reality with a special brand of passivity – *'pure resonant passivity expressively waiting.'* (Eigen, 2018) Not only is Mike never in a rush, he avoids it. This takes me to his equation with Time. Cohen (2021) has written on how time exists as a background object in Mike's thinking and work. It is Mike's phenomenal tolerance for emotional intensities that shapes his equation with time and waiting.

Further, Mike welcomes experiencing the self along with the alterity that works hard to elude it. Alterity or otherness thrives in invisibility. Recently, I wrote about Mike as an artist of the invisible (Masih, 2021) Through excerpts from Mike's works and my own sessions with him, I reflect on Mike's expert use of his multisensory self in sensing and illuminating those invisible aches engraved on the walls of his patients' inner home leaving them haunted. He sees the parts of self that are 'invisible in plain sight!' (in personal communication, Eigen, April 2019) My experience of learning from Mike has been an answer to a question that has often plagued my mind – How does one recognise a person's Otherness without making them an Other to oneself? How Mike welcomes experience has often made me think of the ideas of philosophers Levinas and Merleu-Ponty. We know that Emmanuel Levinas established the importance of collaboration and relationship with the other in the birth of subjectivity. His ideas open the imagination of intersubjectivity by their sharp focus on questions about how we experience ourselves, those around us and the world. These are also concerns that have been addressed notably through works of phenomenologist, Merleu-Ponty, who stressed the pivotal role of the body in our immediate experience of the world around us. In the immediacy of experience, all that is evoked is pre-reflective. Mike holds us in this immediacy of experience and pays close attention to how 'being in the moment' could rattle one's mind and body. He gently but steadily brings into dialogue the pre-reflective and othered parts of the mind, like he invited the 'tyrant' in me for a conversation. However, Mike welcomes experiences that may be experienced as overwhelming while at the same time containing them. This brings to mind a supervisee who Eigen (2004) wrote about in his work, Psychic Deadness. A supervisee reaches out to Mike for help with an abusive couple who survived explosive fighting. His supervisee reached out to Mike when the couple threatened to quit therapy. Mike sensed his supervisee's anxiety to 'do something' to make the couple stay in therapy. One gets a sense of Mike's ease around his limitations as he notes,

> For a time I lost myself in the feeling of pressure, tasting it and smelling it. I did not feel I could come up with anything useful, since this couple found nothing useful. That in itself was freeing. At least I could luxuriate in the impossible situation presented to me, and just savour the particular horror of the moment. I could empathise with my supervisee, who was sinking in pressure.

In the same chapter, Mike reflects on the role of supervision in the revival of psyche. He writes, 'supervision functions to restore the supervisee's psyche. The supervision couple survives the patient-therapist couple.'

Surviving any experience entails experiencing it. Being with Mike teaches me to be in the immediacy of experience while getting comfortable with not-knowing what that experience might evoke in me. I found resonance in Aner Govrin's (Eigen & Govrin, 2007) reflections on being supervised by Mike. As I dive into his accounts, the parts that find special echo with my own experiences are where Mike emerges as deeply interested in shifts, movements and transformations. How does change happen? I agree with Govrin when he notes about Mike that, "talking to him, like reading him, is a transformative experience…the "thing itself" that matters: mere experience, unstructured ideas, rich streams of thoughts, ceaseless movement, a feeling of biblical flood or a rainbow…his listeners have to transform their attentive capacities." Like Govrin, I too have learned (and am still learning) to relish in my unknowingness and give up frantic efforts to fully make sense of what Mike means. Mike facilitates interaction in a 'real experiential sense.' Being in his presence, an image often comes to my mind – Mike welcoming me to look at a work of art that is psychic reality. Approaching psychic reality from an aesthetic vertex, Mike is inviting me to say what this artwork conjured by the psyche is evoking in me. Following these evocations has enlightened me about my own equation with knowing and being known. In Bionian terms, such an exercise has made me confront my own capacity for positive and negative emotional links; L, H and K – love and hatred for knowing psychic reality. Meltzer, following Bion, considered this an essential 'aesthetic conflict,' out which evolves the capacity to 'learn from experience.' Reflecting on the ambiguity inherent in meeting the mother, Meltzer defined aesthetic conflict as 'the aesthetic impact of the outside of the beautiful mother, available to the senses, and the enigmatic inside which must be construed by creative imagination. Everything in art and literature, every analysis, testifies to its perseverance through life.' Meltzer posits that the central experience of pain in aesthetic conflict lies in uncertainty which can be best greeted with a desire to know (K-link).

> In the interplay of joy and pain, engendering the love (L) and hate (H) links of ambivalence, it is the quest for understanding (K-link) that rescues the relationship from impasse. This is the point at which Negative Capability exerts itself, where Beauty and Truth meet.

The tolerance of aesthetic conflict lies at the heart of what Bion, after Keats, has termed 'negative capability': a capacity for uncertainty without irritable reaching for fact and reason. The cloud of unknowing hovers above all encounters between self and other between people and within a person too. This unknowingness carries special intensity in analytic encounters.

In my own work, sometimes, I have wildly recoiled from what I have encountered. In such times, Mike, driven by a K-link, helped me keep my gaze alive, withstanding the discomfort and horrors that it stirred in me. He stares at the horrific long enough until its beauty begins to shine through. He notes that,

> our interest in life, if not thwarted or stunted, will lead us to each other, no matter how foreign or strange we are. We are excited, not only threatened, by difference. We want to nourish and cultivate mutual permeability, creative vulnerability. (Eigen &Govrin, 2007)

One gets a taste of Mike's love for knowing psychic reality and tyranny that thwarts it, in his response to Govrin's question about the need to know –

> Understanding is nourishing. Truth is nourishing. Love of truth, love of understanding: a great nourishing, driving force, but great tyrants too. How much destruction is unleashed by the way we understand things, by truths we live and die for. To sit together and speak about what we do to each other with our truths, the emotional impacts truth has on us: this is one of the contributions therapy can make to culture. The idea that we can do this and keep on doing this without coming to a conclusion, the notion of interminable analysis or therapy, is itself therapeutic, a guard against forcing ourselves and other into tyrannical finality. Another double capacity and need: to focus on what is unbudgeable while working provisionally along lines that yield access.

In the excerpt from my supervision with Mike shared above, it was the tyrannical unbudgeable (and unbridgeable?) in me that Mike welcomed in a bridge of dialogue.

Revival of Psyche

> *'Experience is an endangered species.'*
> *– Eigen, Feeling Matters* (2007)

How did my work with my clients revive, you ask?

Mike, welcoming the tyrant part of me, was experienced by me as an invitation to be benevolently known, even with my tyrannical parts. Elsewhere, I wrote about Mike as an artist of the invisible and wondered,

> what enabled Mike to 'sense' the invisible, whether it is the demonic and/or terrorist part playing hide and seek. It was as if Mike had a multisensory self

at work allowing him to possess a 360 degree vision as well as a scotopic vision. The former lets him see and share various vantage points while the latter makes it possible for him to adapt his vision to the bleakest clinical moments. (Masih, 2021)

Welcoming the experience of the worst part of me opened my psychic apparatus to a host of experience. I began to notice that my mind was also turning into a multi-sensorial apparatus. When I sat with my clients I was sensing their presence through what my eyes saw, my ears heard, my nose smelled, my skin felt, my body spoke and what was evoked in my mind.

My altered psychic state became starkly evident to me in session with one client. I call him Ben as he reminds me of Mike's patient, Ben from Coming Through the Whirlwind (Eigen, 1992). My client, Ben, was a 35-year-old professional life coach. People known to him experienced him as "full of himself." Psychotherapists may address him as narcissistic. He was well read and knowledgeable about psychotherapy and how trauma affects the mind in many ways, he was like me. He extended his use of intellectual theoretical knowledge as a life coach to our work. Session after session he felt enthralled teaching me his wisdom. I felt an impasse in that the space of the session was saturated with content that was bereft of meaning. I felt helpless to do anything about the impasse. Both of us fuelled this meaninglessness. In one session, weeks after Mike created an essential turbulence in me, the unbudgeable impasse in my work with Ben was also dislodged.

Ben walked into the room, greeted me and sat on the chair. He began to speak about his day, his work with a client whom he helped to feel more confident and less ashamed. He then went on to speak at length about his own shame, a punitive maternal internal voice of his mother's that stifled him.

Ben: *I thought I worked on this part of my mother that lives inside me. I know it has to do with my past.*

In a nearly sleepy state, with my eyes closed, with my mouth opened, these words sprouted out:

Me: *You know a lot. But do you suffer what you know?*

Both of us turned and looked at each other.
Where did that come from?
We then looked away to look within, to reflect.
My own internal dialogue:
Where did that come from?
Does he suffer what he knows? He does not.
Do I suffer what I know? I do not.
Our arrogance and the arrogance of others who resided in us kept us from suffering what we knew to be our truth.
We are so similar in some ways!

What does it mean to suffer what one knows?
How do I suffer what I know?

I instantly felt lonely. The heart, enclosed in my chest cavity, ached. I breathed deeply to soothe it and turned to look at Ben. He was clutching his chest and breathing deeply, profusely. In a rather dramatic way, Ben covered his face with his palms and yelled,

Ben: Fuck! What did you say?! Fuck! (struggling to breath) There is something there!

For some time Ben was breathing heavily, suffering the emotional experience of holding his breath around judgemental objects. We sat together, breathing. Each in touch with their pain. Eaton (2015) wrote, 'Breathing links inside and outside, mind and body, and even self and other. Breathing creates a basic rhythm. This basic rhythm emerges and is elaborated unconsciously in the body's experience of self, other, and world.'

In the space Ben and I shared, breathing was welcomed, along with the body and dreaming. I breathed through emotional knowledge of how my fear of losing loved ones kept me from being alive to the impact of the other on me. After some chest aches, many deep breaths and a few tears Ben and I looked at each other. I was feeling again in the presence of someone. We were both teary. He was looking right into my eyes and I let him. I was not unnerved by his gaze. As we held this gaze, I noticed his beige skin turn red and then almost crimson. I smiled and he smiled back. Then hiding his face behind his palms he said:

Ben: Something is coming up but I don't know if I should say it.
Me: Hmm… Something that has been hidden?
Ben: Yes! I don't know. Urgg! Do we have time?

There are two table clocks in the room. One faces me and the other faces him. I saw that there were still seven minutes left in the session. I turned to look at the clock facing him. It had stopped working a few minutes ago.

Me: Oh! It seems time stood still for you there!

I was surprised to witness my playful use of factual truth to convey an emotional one.

Ben laughed.

Me: But I can tell you that we still have seven minutes before the session ends.
Ben: Okay. I will say it. What will happen if I say it?
Me: Hmm…There is only one way to find out!

Where did this audacity come from? – I wondered.

Ben: Okay. I am going to say it...(sighing) *Your beauty...*
Me: Hmm...mm? What about it?
Ben: (Sighs) *Okay! I think you are very attractive, beautiful even and I have not said it because I felt ashamed thinking that you will judge me.*

I could see he was moved by the experience we shared and carried an appreciation for the beauty of that experience. At this point, this appreciation could only be translated inside him in terms of the physical beauty of someone who could enable an experience of deep emotional resonance.

Me: *If you were to be touched by beauty and recognise it, you shall be judged... for?*
Ben: *If I see beauty I might destroy it*
Me: *Or...*
Ben: *be destroyed by it...Woah! I never knew this!*
Me: *Hmm...welcome to not-knowing.*

The session ended. After this session, Ben decided to go for a drive. This was his first drive in many years of prioritising making money for survival, very similar to how I had prioritised surviving over living. He drove towards the hills and saw many waterfalls on his way. He then parked his car on the side of the road and sat on the roof of his car, relishing the sight of a rainbow. In the next session, he spoke about the rainfall from when we last met. I thought of the tears that fell and my own falls as a therapist. He then showed me a picture on his phone of a view he enjoyed and captured. He held his phone for both of us to be touched by the beauty of the view – A majestic vibrant rainbow arch stood at the horizon, behind a lush green field of grass that glowed as last rays of the setting sun fell on it. As I sat there soaking in the beauty of what I saw, an excerpt from the fields of experience Mike opens in his writing came rushing to my mind like wind and I murmured under my breath – Ah, Strawberries!

References

Bion, W. (1985). *All My Sins Remembered: Another Part of a Life.* Abingdon: Fleetwood Press.

Cohen, K. (2021). On the Importance of Time as a Background Object. In *Healing, Rebirth and the Work of Michael Eigen: Collected Essays on a Pioneer in Psychoanalysis.* Edited by Fuchsman, Ken & Cohen, Keri S. New York: Routledge.

Eaton, J. (2015). Becoming a welcoming object: Personal notes on Michael Eigen's impact. In *Living Moments: On the Work of Michael Eigen.* Edited By Bloch, Stephen & Daws, Loray (pp.131–148). London: Routledge.

Eigen, M. (1992). *Coming Through the Whirlwind: Case Studies in Psychotherapy.* Wilmette, IL: Chiron Publications.

———. (2004). *Psychic Deadness* (1st ed.). Routledge.

———. (2018). *Feeling Matters.* London: Routledge.

———. (2021). Rebirth: It's been around a long time. In *Healing, Rebirth and the Work of Michael Eigen: Collected Essays on a Pioneer in Psychoanalysis*. Edited by Fuchsman, Ken & Cohen, Keri S. New York: Routledge.

Eigen, M., & Govrin, A. (2007). *Conversations with Michael Eigen* (1st ed.). Routledge.

Masih, S. (2021). Reading the works of Michael Eigen: Artist of the invisible. In *Healing, Rebirth and the Work of Michael Eigen: Collected Essays on a Pioneer in Psychoanalysis*. Edited by Fuchsman, Ken & Cohen, Keri S. London: Routledge.

Rumi, J. (2004). *The Essential Rumi*, C. Barks (Trans.). (p. 109). New York: Harper Collins.

Chapter 9

Welcoming the Eye/I of the Storm

A Homecoming Story

Epsita Sandhu

During these last few years, to live in the world has meant learning how not to die. Come back home, for there is something deadly in the air, spreading through touch and through breath. It is no longer safe for stranger bodies to touch or to breathe in. Come back home. To familiar, safer bodies. To bodies that have birthed you, to bodies that can devour you. We will keep you safe, not dead. Being alive is too much; it will certainly kill you. Come back home.

Come back home.
Welcome, welcome back.
For some, homecoming has been a séance with familiar haunting voices.
What does it mean, to come back to beckoning ghosts of the undead, to re-discover the haunting of your house?

To learn how you carry it all in your body? To learn that home has been on your back, like a host of spirits with unfinished business which can only speak in riddles? Or like the shards of a turtle's broken shell, which penetrate into the soft tissue underneath, damaging and poisoning internal organs, blood and pus oozing out and spilling along its skin, tracing blueprints of locked rooms and barricaded corridors where you were first touched in ways that have not ceased to hurt yet. He's not dying yet, the turtle. He stands very still and heaves in agony. To move is to be assaulted by unnerving pain.

To come home for Aman, like so many of us, was to be called to witness, in an uncanny moment, the outside of his insides.

He had just crossed over the precipice of 30 when he came to therapy. He was a freelancer working in a competitive artistic industry, and I was a student and trainee at the community low-fee clinic at my university, called *Ehsaas*. His life was paced faster than his breath could catch up with. Mine was slow, almost too slow and heavy, as intensive as psychoanalytic training can be. He was a queer man, highly literate about the cultural forces seeping in his profession that perpetuate and sustain marginalization of his oppressed caste identity while performing a brand of popular, non-disruptive progressiveness. He was surrounded by a circus-like, dizzying social life composed largely of caste-privileged, elite Delhi

DOI: 10.4324/9781003322993-9

socialites and had an active work and sex life, all of which he felt disconnected from. I was a cis-straight, caste-privileged, middle-class woman, whose energies remained neatly bracketed within the routine of academic and clinical work. Our lives were very different from one another.

Yet, we've been working together for four years now, with sessions missed every few weeks being part of the way in which he regulates the intensity of the work. Among many caesurae that we have survived together, one was the shift to a virtual space as we all transitioned into the new normal of the COVID-19 pandemic. He took a long break from therapy after he returned to his hometown to his mother and sister. I had a homecoming too, much like many younger adults at the time.

Throughout our work, I often wondered if therapy was doing him any good. He came with a history of relational and sexual trauma sustained when he was a child and in his youth. Often, it felt like there was a lifetime of catastrophes that we needed to touch upon. Yet, his focus remained on the problems of not being able to build a stellar career, not being able to do the work he could feel proud of, and not being free enough of the pendulum of anxiety and numbness that kept him suspended yet afloat. An endless flagellation of *nots*. He also felt *not* in enough trouble to be able to go any deeper. He had done all the narrativizing he needed to do about his 'past' trauma. He did *not* see how talking about any of that could help him.

This paper is about my witnessing of his return to the (k)nots that arise from the depths of homecoming and welcoming the disentanglements of his roots from close quarters, while I was thrown in the jumble of my own. 'When two personalities meet, an emotional storm is created' (Bion, 1994). We were two people whose weather systems were storming with the same pressure of a collision between past and present.

This paper will highlight how becoming a welcoming object for the undercurrents of my own emotional climate has allowed for my work with Aman and our therapeutic space to become an eye[1] of his storm.

Returning home sponsored a retracing of the cracks in its floors and in our shells. It's been about remembering pain from the outside in, encountering the familiar liminal voices that echo through those cracks. It's been about learning to witness them and welcome them when they feel like intruders let back in through the collapse of the larger world as we knew it and the shells we had built to survive in it – a shockshell is better than none. This paper is about the beginning of a reacquaintance with pain to recognize its capacities to sustain the survival of thinking-feeling processes disrupted by trauma. For 'a psychology looking at only at what interrupts is incomplete or unbalanced' (Eaton, 2015).

The First Meeting

Ten minutes late for our first appointment, and after being lost on the way, Aman did not know how he made it to Ehsaas.

He had come here to seek help with a feeling of pervasive dread. Time had passed him by. He was in his 30s and not the success he thought he was supposed to be. He was living in a cheap apartment his mother had arranged for him with a landlord whose micro-aggressive queerphobic and caste-phobic prejudices made Aman feel trapped and persecuted in his own living space.

'Friends from work' and strictly casual sexual dalliances would routinely flock to his home in throngs, but he would find himself perched in a corner and drown out the noise in an alcohol-induced hum. His very words in the room with me were barely more than a mumble, and constantly, swaying at the edge of his seat, he barricaded his mouth with a quivering hand.

He felt used by his employers and lauded for his ideas, which were then misrepresented in the final product. He felt that he wouldn't still be stuck here if it weren't for something that was terribly wrong with him. Why, he expected himself to have established his own brand by now. Instead, he is *still* a queer man struggling to build a livable life in a hostile world, *still* traumatized from multiple instances of sexual assault and years of sustaining complex trauma as a child and in his youth.

> I have talked it all out in therapy before, worked it out that I probably wasn't raped or even if it was … assault, I probably seduced them, or maybe later turned it into a seduction in my head to cope, something like that … I don't know. he let out the shakiest breath, 'I don't know if this will help'.

By the end, I was left wondering about that too. I gasped for air. It felt as though I had been thrown in tar, unable to move, unable to even hope that there was a way out. I stepped into the corridor of our community clinic and looked up at the board hanging over the entrance. *'Ehsaas'* refers to a taste of feeling, an opening into experience. I struggled to imagine how we would even begin to enter these spaces with what had already been worked out, or in so many knotted ways. 'Not a rape', 'not trauma', just knots and knots in which his experiences seemed to be tied up to dismissive, exploitative, persecuting forces in self and others. Tongue-tied, Aman's voice was only a muffled scream, echoing through repeated erasures and rewritings of narratives that consistently seemed to serve the 'expected', not the truth of his lived experience.

How did he, indeed, make it here?

Home Is Where the Heart Aches

For the first several months of our work, when we could still meet in person at the clinic, Aman would often miss our sessions. It made him anxious to leave home. He didn't feel safe in public spaces where he had experienced multiple instances of being harassed and even violently assaulted. But even as he told me about being groped in buses and trains and, at least once, being attacked by a group of taxi drivers, it felt as though he didn't know if these were real events or not. Nor did his friends and family.

The fact that it incarcerated Aman to his flat made it real enough for me. Traumatic memories tend to be pixelated with dissociative and repressive processes anyway. What if there were memories and more importantly, lived feelings of assault, attack, and violation, that percolated into his present, in real and perceived threats to his safety? In an immensely facilitating quip in supervision, Dr. Masih's words helped to hold space for these complexities in our work: 'Fantasies are just as real in psychic material as memories'.

Persecutory figures kept him from being in therapy. Yet, Aman persisted. He told me about his early life. He hailed from a small town and had to fight his parents tooth and nail to be able to extricate himself from his fate as their son. Even as a child, he'd been as honest as he could about being attracted to other boys. He'd even told his mother about his uncle and the many times he had been abused by him. He'd never shied away from being more interested in pursuing art and developing a creative life than stepping into his father's or mother's shoes or their aspirations for him to live as a straight man with a stable government job and a 'respectable' life in the community.

The range of his experiences were all always met with either dismissal or punishment. What he was saying was *not* true; he would come around eventually. In the meantime, he could always be beaten or berated into good behavior.

It seemed, however, that Aman was made of stronger stuff. He created caverns where he could exist as himself – hidden, but in plain sight. He would lose himself in books and draw for hours. He would bring boys home, hold hands with them, and exchange kisses in his room. His mother could have caught him, might even have known. It seemed like he wanted to be found.

Aman openly chose a training program in the arts, despite enraged opposition from his family, as far away from his hometown as he could. It was shortly after he finished that he lost his father. He knows, in theory, that his grief for his father would only be as complicated as his relationship with him had been. But he didn't know how talking about him now could help.

There's something to be said, perhaps, for the quiet intensity of the task of welcoming resistance. Aman, I learned, didn't wish to talk about the past because the present was perhaps too fragile.

He had fought so fervently to arrive where he had come, a big open city where he perhaps hoped to find a dream that could take him beyond what he *had* tolerated (Eaton, 2015), only to find that he couldn't step beyond the threshold of a hostile rented home that still connected him to his mother. And that for reasons he couldn't clearly fathom or resonate with, he just couldn't bring himself to live up to the aspirations he had hoped would carry him over.

How could we then talk about what he had indeed carried over with him across the thresholds he had managed to cross? He seemed to be entrenched in an unending quagmire.

Aman would soon find himself returning to the origins of this quicksand in real time. Except this time, he'd be carrying me, a witness, over as well.

Pain Seeks Feeling

Shortly after Aman relocated, he began to talk about the return of a liminal pain in his body. He had been used to being in physical discomfort and pushing on anyway since he had been little. As an adult, he had learned how to manage it. He would work himself into exhaustion when he could, then push through that exhaustion too. At other times, he would use alcohol and weed to numb himself. Most importantly, there was a part of him that didn't believe in the reality of this pain.

To think that therapy could be working when pain and its incessant cacophony in the body are gone is to be left still in silence, whose meaning one must learn to listen for. While neuropathic pain allows Aman to express the need to be still, emotional pain is more easily dismissed as meaningless.

'Being in pain and not talking about it and still being functional' is a familiar roadmap to his *being*.[2] Working to translate pain, perhaps, is new territory. He seems just as surprised as I am that he hasn't missed any sessions lately and perhaps actually wants to talk here.

I wonder if, for once, his body does not need to hold and be gripped by a pain that a mind (mine? His?) is beginning to be able to think about. Yet, release can also feel like loss.

Aman makes me wonder what it means to survive the trauma. If trauma can be seen as an impact that disrupts thinking and feeling processes (Eaton, 2015), how do we make it, then, anyway, and what does it make of us, what do we make of it? Can the embodied psyche, in a flourish of inversion, create an exoskeleton of unthinkable pain where our 'lovely bones' have been arrested/suspended in growth?[3]

What would be the cost of shedding this shell?

He thinks of his mother, how he cannot be the son she wants.

A: We fight all the time, mother and I. I've come out to her a thousand times! Fighting with her about my choices again and again brings back the neuropathic pain. If I cannot marry, in sometime, mother will throw me out. I can't date anyone I might actually like. And to ask that I be left to die alone in silence is also too much. I don't even necessarily want a husband, or wife, or children. They're not in my daydreams. That would be irresponsible, dumb! When I broke up with my ex all those years ago, It was as though I'd been holding my breath all this while with every breath I would take.

Ambivalent breathing! Aman takes in a breath but holds it in place. Eaton (2015) describes breathing as an unconscious linking device, connecting the outside and the inside, the self and the other. Aman's breathing alerts us to these links, which thread through his relational experiences.

E: Perhaps you want to contact something, but also don't. The other could facilitate a contact within'

A: I don't know if anyone would want to listen to me, or read anything I have to say. When I reach for words, I feel less panicky. But why would anyone care, my own mother doesn't care

E: Your loyalties are strong. Do you care, when she doesn't?

A: If I can't make her happy, how can I ask to be happy and okay?

Aman cannot allow himself the right to be pain-free, a vicious morality. Eigen alerts us to primitive fears and destructive urges that can take the form of ethical persecution (1996). Not only are vital parts of Aman always threatened by persecution, but their entrapment in obligated/persecuted survival has also been vehemently justified. It seems that we are not always aware of how righteous we can be in self-torment, hating obligations that we keep anyway.

E: I think when you say you don't deserve to be happy because you can't give your mother the son she wants, as painful as that is, I think it keeps you from seeing that perhaps in her you may never have the mother you need.
A: It feels selfish to say that she will never be the mother I need her to be because there are parts of me that she will never understand. Once I know I start living, I know I will have to fight with mother.

What's the point in talking about gender and queerness here, in his hometown?, he wonders. With a casual fell stroke, Aman is capable of erasing all his narratives. Growing up queer is at the core of who he is, he says, there's nothing he can do about it.

I'm drawn into the inertia, and I don't resist it. Therapy really cannot, in many ways, 'do anything about it'. Making room for Aman's aliveness and deadness, to value it, is an unprecedented way of being. With every session, I'm left wondering if any of the work we do matters. Sometimes just showing up seems beyond possible and bearable; one doesn't know what to do with it. With Aman, I cannot unsee that I'm welcoming someone unwelcomed (Eaton, 2015), something I cannot always see.

E: It's so important to you that you could be *her* son, a very deep and heartfelt wish
A: It comes at a price that's not mine to give
E: What do *you* want from her?
A: I just want her to accept me. See my choices and not be disgusted by them. It's not a lot to ask for but it is. I cannot love anyone. She is disgusted by me. She hides it when I'm around, but she can't really.

I can't be anything here. But I don't want to leave! I want to stay. The thing is, I'm not ashamed of being gay. It's them! Why should I leave?

I'm not looking for an apology or salvation. I just want some acknowledgment. How many times can I say it? For now, I say nothing.

Aman and his mother speak to each other in riddles. His body expresses pain, and his words a rage born of his unmet need to have that pain (and its scourged endeavors for pleasure, connection, and creativity) acknowledged and maybe even loved. I suspect that it is not shame that keeps him in this paralysis with his mother and motherland. It might just be (1) an anger whose intensities render it scattered, muted, turned inwards, and perhaps even (2) love, reworked into a Kleinian envy of the mother, who seems to be holding back something he needs and something that's hers and only hers to give.

In how many ways, then, can he scream in agony? How many times? Eigen talks about screaming that, without a frame of reference, can turn to eternal screaming and there can emerge as a state of being, a feeler of pain. This primordial feeler of pain, Eigen writes, 'grows into an I-You story or scene or narrative' (p. 45, 1999). These stories may become fixed and provide a scaffold for what he calls a 'pain nucleus'.

'Part of therapy is to awaken the emotional nucleus itself, the emotion in subject-object casting' (1999, p. 45). Physical pain, or neuropathic pain, is a language, a signifier for an emotional I-you story the Aman has been typecast in where the (m)other is an obstructive object. She persecutes both a desire for pleasure and meaningful contact with pain. When Eigen tells us that one can get caught up in an I-You catastrophe, he describes the quality of a possible transformation,

> For the moment, Clea sees part I-vs.-You catastrophes that block and taint her life and gets a breath of affect as such. Enemies are real. They won't go away, One needs to protect oneself. But to free core feeling from painful contraction is a breath of fresh air.

For a long time in my work with him, Aman and I have only been *in* pain together. Post every session, whether they were in person at Ehsaas or through a screen, I would be left feeling choked up, an ache in my back from hunching toward the screen, trying to listen to his ever-softening voice with which he 'says nothing'. Eigen, with his favor of feeling, has helped me to have faith in the value of this resonance. He may be less interested in finding reasons and more interested in being the feeler of pain with his patient. I felt as though I didn't have a choice. 'Reasons', traces of the many origins of trauma in Aman's life, just felt dry and dead. They deadened, feeling even more. Only the pain was real and accessible. It's arrival in his body was indeed an opening, but only the beginning of a search for the I-You story he'd been in.

'Daring to speak is one of the most important acts in re-establishing a human dimension otherwise often crushed in the aftermath of violence' (Eaton, 2015). Perhaps suppression of 'real language needed to sustain the possibility of thinking, exploring, fathoming, and working through suffering that it sows' (Eaton, 2015) could also be an indication that violence is afoot.

Aman has dared to articulate many parts of himself, despite terrible violence. Yet he has also carried unspeakable, unthinkable secrets, his own and others', that seem to be killing people in the silence, like his cousin, who, between Sarkari Naukri and death, was lost to the latter, or the numerous other men, his father included, whose unlived lives in the performativity of hypermasculinity Aman was only too aware of. His eyes are wide open. How is mother so blind? How can she not see the nightmare he screams in?

How do you reconcile that?

A: (In a whisper) I don't think I can. Whatever person I am supposed to be, that she needs me to be, I've put it on hold. I can't walk away from it either. I don't want to walk away from it

E: What's keeping you here?

A: Here, I can learn how to shut doors. Learn how to occupy space. Wherever I've gone, its to do that.

Aman illuminates the pull toward catastrophe, the place where structures break down to violate being, and the broken is swallowed in so that we may familiarize with the contours of the debris. The Winnicotian maternal environment fails to keep the 'too-much' out, and the remains are taken in, impinging play but informing the construction of false selves. The only room that can feel like one's own is a bomb shelter.

A: It would've been easier if I hated her. But I don't. I love her. I hate that I'm in pain. I hate that I have to choose between her and a life that she wouldn't understand. I'm holding onto her because I need care, but at the same time it seems like something I cannot ask for. It feels trivial, needing these things from her. The least I can do is remain alive, barely. Even that is painful. It feels like I am made wrong.

Human Sacrifice

Is Aman's pain as much a communication as it is a concealment? What is he hiding in his body?

In Eaton's study of how Eigen facilitates becoming a welcoming object, he traces the movement from welcoming the body to welcoming the emotional storm. This progression inspires a tremulous opening. It's as though the instruments of emotional processing that have been disrupted by traumatic experience throw static, broken frequencies through the body into the screaming emotional storms that follow the trauma. Can we stay with the disjointed staccato that comes and goes in a rhythm of breakdown and emergence toward repair?

Aman's pain emerges in the body to give voice to injuries forgotten and forbidden to thought, then is lost to render a somatic silence that demands we think of what the pain meant to say and what needs to be said even though the pain is gone. Perhaps the dulling of bodily pain renders psychic pain clamant or claimable.

This moment in our work is where a key idea finds its expression: In complex ways, the 'I' discerns itself from the mind and the body. A 'basic pathological structure of our day', comprises a 'detached, covertly transcendental, steel-like mental ego vis-à-vis an explosive-fusional body-ego' (1992, p. xv).

Aman tries to transcend his body, other it altogether, leave it behind, now that the grip of pain has softened. As if its lived history has been rendered wordless/worthless too. Yet, as he feels and expresses an anger toward this body that has failed its function of holding pain close, he seems to be mourning, and perhaps therefore dreaming, the function of his pain. Like an armor, it keeps him alive by obstructing touch, being violent, and perhaps obstructive too. It keeps out as well, the 'obligation to survive' that he hates. Is this an obligation to hatch? To be touched by something outside of his own externalized internal?

A: I don't know how to be happy

E: Could you bear to be happy?

A: No. No ... I feel guilty. I increasingly feel like there is no point to being alive, I can't make it happen. Even if I could, in all those scenarios where I could make a life worth living, I couldn't dare to ask for happiness. I want to be successful, I have some ideas, but what is the point If I never work on them. I find that I am increasingly unwilling to make the effort. My body doesn't move

E: Maybe you use these ideas to torment yourself, your body

A: Maybe that's another way of self-harm. The fact that I can't bring myself to do a job, makes me feel ... not less, but somehow not right. I literally just get out of the house for doctor's visits and funerals

E: All your movement exists between death and not dying

He hopes that his mother will arrive someday and support him to live the life he wants to live. Someday she will recognize his long dalliance with deadness and yearning for aliveness. Someday, perhaps, she will welcome him into a home where he does not need barricades around his room.

A: I can't do it on my own. I've made my quicksand and now I must lie in it!

Aman talks of a sinking feeling, sinking in the presence of a witness who refuses to help and expects him to pull himself out. An impossible other. I wonder if he feels that way about me too. Is it even possible for me to draw him out as he draws me in? I find myself praying after our sessions. It was an unusual ritual for me. I pray that someday he'll feel safe, creative, and open. But before any of that, in the here and now, there is the quicksand of forever-numbing pain. I wonder if we can feel safe, creative, and open while we feel pain. His pain, after all, opens me to prayer – something to hold onto as I join him in the despair. Maybe our psyche too could come together through catastrophe (Eigen, 1999).

We return to the torment. Aman's pain both obliterates him and keeps him from vanishing. He seems to keep himself barely alive through contact with art. Anything that moves him also hurts. It fills him with inspiration, which collapses in the face of the increasing nothingness and the unwillingness/incapacity to pull himself out and move. His mind is moved, and his body freezes. He is caught in circles. He feels he should be judged! He waits for the pain to come.

A: I seem to be the least responsible stakeholder in my life. I don't know for how long I've had this thought. But I wake up hoping I was dead, and as I go to sleep, I imagine huge knives chopping me up, making sure there is no trace left of me. I'm not very good at living

E: What have you done? What are you punishing yourself for?

A: For not dying yet. I expected happiness a long time ago and that was asking too much

Aman lost his cousin to suicide only a few months ago. He was also gay, and being pressured to choose the same 'life', Aman resists. Unlike his cousin, he had tried to get away to pursue a discovery of his own self. The crumbling of whatever he had been trying to build had begun much before the pandemic, but his return home, I imagine, must have felt like every possibility of aliveness – of happiness – had been chopped down. His enemies, the killers in his dreams, were real, and so was death at their/his hands.

In *Psychic Deadness* (1996), Eigen elaborated on Klein's ideas around deadness and traces the many displacements of the death drive in its 'centripetal' and 'centrifugal' forces. Persecutors on the outside are introjected, he suggests, and they join forces with the destructive impulses within. One's internal landscape becomes hostile, poisoned by the toxic nourishment, if you will. A quicksand that destroys via engulfment. I wonder, however, if persecution and punishment may be differentiated as expressions of this destruction. To be persecuted is to be harassed in order to afflict injury (Mirriam-Webster, n.d.), usually on the grounds of who or what one is, not merely what one does. It may also be different from annihilation since it doesn't quite afford us a release into death. No, our persecutors seem to mock us by the relentlessly extending limits of what we can bear to survive. The other taunts us by the very tenacity with which breath refuses to leave our body, no matter how famished, tormented, or degraded it may become.

'The worst violation is tantalization', writes Eigen (1992, p. 18),

> To tantalise is to tie personality into knots, to turn it into a yo-yo, or to send it into a steady spin to nowhere. Tantalization keeps the personality on the edge of disintegration. One suffers a terror of disintegration or worse, is treated to increasing doses of disintegration process which never ends. Since the personality becomes obsessed with its own disintegration, it does not have the chance to believe in or experience a renewal through unintegration or chaos. Tantalization offers a macabre version of play which makes one cynical. It forecloses the kind of faith that enables a healing letting go.

Aman's 'happiness' would probably be predicated by this kind of 'unintegration or chaos'. It is indeed too much. It comes also at a price that is too much to pay, a letting go of the tantalizing mother (inside/outside) whose persecution keeps him in his cynical (k)nots.

A: How can I be happy if she can't be happy with me and my choices?

She demands a sacrifice, and he does not fight it. Why not?

Aman's father was someone he could fight with. He could *exist* in opposition to his father. I picture a taut string, unknotted. Aman was fighting to breathe, but he was not frozen – tethered perhaps – but he could move. Hate between his father and him sustained or brought some life. Hate from his mother just stops short of killing him.

His father didn't survive some of the forces of suffocation that men like Aman and his cousins face. It's not just their sexuality, but the very human, vulnerable, sensitive, and creative parts of men that also do not thrive at home. Perhaps Aman needs his father to be alive, and so hasn't mourned him enough. Mourning needs us to come to terms with a loss as fully as we can, after all. And Aman's father, too, from the outside-inside, continues to beat him into senseless incapacity.

Responsible people in Aman's life negate his being, condemning and turning a blind eye to his chances/scenarios of experiencing fulfillment, pleasure, meaning in pain, sex, love, solitude, etc. Responsible people see him as *not* enough. They do not *see* him enough.

When his father was alive, Aman could still sneak past his 'responsible negation' and fight for his life.

He worries that he might be blaming his mother for too much. I wonder if we blame people as part of our connection with them. Perhaps ceasing to blame can also feel like a severance, a 'healing letting go'. In a culture such as ours, perhaps even more so than others, being a self has a strong communal tone. Not being supported, loved, and accepted for your choices is not only deeply painful; it is annihilating. Without it, Aman is stuck in what he describes as a 'circularity' of depression.

What does he need to break free from this circle of pain?

'Love', he whispers, 'I need love. I think I secretly know that I don't hate them. I love them. I need them. But I need so much from people. I am stuck depending on them instead'.

Knots after knots after knots, we welcome them all.

Unbeknownst to Aman, my own history with love has been tethered with violence. When I was just at the turn of my adolescence, my body was beginning to change and I felt the first flutters of desire. I remember being told by my mother, 'If your father ever caught you with a boy, he will first kill you and then kill himself'. The words lodged themselves deep within my insides; flutterings turned to shivers of panic. My sexuality was utterly forbidden, it could get me killed, and it could kill my father. This isn't an unusual story. In the culture that I grew up in, women's bodies are a thing both endangered and of danger. Most women in my generation, despite being from 'modern, educated, urban families', learn quickly the necessity of a double life if they're to have their needs for intimacy met. Some dare to fight for it, and others don't. Coming back to our childhood homes during the pandemic has also meant a resubmission to the explicit and implicit ways in which our sexualities are held under duress by patriarchal structures. But perhaps most painfully, it has meant to remember the often violent and surveillant ways in which this regime is put into practice by the people who are also our objects of love and safety. As adult children, it is heartbreaking to see that a parent can be so afraid of things they do not or do not wish to understand that their love becomes conditional on your own unfulfillment. There is love here, just not one that can hold you in your entirety. Learning how to grow a mind-body of your own can then mean learning how to sever cords with the other's insidious mindlessness.

Aman and I could not have more different lives, and yet each of ours has been a homecoming, sponsoring similar bereavements. I find myself moving with him into painful unchartered territories, hoping that I can be a witness to the tenacity of his frozenness by learning how to thaw some of my own.

E: Your parents perhaps did not have enough of what you needed. Maybe you lean into a 'dependence' on them to deny that they're limited. It's too painful to see that they're not enough. You must be too much. You must be *not* enough.

A: I have been let down by them. Why couldn't I bring that to therapy? I'm surprised at myself that … I know its not theirs to give, love, acceptance, whatever, but I just haven't been able to accept that. How could they not find it? I'm just resentful … and I think I turned it in. And it's so heavy. I'd do anything, anything to feel lighter.

I share with him a sudden association: 'We create gods and monsters to give shape and form to something that will hold us against chaos, the catastrophe of un-integration, but also life-threatening deficits. To keep them alive, however, something must be repeatedly killed'.

A: A human sacrifice.

And so, Aman does not die, or live. He lives as a human sacrifice.

Rudhali – Welcoming Mourning

A: I don't know if I can take it, physically, to not be in pain.

In some rural communities, even to this day, there are women whose sole task is to arrive at funerals and mourn for the dead. In Rajasthan, a state with a rich aristocratic culture and one where I spent some years of my childhood, these women were called Rudhalis. For families that belonged to an opulent class and caste, any display of grief was considered most abominable. They would then call upon these women, who would break their bangles, smear their faces with dust and ashes and tears, and wail with anguish, so that the soul of the departed would know itself to be properly grieved.

I share with him what I can make of my reverie. Aman, in my imagination, is cleansing his family of generations of grief. Surrounded by funerals, performances of grief, he seems to be the only one asking, who or what has died here? How were they killed? For what? He seems to be the only one feeling something real. Rage, disappointment, and horror. He can't bear to live in a world where death runs in silent circles around him. Except that he does bear it, and he does become a living, curious, even compassionate witness to the dying.

He says that sometimes he feels as though he cannot remember what he's mourning. As if the memory, or perhaps language for it, is dead too. And he's just left feeling sad. I tell him that's a trace we can look at – this feeling of sadness.

A: If that were my actual job, I'd be so good at it (he chuckles) to be sad about things

Suddenly he brightens, and the gathering storms part just a little bit.

I smile too, while my eyes begin to well ever so slightly. A rainbow moment for the body and soul. Not dying yet, are we?

E: It takes work, doesn't it, to feel such sadness, really feel it. It's the work of your life, perhaps.

It certainly seems to be mine.

Suddenly, he says that he often struggles to look at the screen. 'What's to be sad about? What's being destroyed? I seem to be just telling you, well, another sad story, but maybe it isn't even that sad?'

E: As long as you don't look at the screen, you don't grasp at whatever's on it. Perhaps you don't grasp me, listening to your sadness, and I escape destruction.

Quietly, he mumbles, reminding me of the Aman I'd met in Ehsaas all those years ago: 'If I don't grasp at something, I will have nothing to mourn'.

How much have we survived? Several missed sessions punctuate our work. Sometimes they feel like necessary caesuras, 'breathers', 'pain relievers'. I was relieved of witnessing the pain Aman would rather be able to diminish than have observed, understood, and acknowledged as real. But now, I'm being told that the eyes in the storm have been watching me. I could be destroyed too. Will I make it?

'If I don't make anything, if I don't love anything, perhaps the pain would stop'

Yet we make these connections together, however slowly, cautiously, and surreptitiously. Something grows/glows in the dark. The pain doesn't stop. It comes into sharper focus. There may be no other way.

Satisfactions can also feel like losses one could wish to cut. A temporary severance from need and dependence. To not need that which one loves, one wants, one created or discovers, may also be a painful bereavement.

A: I feel like for a while, maybe I don't want to want things'

About Desire

Queer sexual encounters in a community like Aman's are always secrets percolating with shame that Aman feels burdened by. The shame of the other for wanting him (not desiring, just wanting) for their own sexuality annihilates any possibility of any real intimacy. Aman does not imagine the need for a closeness that crosses the boundaries of sex. If you know each other's bodies closely, pleasures, and dissatisfactions, this does not have to facilitate or even permit emotional, relational closeness.

'I'm surprised I never talk about sex in therapy', suddenly he wonders out loud, smiling. I smile too. And why not? And why now?

Perhaps Aman is testing the boundaries of our conversation too. What words touch how much, how little, or too much? Would sex break through whatever sincerity we have experienced together? Could this become another encounter where 'this is not what' he wanted? Will it add too much of a touch of real to our space where we use even our words with such caution?

A: I don't know why. Maybe the stories are too graphic, and I'd feel judged. Maybe I'd just feel silly saying it. It just doesn't come up. It seems frivolous too. Elsewhere I don't shut up about sex. Here in therapy, what else do I say except that I don't even enjoy it, that it leaves me feeling violated. "violated" isn't event the right word and I wouldn't know what to say either

E: We wouldn't know which words to use for sex until we talk about it. Listening to you, I feel as though it's anything but frivolous. But perhaps that's exactly why we need to dismiss it as that?

A: If I took it too seriously ... I'd just feel like, oh my god, is everyone trying to violate me? What is it, that people just don't know how to have sex anymore? They just don't know about boundaries here. Sometimes people do come to me because they want to have an emotional experience. They just want to cry or be held. But then, I just envy them. They feel safe with me. And I can't seem to have that.

E: You wish to feel safety, connection, pleasure while having sex. But it also feels too much to ask for. There seems to be a price to pay.

'Yeah', his voice cracks. 'I'm not allowed that. If I were to fall in love, be with someone, I'd have to choose between my entire life, my family here, and that person'.

When Aman brings someone over to his room, sex may or may not happen. His mother seems to know but also wishes to not know. She casts her disapproval across closed doors. What does she forbid for Aman? It's not just the act of sex with a man, or a woman he's not married to, but it's play, frivolity, intimacy, pleasure, and love. So much of what makes life worth living.

I feel the jab of what follows.

A: it's just disrespectful- to think that that's all there is to a gay person's sex life. Just meaningless liaisons with other men, to be kept out of a marriage, out of respectable things people do

Aman doesn't wish to tear himself away from the home he grew up in, even as it feels like a broken place whose shards impale him or cause him to shrink his being. It's a part of him, and he is a part of it.

Sex, perhaps, could bring him closer to being seen and understood, naked and clothed in ways that he needs. Perhaps therapy could too. These are spaces where we could set our own pace, start when he wants, stop when he wants, and get a feel for boundaries. How much is too much to bear or to ask for? What words feel right, and what words are too much? Every session he has missed, every session he has cut short, every time he has chosen to keep something out of reach for me, might just have been his way of teaching me more about what he needs from intimacy and distance, usually encoded in pain.

A: I've never seen sex to be just physical, its always about the mind and the body, how one feels

When Aman insists that he's not here, it feels real. But he's, indeed, there too. There are feelings that have been hidden in the nots. Not close, not safe, not satisfied. These *are* feelings his body lives again and again with every sexual encounter. I wonder if we welcome them as un-(k)nots.

E: And disappointment in sex, that's a part of what you feel

A repeated echo of being touched *wrong* runs through his life. Until we make room for that, there can be no calibrations. Loving touch is a sensitive touch, respectful of how it can hurt. Perhaps to make room for pleasure, we must learn the voice and language of pain. In Aman's body-mind, pain has been a marker of breakdown of communication in the wake of repeated trauma and a sensation that orients him. It has been a dissolution of edges around the here and now, so the past-present is an unthinkable but lived continuum. It has been a barricade too, against touch of all kinds. It has given screams to what cannot be dreamed – the past and the future. Touching it through words has rendered a mourning possible.

Coming home has meant to learn to welcome a recognition of the fibrous pain – inside and outside – that sustains Aman's history, traps him in the present, and may just open a desire for a future too.

It's always been here. It's been here all along.

Notes

1 A place of calm in a storm, a place from where to witness it.
2 Being as a noun and as a verb, a sense of identity/self and a gesture of sentient, alive existence.
3 This is a reference to the novel 'The Lovely Bones' by Alice Sebold. In the book, a preteen girl is brutally assaulted and murdered by a seemingly unthreatening, friendly man new to her neighbourhood. She wakes into an afterlife, a sort of transitional space between existence and non-existence, from where she continues to witness the lives of

her friends and family, as well as her murderer in the wake of her death. The title, as we learn in her final reflections at the end of the story, is a reference to both her bones, that eventually help in tracking the perpetrator, and the bones of her loved ones, as well as a network of 'tenuous' connections within and between them as they grieve for what they lost with her, that continue to 'grow' around her absence. The story is a study in the ways in which we survive and are born through the ruptures of painful, traumatic experiences, as well as 'ordinary' catastrophes of death and loss. Despite everything, as Eigen (2016) reassures us about a 'pulsating pain, a rhythm of existence', life seems to 'grow wherever we can'.

References

Bion, W. R. (2019). *Complete works of W.R. Bion volume 10*. Routledge.

Eaton, J. L. (2015). Becoming the welcoming object- personal notes on Michael Eigen's impact. In S. Bloch & L. Daws (Eds.), *Living moments: On the work of Michael Eigen* (Vol. 10, pp. 131–147). London: Routledge.

Eigen, M. (1992). *Coming through the whirlwind: Case studies in Psychotherapy*. Chiron Publications.

Eigen, M. (2004). *Psychic deadness*. Karnac Books.

Eigen, M. (2005). *Emotional storm*. Wesleyan University Press.

Merriam-Webster. (n.d.). *Persecution definition & meaning*. Merriam-Webster. Retrieved March 6, 2023, from https://www.merriam-webster.com/dictionary/persecution.

Chapter 10

Listening in with Michael Eigen

Isolde Keilhofer

Part of psychoanalytic listening conveys the deeply felt message that the pain you speak of is real – more real than you or anyone, so far, can bear. (Eigen, 2002a, p. 10).

Michael Eigen's writing is expansive, spans decades, and offers a generosity of clinical riches that reach into the depth of the psyche and the music thereof. Throughout his work, Eigen encourages readers to pull on threads of their own interest. An invitation and herein a response in wonder of psychoanalytic listening. How does a psychoanalyst tune into the harmony, the cacophony, and the silence of this music of the psyche? *Listening in with* Eigen opens possibilities.

Beginnings, as Eigen often cites, can be challenging. In one beginning of what would evolve into psychoanalysis, the first patient, Anna O, working with Breuer and he turning to Freud for counsel, deemed it a *talking cure*. For Eigen, psychoanalysis extends further into a writing cure and also into a listening cure. "Psychoanalysis," he writes, "is a voice for the excluded" (Eigen, 2001a, p. 12). In the context of childhood isolation of unheard pain, he explains in an interview:

I've spent my life listening to others, keenly aware I am listening to myself as well, that the other is me, that we are working with damage we share and inflict. My writing is a kind of listening as well as a longing to be heard. I've been touched to find my voice touches others who need it. They hear the wound the writing comes from. (Eigen, 2007, p. 89)

Musical references abound throughout Eigen's writing. He builds on the work of Freud, Klein, Winnicott, and Bion, among so many other writers and so many other fields of inquiry, like a scholarly jazz musician (Keilhofer, 2015). He is a jazz musician "…born into music" (Eigen, 2011, p. 127). With Eigen, one learns about building capacity through ongoing practice, practice, practice, beginning again and again and again. Playing it by ear. A basic rhythm of breakdown and recovery, its' many permutations and damages, is essential to his work (Eigen, 2002). One important back and forth is between injury and recovery; at times, the rhythm gets jammed. "Something off in the music of the psyche" (Eigen, 2011, p. 123).

DOI: 10.4324/9781003322993-10

An important note too on language. Anna O, whom Lothaine calls the co-discoverer of psychoanalysis, used the phrase *talking cure*, in English, not in her native German, to describe the process of symptom relief that came from speaking persistently and consistently to her trusted physician, Breuer. Interesting, too, are the shifts in language Anna O utilized or needed in order to speak, remember, and register her traumas. This *talking cure* foreshadowed an essential technique of psychoanalysis: free association, freely saying what comes to mind without critical judgment or censorship. The term cure (Kur in German), however, in the 1880s referred to the treatment itself not to a successful termination of treatment as a cure is defined today (Lothaine, 2006). Psychoanalysis is a process, and the outcome is unknown.

In attracting many foreign travelers to his practice, Freud listened to analysands in numerous languages. Lacan listened to registers of language, to wordplay. Bion also listened to silences, noting their many languages (Bion, 1990). Eigen, too, listens to the multiple meanings contained in words and their evocative dimensions. He writes,

> Look what language does: ear in tear, hear, heart, fear, sear, dear, learn. How important hearing is. By using the couch, Freud tries to play down visual control, dominance, and mastery in order to touch a hearing–feeling dimension, between mastery and mystery. (Eigen, 2016a, p. 285)

Freud emphasized the analyst's role of receptivity, likening the analyst's listening attunement to a telephone receiver, newly invented in his time, adjusting to the frequency of the transmission or to unconscious signals (Freud, 1912). In his Seoul seminar (2010), a century later, Eigen playfully emphasizes this too: "I love the big ears of the Buddha … I think that's what psychoanalysis ought to use for its logo. Like a new way of listening, a new way of hearing oneself" (Eigen, 2010, p. 16).

Psychoanalysis has many difficult beginnings; two of note are connected with Theodor Reik, one of Freud's first and favored students. Reik was a pioneer in writing about psychoanalytic listening beyond conscious perception, most famously in his classic *Listening with the Third Ear* (1948). He expanded upon Freud's concept of even hovering attention to encompass and highly value the analyst's inner experience and the unconscious communication between analysand and analyst, a prescient intersubjectivity. In addition to theoretical starts, Reik also instituted a very practical one. Reik, with a doctorate in literature, after immigrating to the United States from war-torn Europe and then facing rejection to practice as a psychoanalyst by the established American medical psychoanalytic monopoly, fought for and founded the first lay psychoanalytic training institute and its adjacent low-fee clinic in New York.[1] Yet, despite such a far-reaching legacy for non-medical psychoanalysis and despite or because of becoming a prolific and widely read popular author in his own time, Reik is scarcely referenced and currently barely taught in his own institute (Safran, 2011). An institute that Eigen joined many decades after its founding.

In Eigen's writing, there is also a scant mention of Reik, except for an exceptionally important reference via Bion. Eigen relates how in Bion's New York seminars in the 1970s, the only American analyst Bion made reference to was Reik, especially Reik's interest in surprise and the use of intuition in analytic sessions (Eigen, 2014). Although separated by decades and leaving Bloom's anxiety of influence aside, an affinity between Reik and Eigen is found in their deep interest in the psyche and their creative writing styles, each expressed with a unique élan. Reik uses a self-confessional analysis, whereas Eigen's writing style, although at times generously personal, is more dialogical in nature. Both present a jargon-free psychoanalysis that is accessible, welcoming, inclusive, and free associative. Both reach a broad audience. An essential point of connection, however, spanning through this space-time barrier and/or continuum, is the focus in their clinical work on the experience *in* and *of* a session, the phenomenological underbelly of psychoanalytic listening.

An important new dimension, another beginning perhaps, in psychoanalysis opened with what Ogden calls a gradual but radical shift from epistemological psychoanalysis to an ontological psychoanalysis. The former involves knowing, understanding, and interpreting, and the latter involves being, becoming, and waiting. Of course, there is always an overlap. For Ogden, Freud and Klein are "principal authors" of the former, while Winnicott and Bion are "principal architects" of the latter. Ogden writes:

> From the perspective of ontological psychoanalysis, it is not the knowledge arrived at by patient and analyst that is the central point; rather, it is the patient's experience ... in which the patient is engaged not predominantly in searching for self-understanding, but in experiencing the process of becoming more fully himself. (Ogden, 2019, p. 665)

Understanding versus discovering. Eigen writes of Bion: "He opts for a primacy of perception and attention over memory and knowledge as the analyst's most basic working orientation" (Eigen, 1981, p. 424). Of his own work: "I'm not a theorist. For me, it's all expressive. Phenomenological" (Eigen, 2016, p. 128). In other words, "...my desire is not to 'solve' anything, but to open fields of experiencing" (Eigen, 2007, p. 130).

Experiencing curiosity, especially about beginnings, brings to mind primal scenes and very early listening exposures. The Freudian primal scene refers to fantasy and real observation around parental intercourse. "Who is doing what to whom?" (Eigen, 2002, p. 733) For Freud, in different ways, this scene could lead a child to interpret coitus as an act of aggression, to excessive excitation arousing excessive anxiety (lodged in the body as symptoms), or to the advent of infantile sexual theories, which sparked or hindered curiosity. The experience for Eigen conjures up a mixture of creativity and destruction, a birth and murder scene, perhaps that can later be met with a faith in a rhythm of rebirth (failed, partial, ongoing) (Eigen, 2002). Eigen, on a very personal note, writes:

> My work as a patient is what made me an analyst. But many factors went into making me a patient. I slept in a crib in my parents' room until age five. From

the earliest age, I listened for sounds in the night. I have never stopped listening. Some of my earliest dreams were primal-scene dreams. (Eigen, 2001, p. 158)

In Dora's case, Freud writes: "Children, in such circumstances, divine something sexual in the uncanny sounds that reach their ears" (Freud, 1905, p. 80). Freud also learned from this early failed treatment that battling with a patient over the correctness of his interpretations and convictions rightly undermined the "sympathetic inquiry" he had in mind. *He did not make space for Dora to discover for herself the impact of her experiences.* Primal scenes invoke a spectrum of responses, whether locked into a parental bedroom, forever wanting to break free, or locked outside a door, forever wanting to break in, and all the variations in-between, of gleaning the divine/uncanny.

It is also essential to highlight Eigen's statement: "My work as a patient made me an analyst." It is a unique advantage of psychoanalytic training that one is required to undergo their own analysis. Experiencing from the inside out not only the strength of resistance and transference and dreamwork but most intrinsically the healing power of being heard. Conversely, being in therapy leads some to psychoanalytic training. Eigen writes of his regret about giving up playing music: "I plunged into psychoanalysis, hooked by psychic life, and never came out" (Eigen, 2011, p. 128). Although in Freud's time analyses were quite short, just a few years at most, Freud stressed ongoing check-ins for the analyst,

> Every analyst ought periodically himself to submit to analysis, at intervals of, say, five years, without any feeling of shame in so doing. This is as much as to say that not only the patient's analysis but that of the analyst himself is a task which is never finished. (Freud, 1937, p. 402)

From one perspective, or vertex, to use Bion's word, the journey from early to late Freud, from Freud to Eigen, of exploring the curative power of psychoanalytic treatment is perhaps a journey from hubris to humility.

Silence and creative waiting are essential components in the acoustic landscape of the analytic space. Eigen writes: "In Winnicott's writings, non-intrusiveness is often linked with the analyst's silence and capacity to wait" (Eigen, 1996, p. 79). Eshel adds the hearing heart (Eshel, 2016). Levine puts it bluntly: "You help the person free associate and get out of the way" (Levine, 2023). For Reik, "psychoanalysis shows the power of the word and the power of silence" (Reik, 1968, p. 173). Screams are silent too. Eigen writes: "In therapy, the lost scream surfaces because it has a partner, someone who hears it. A therapist knows about soul screams" (Eigen, 2002c, p. 152). With patience, one can hear the echo of childhood screams and the echo of intergenerational traumas not yet spoken (Davoine and Gaudilliere, 2004, Keilhofer, 2014). At times, the echo of former patients is met with an aha moment that comes years too late, with pangs of lament. Echo, in Greek mythology, could not make herself heard nor seen with Narcissus, both failing to make relational contact (Teitelbaum, 2010). The multiplicity of layers encompasses full to empty, pregnant to void.

An analytic session offers a pause, an essential element of music as well, a pause for Bion's attention and perception (Bion, 1990). "Now that I hear myself say it out loud" is a refrain heard from numerous patients in numerous sessions in innumerable ways. "Now that I am talking about it." "Now that I am thinking about it." "I haven't made the connection till saying it just now." "Now I'm hearing myself." "What comes up for me when saying that out loud … [.]" "There is something I have to tell you." A receptive, embodied, listening encounter opening possibilities.

As with beginnings, endings can be challenging. In Eigen's work, a steadfast, yet also ineffable, background of support nourishes psychoanalytic soundings, and it is perhaps fitting to end on a foreground of musical note. In Emotional Storm (2005), a passionate book, Eigen relates an anecdote in the afterward that is bursting with further ideas:

> I feel a little like John Coltrane, famous for endless sax solos, asking Miles Davis, a great trumpet man, how he knows when to end. 'Just put your horn down, man. Put your horn down,' Davis answered. Easier said than done. (Eigen, 2005, p. 213)

Eigen's solos reverberate beyond the page and openheartedly invite and spark those so inclined to pick up their horns of choice as well. Voices of the excluded, calling and responding, through time.

Note

1 Founded in 1948 The National Psychological Association for Psychoanalysis is still in operation, as is the Theodor Reik Clinical Center. Freud had already written *The Question of Lay Analysis* in 1926 on this important topic with Reik in mind.

References

Bion, W. R. (1990). *Brazilian Lectures: 1973 Sao Paulo, 1974 Rio De Janeiro/Sao Paulo*. London: Karnac.
Bion, W. R. (1991). *Cogitations*. Karnac Books. Kindle Edition.
Davoine, F. & Gaudillieère, J. (2004). *History beyond Trauma: Whereof One Cannot Speak, Thereof One Cannot Stay Silent*. New York: Other Press.
Eigen, M. (1981). The Area of Faith in Winnicott, Lacan and Bion. *International Journal of Psychoanalysis* 62:413–433.
Eigen, M. (1996). *Psychic Deadness*. London: Jason Aronson Inc.
Eigen, M. (2001). *Damaged Bonds*. London: H. Karnac (Books) Ltd.
Eigen, M. (2001a). *Ecstasy*. Middletown, CT: Wesleyan University Press.
Eigen, M. (2002). A Basic Rhythm. *Psychoanalytic Review* 89:721–740.
Eigen, M. (2002a). Half and Half. *Fort Da* 8:7–17.
Eigen, M. (2002c). *Rage*. Middletown, CT: Wesleyan University Press.

Eigen, M. (2005). *Emotional Storm*. Middletown, CT: Wesleyan University Press.

Eigen, M. & Govrin, A. (2007). *Conversations with Michael Eigen*. London: Karnac Books Ltd.

Eigen, M. (2010). *Eigen in Seoul: Volume One, Madness and Murder*. London: Karnac Books Ltd.

Eigen, M. (2011). *Contact with the Depths*. London: Karnac Books Ltd.

Eigen, M. (2014). *Faith*. London: Karnac Books Ltd.

Eigen, M. (2016). *Image, Sense, Infinities, and Everyday Life*. London: Karnac.

Eigen, M. (2016a). *Under the Totem: In Search of a Path*. London: Karnac.

Eigen, M. (2020). *Dialogues with Michael Eigen: Ed. Loray Daws*. Psyche Singing, NY: Routledge.

Eshel, O. (2016). The Vanished Last Scream: Winnicott-Bion-Eigen. *IJP Open – Open Peer Review and Debate* 3:1–32.

Freud, S. (1905). Fragment of an Analysis of a Case of Hysteria (1905 [1901]). *The Standard Edition of the Complete Psychological Works of Sigmund Freud* 7:1–122.

Freud, S. (1912). Recommendations to Physicians Practicing Psychoanalysis. *The Standard Edition of the Complete Psychological Works of Sigmund Freud* 12:109–120.

Freud, S. (1937). Analysis Terminable and Interminable. *International Journal of Psychoanalysis* 18:373–405.

Keilhofer, I. (2014). "Freud's 'On Transience' and the Eternal Wounds of War" in *Other/Wise Uncut*, Vol. 2, Fall 2014. https://ifpe.files.wordpress.com/2014/10/isolde-keilhofer.pdf

Keilhofer, I. (2015). "Unwanted: Deadened Aliveness" in *Other/Wise*, Volume 1, Summer 2015. https://ifpe.wordpress.com/2015/07/01/unwanted-deadened-aliveness/

Levine, H. B. (2023). *Bion and Beyond: Towards a Psychoanalysis for the 21st Century [Paper Presentation]*. Massachusetts Institute for Psychoanalysis, Watertown, MA, US.

Lothane, Z. (2006). Freud's Legacy—Is It Still with Us? *Psychoanalytic Psychology* 23:285–301.

Ogden, T. H. (2019). Ontological Psychoanalysis or "What Do You Want to Be When You Grow Up?". *Psychoanalytic Quarterly* 88:661–684.

Reik, T. (1948). *Listening with the Third Ear: The Inner Experience of a Psychoanalyst*. New York: Farrar, Straus.

Reik, T. & Altman, K. M. (1968). The Psychological Meaning of Silence. *Psychoanalytic Review* 55:172–186.

Safran, J. D. (2011). Theodor Reik's Listening with the Third Ear and the Role of Self-Analysis in Contemporary Psychoanalytic Thinking. *Psychoanalytic Review* 98:205–216.

Teitelbaum, S. (2010). *The Echo Injury: Narcissus and Echo on Line and the Loss of Body Cues in Electronic Communication [Paper Presentation]*. IAARP 2010. San Francisco, US. https://ifpe.files.wordpress.com/2011/10/the-echo-injury3.pdf

Chapter 11

Faces of the Welcoming Object

Musings on Midlife, Madness, and Mysticism – Welcoming and Being Welcomed

Marian Campbell

> "A deep commitment to welcoming runs like an underground river through all of Eigen's work."
>
> (Eaton, 2015, p. 133).

Michael Eigen welcomes faith and spirituality into the field of psychoanalysis; in fact, he welcomes himself, with all the pulsing particularities of his heart, mind, and soul, carving a unique Eigen-shaped space into the field of psychoanalysis and into the lives of his many readers, inviting us to do the same, to find our unique shapes as we open to and evolve in O.

I love the stories Eigen tells of meeting Winnicott and Bion as a young man and his surprised and enduring impression of being accepted by both men, each in their own way. This must have had a profound effect on how he has been able to write with such intimate and perceptive sensitivity and passion about the living, struggling essence from which each man was seeking and working, but also on how he has integrated and channeled their work through his own being and becoming to produce writing that is profoundly and uniquely Eigenesque. His is no dry explication of another theorist's body of work! And so, while I benefit enormously from a range of writers from the fields of Jungian psychology, psychoanalysis, and relational psychoanalysis, it is to Eigen I turn for comfort and encouragement, for rest and hope, where my soul breathes a sigh of relief in the complex simplicity that there is impact and coming through, where the how is more important than the why, where I find the fine tracings of my own inner psychoanalytic mystic, and where I am inspired by his deep commitment to welcoming, opening to experience, even when the experience is of being unable to be welcoming or to be unwelcomed.

A Rhythm of Faith

> What matters most is not the state or moment one is stuck in, but the loss of movement, the pulsation at the boundary, the crossing. The patient grows in the ability to cross over. (Eigen, 1998, p. 59)

DOI: 10.4324/9781003322993-11

It seems to me that the 'psychoanalytic mystic' and the 'welcoming object' are intertwined, and crucial to both is Eigen's rhythm of faith, "a kind of constant conjunction, crucifixion-resurrection" (Eigen, 2011, p. 110). Eigen describes this as an "*inner sequence in normal living*" (Eigen, 2011, p. 4), which is inescapable and which we need to help our patients make room for. In Eigen's unique experiential articulations of this movement 'between,' I sense no privileging of one state above another, no striving toward the end of some linear progression, no neat packaging of how things are or should be or should become, only an emphasis on faith and movement, as much or as little as our damaged selves can muster, in the Grace of coming through. Eigen is not interested in structures and explanations so much as in the experience of personal encounters with *impact* (Eigen, 1986).

Whether welcomed or not, known about or not, transformations in O/God/reality always happen in unknown ways - we cannot avoid them (Eigen, 2011, p. 59). But our shifting capacity consciously to welcome them and to be open to them-this seems crucial to our own impact on these transformations in O; it potentially changes our transformations and changes our being in O. But to be open and to engage in mutual impact takes faith. Eigen (2011) suggests that faith in O and transformations in O are related because faith in O is the background support to the psyche to allow an openness that lets transformations in O do its work. Eigen refers to Job as an example. Job has just been shattered by God, and yet in the course of their mutual impact, "he cries, 'Lord, though You slay me, yet will I trust you.' That is F in O." (Eigen, 2011, p. 62).

This faith seems to serve Job as a subject in the face of the implacably wholly Other. Job's is not a blind or sacrificial faith, an abject submission. He does not even initially surrender. Stripped of everything and treated like an abject object in what is described as a wager between God and Satan, he calls out and objects from his position as a hu/man in relationship to God; he challenges God even though he was always destined eventually to surrender in awe to something so inconceivably and unknowably bigger than himself. And when he comes through, he finds Grace – more abundant than all he has lost: crucifixion-resurrection. Job by no means welcomes his experience of such abject suffering, but he remains open to, in fact, depends on, and appeals to his personal relationship to God/reality, even as he is all but annihilated. The flow of the story suggests that it is his objection, his appeal from a place of his own valued subjectivity (despite the advice of his friends simply to submit), that evokes God's awesome display of power. And then the transformative moment happens where Job is "brought to silence in the face of God's presence, a point of contact, essence to essence" (Eigen, 2018, p. 32), and at that point Job cries, "Now I know you in my flesh." There is a mutual impact - even as God transforms Job, he is also transformed by Job. Jung (2002) writes about Job very much in the context of midlife psychology and suggests that in this traumatic encounter, Job has seen the back of God and has seen God in a way that transforms God's sense of himself (the unconscious becoming conscious). This leads directly to the necessity for the coming of Christ, for the transformation of the God-image to include compassionate wisdom; Sophia, the feminine face of God, and is presaged in the interesting and easily missed little detail that once Job is restored in Grace, even his daughters will inherit (Edinger, 1992). Eigen refers to Jung's ideas, reflecting on the coming of the Shekhinah, a divine wedding, "a linking image between broken, fragmented, dissociated parts of existence" (Eigen, 2018, p. 33). Jung's God/Self is not O, but it does function to mediate the mystery of ultimate reality by pressing the individual to become more of herself. Stevens Sullivan (2010, pp. 50–51) writes that the concept of Jung's Self "suggests that behind O's apparent cosmic indifference lies an interdependent harmony that we can never understand or map," and that makes "each of us an infinitesimal but meaningful part of the whole."

Job seems to wrestle for the right to an I-Thou relationship with God/reality, even at the point of imminent annihilation. Orange (2010, p. 18) describes this central concept of Martin Buber's philosophy as "a personally intimate encounter or meeting between I and Thou, which differs radically from all I-It relations, in which we regard others as a thing." And, I would add, that "I" also claims the position of a subject, not a thing in the face of the Other. In the story of Job, God remains a personal Thou even in his awesome show of implacable power and Otherness, and Job holds onto an "I" in the face of that terrifying Thou. It's not that Job's I-response changes God as an object, but it changes the experiential nature of the encounter. *O is an encounter, not an object.* In answer to the question of why we should have faith in a reality that we do not know and that is going to destroy us as surely as it created us, Eigen writes, "The idea of faith for Bion has something to do with being alive now. Am I alive now no matter what the reality is? Am I living my reality, whatever it is, whatever it does?" (Eigen, 2011, p. 62). There is something wild and elemental, yet so intimately personal, in this story of Job and in this faith in O. It is powerfully depicted in all its movement and drama in a series of drawings by William Blake (Edinger, 1992). It brings to mind these lines from Rilke's (2007) magnificent poem about grief called *Pushing Through*, "You be the master: make yourself fierce, break in: then your great transforming will happen to me, and my great grief will happen to you."

This moves me in my evolving sense of the welcoming object, especially as many of my patients and I find-lose ourselves in the throes of middle age. And it reminds me too that this is not a once-off dramatic climax in a linear storyline with a happy-ever-after – this is the repeated drama of being alive in every moment, the inescapable sequence of normal living, a "rhythm back and forth between pleasure-pain, joy-suffering, something good one moment, then something takes it away" (Eigen, 2011, p. 4).

Welcoming in Midlife

So the question isn't "Am I going to die?" I am going to die and not too long from now. The question is "Am I alive now?"- and what would that mean, to be alive now? That's the real question. (Eigen, 2011, p. 62).

This question seems especially pertinent to me in midlife. As a Jungian analyst, I am well versed in and inspired by the K of midlife. Jungian psychology is primarily a psychology for the second half of life. However, welcoming the O of midlife is something completely different. In my own and my patients' lives, I witness firsthand how midlife can be an invitation and catalyst, perhaps like no preceding developmental stage, to face our relating to and in O. In the face of diverse vicissitudes, including suddenly visible aging and vulnerability, 'empty nests,' unexpected divorces, parents aging and dying, and the onset of chronic illness, patients wonder what they have done with this one precious life and what is still possible. James Hollis (2006) is probably the most accessible and well-known Jungian writer on midlife and describes with compassion and thoughtfulness the threshold experience that it is, especially for those who are for the first time facing the traumatic awareness of the apparent waste of an 'unlived life.' Hollis describes how midlife ushers in a strong psychic pressure from what Jung has called the Self (the Jungian organizing principle of the psyche) consciously and intentionally to take up the task of individuation, to search for meaning/spirituality in the second half of life, and to wrestle with the question of whether we are related to the infinite or not.

I am also particularly interested in what women writers are saying, in increasingly confident voices, about midlife and menopause. Sharon Blackie's *Hagitude* (2022) is a beautiful exploration of myths for contemporary menopausal women in which she includes a special place for childless and/or single women, those whose subjectivity is most invisible in our society. In this liminal space where body and psyche are undergoing relentless transformations, anger, 'madness,' and rage (alongside grief) seem both inevitable and necessary expressions of faith in O for women to break through compliance to historically impinging realities and finally to surrender to a self and a self-with-others that is still emergent and both dreaded and longed for. Women writers pay keen attention to the lived realities of middle-aged women in sexist and ageist societies. Single or childless women face even more constraints as identity, belonging, and socializing occur primarily in the context of couples and nuclear families with children and grandchildren. In South Africa, various constraints are exacerbated by a threatening environment of extremely high rates of gender-based violence, where even life-affirming activities such as walking or holidaying in nature or attending cultural events at night are best not undertaken alone.

What does it mean to remain alive in the face of the subjective realities of loss, regret, powerlessness, mortality, threat, and exclusion? Annie Dillard (2016), in her lovely essay, *The Weasel*, writes about unexpectedly meeting a weasel one evening at her favorite Hollins Pond. She remembers a story about a man who shoots an eagle out of the sky and attached to the eagle's throat, he finds the skull of a weasel, which had presumably, even at this moment of his fateful death, instinctively swiveled around and sunk his jaws into the eagle's throat. Staring into the weasel's eyes, Dillard wishes she could learn this from him: "to stalk your *calling* in a certain skilled and supple way, to locate this tender and live spot and plug into that pulse" (p. 38, italics mine). She describes this as "yielding, not fighting", "yielding at every moment to the perfect freedom of single necessity" (p. 38). I wonder, what is a necessity at midlife other than who you have become so far, nakedly meeting the reality of your life at this moment as best you can?

Ivy

I would like to explore some of these threads further through a composite case of a 54-year-old woman I shall call Ivy.

Ivy returned to therapy almost a decade after a lengthy analysis in her late 30s and early 40s with a clinician who had since retired. Essentially, Ivy came because she was struggling to hold onto a faith that could support her to remain open to her lived experience. Reminiscent of Dillard's (2016) weasel story, Ivy said as much that she wanted to "rescue her destiny from the maw of fate." Outwardly, Ivy was a single professional woman who, despite significant adversity in her earlier life, had managed to carve out a reasonable life for herself. She had an adopted son who lived abroad, supportive friends and colleagues, and a modest income from a stable career. She had also recently been diagnosed with a chronic and potentially debilitating autoimmune disease. I liked Ivy and felt we could have been friends in other circumstances. She was insightful, humorous, and kind, and it was clear to me that in her previous therapy, she had managed, within the context of a profound and creative transference, to allow deep suffering and grief around the traumas and deprivations of her childhood. From her story, I could sense that she had come through a *crucifixion-resurrection experience* (Campbell, 2015), and when her therapist retired, Ivy felt more able to live a fuller life, one less curtailed by the sequelae of her original traumas. She particularly hoped to find a partner and develop her creativity. But a decade later, despite her best efforts, she now faced a frightening diagnosis and felt lost and alienated in her own life. Her once-pregnant future felt aborted, and her life empty - as empty as the childhood she thought she had left behind.

Ivy felt trapped, feeling both responsible for herself and her life and also utterly at a loss about how to shoulder that responsibility in a way that brought some redemption. I started noticing an underlying flat, exhausted mood and a sense of shamed defeat in her sessions. I soon realized that the exhaustion came from this responsibility she shouldered of relentlessly initiating her own aliveness. She brought the following quote she found on *Marginalia* (Popova, 2022) from D.H. Lawrence's 1923 novel, *Kangaroo*: "The secret of all life is obedience: obedience to the urge that arises in the soul, the urge that is life itself, urging us to new gestures, new embraces, new emotions, new combinations, new creations." Ivy felt desperately unable to be obedient to the urge of her soul in the apparent absence of any environmental provision - she felt at the end of her own resources. Despite her best efforts, she needed something from life - some gift, some grace - that she could not provide for herself. Her desires felt constantly and shamefully thwarted by a sense of deprivation. This dilemma became a silent scream that she could not even mouth into the universe. It felt like a vacuum rather than an articulation, an infinite absence rather than an idiomatic expression of identity. Hopes/dreams had become too far removed from reality, and the space in-between, which she had at one time imagined as challenging and creative, had become so cavernous that Ivy had become lost.

I-Thou in the Space Between

Slowly, over time, Ivy showed unexpected bursts of explosive anger in our sessions. They were jolting and discomforting, but I welcomed them as signs of potential vitality. However, the anger quickly dissipated into what felt like a sullen despair, as though she couldn't see the point in anger or even at whom it should/could be directed. But she *was* enraged at something or someone; I could feel it in the deadening cynicism that often underlined the mood in the room. At times, I sensed that Ivy had become oppressively stuck in a depressive position without the revitalizing base material of the primary processes that could provide a substrate on which the alchemy of her transformation could get to work. I wondered whether she needed to contact an inner Job, Job's "I," from which to stand and meet her life, to "Assail God's hearing with gull-screech knifeblades" (Levertov, 1992, p. 251). It started emerging from our infrequent but powerful experiences with Ivy's anger in the room that her ambivalence was not so much that she feared it could be destructive of her objects but that it was useless in the face of the implacable Other. Even worse, it made her feel shamed and abject that her dependency needs and feelings were ignored by life. It felt that in those moments, Ivy experienced herself in an it-Thou relationship, perhaps even an it-It relationship. I wondered whether, in the loss of her therapist and absence of a consistent, dependable figure, having not been able to find/create the intimate love relationships or familial environment she craved, she had been unable to hold onto an internalized background holding presence and become, again, an 'Orphan of the Real' (Grotstein, 2007, p. 313) she had been in her childhood. According to Grotstein, such 'orphans,' due to hypersensitivity and/or traumatic abruption, experience the real without the protective blanket of imagination or symbolization, of reverie, and unconscious processes in creating meaning. He refers to "the demoralization that accrues from a failure to develop a background presence of primary identification as the initializing experience of containment, otherwise known as being *blessed*" (2007, p. 313).

Having made a new beginning after her last therapy and felt a life-giving reorganization in her personality, something was goading her back to a hardening, a deadening organization around an aspect of her trauma, an emphasis on self-agency and shame at overwhelm/failure as an early survival response to failure in the holding environment. She seemed to be trying to move this historically unsupportive inter/intrapersonal environment to an inner-outer holding Self/God, a vital midlife task, according to Jung. Still, old destructive patterns were interfering with the shift. She felt stuck in time, in suspended animation where the present is hollowed out between a past and a future that both feel irredeemable.

Some more light was shed on this impasse when Ivy remembered what she called a "spiritual trauma" in her adolescence. She had become an earnestly committed 'born-again' Christian in high school. Her experience then had been of a deeply personal, safe, and loving relationship with Jesus, but in retrospect, it was clear that it had actually entailed an austere emptying out of herself in which she sacrificed normal adolescent desires, rebellions, and experimentations for devoted compliance to 'goodness', service, and worship. By the time she started realizing the damage done - the cruel and unnecessary shallowing out of her developing self - she had already lost her adolescence. She had felt deeply betrayed. Thinking back, Ivy felt that her earnestness, her vulnerable love, and her innate capacity for mysticism had been exploited by the church and by God, if he existed at all, and had left her deeply distrustful of intimacy and spirituality. Apart from severe early parental failings, here was another origin of a cruelly failing I-Thou relationship where no subjective "I" had been allowed and where the personal had not been safe at all. Perhaps now an impersonal, implacable Other was a preferable suffering to a personal, murderous Other?

An Emergent "I"

Meanwhile, another interesting piece of Ivy's puzzle was emerging. She frequently set whole weekends aside to be alone - declining invitations, making no appointments, and even shopping for food seeming an intrusion. She anticipated this time with some relief and expectancy, looking forward to a sense of spaciousness and to seeing the way the light falls into the spaces of her home. In this *waiting space*, Ivy said she is never bored and seldom lonely for any human she knows. She potters and rests, but she also longs for something. I find it remarkable and poignant that she is persecuted by the emptiness of her life, yet she empties space within which to wait to be met. Something also happens to time in this space - as the day progresses, Ivy often feels that time is moving too fast and is running out, and she feels anxious and disappointed. This experience of time is interesting. Ordinarily, waiting can feel long and tedious, even endless - hence the expression "killing time". Yet here, it seems that endless spaciousness of time is perhaps necessary to keep up hope of being met. Perhaps linear time is concretized, where what she really needs to access is a sort of 'out of time,' an attitude that allows time to circle around and back on itself, a timeless presence.

What/whom is she waiting for? The obvious association is with a Beckett play, like *Waiting for Godot*, waiting for something important to show up (Eigen, 2011). Is she waiting for soundings from Jung's objective psyche? Winnicott's incommunicado self? Is she waiting for something from outside? Inside?

I think of Winnicott's (2005) patient described in *Playing and Reality*, a woman who, after a long analytic treatment, comes to him for weekly sessions of indefinite length, reaching three hours at a time. He provides a supportive, reflective environment wherein she can reach toward resting in an unintegrated state from which "the individual can come together and exist as a unit, not as a defence against anxiety but as an expression of I AM, I am alive, I am myself" (2005, p. 76). Winnicott describes how, in her formless searching, what is essential is not her finding answers so much as realizing the creativity of the self in the "me" that asks the questions. This is Winnicott's "Sabbath point of personality" (Eigen, 1998, p. 46), where below the ubiquitous conflicts of the personality, one can dip into the "inexhaustible background of formlessness and more forming" (p. 46), into "unknown, boundless presence" (Eigen, 2011, p. 22) at the sacred core of our aloneness. Yet this is not an experiential given; when support for that basic aloneness falters, the emergent self-feeling can feel like it is facing

disaster rather than coming into being. Thus, Winnicott also "provides for experiencing unreality, nonbeing, deadness, so that an aliveness one can say 'yes' to has a chance of emerging" (Eigen, 1998, p. 58). I wonder whether Ivy was intuitively trying to create space and time for an experience of unintegration, to find that boundless presence from which the creative self she needed in order to face her life again could emerge. Undoubtedly, she would need to use me to re-find her relationship to the infinite other, but it was not essentially about creating a transitional space between therapist and patient but between Ivy as an I in connection to the Thou of life. Perhaps her previous experience in therapy had helped her internalize a sense of a supportive background presence, but faced afresh with overwhelming life experiences, she found herself again unable to maintain faith in the fluctuations of presence-absence/personal-implacable. In her despair and her acute sensitivity to absence, indifference, and life not coming through for her, she cannot remain open; she is compelled to close the gap too quickly, and she forecloses on the emergence of something from formlessness. I see this in sessions where Ivy always feels they are too short, and even when she gratefully experiences small transformations, a flush of tears, or a single spontaneous affective movement, she seems almost to "bank" it and move on as though unable to tolerate the precariously expectant waiting for something taking shape to develop further, or worse, to disappear on her, so she disengages first. There have been traumas to union as well as to separateness, and so the moving between is paralyzed, neither feeling safely possible - frozen midway. And yet here she is, trying again to make room for movement.

Beyond Object Usage

Ann Ulanov is a Jungian analyst and theologian who also welcomes spirituality in psychoanalysis. In her book about psyche and religion/spirituality called *Finding Space* (Ulanov, 2005), she emphasizes the intensity of lived experience and suggests that "we must change our description of Christianity or any other religion from categories of investigation to capacities for experiencing" (p. 9).

Ulanov uses Winnicott's transitional space to describe the playful back-and-forth movement between our subjective God-images (a me-God that confers a sense of self on us that we ourselves help to create) and our objective God-images (an independent, not-me God that confronts us rather than reflects us) that is necessary for our experience to feel real and alive. Then she adds a further step: with deeper psychic experiencing and the death of our God-images comes a crossing over from object relating to object usage, a precarious crossing, a looming gap where a loss of self and a loss of faith in God can coincide. But if we can bear the gap without collapsing the tension, the integrative forces of the psyche that Winnicott believed mirror the integrative forces at the heart of reality emerge: something new arrives, an objective-subject God "comes toward me as the Subject who sees me as a subject, entering my life in every intimate way" (p. 36) in a space of meeting. Ulanov describes this as glimpsing "resurrection" (p. 12).

Ulanov emphasizes the faith the child develops from object usage through repeated experiences of the objective, loving mother surviving destruction and extrapolating to our religious experience. Eigen, however, reminds us that object usage doesn't always result in an affirmation of our subjectivity and the goodness of the Other, but in "the felt realization that the other (of time, parent, world, etc.) is not knowable and cannot actually be 'used' in any way" (Malater, 2015, p. 61). Malater continues that in the time of psychoanalysis, the patient "begins to see that what he needs is to be in the time of openness, forever approaching another who is never fully known" (p. 62). In this vein, Grotstein (2000) posited a 'transcendent position' in which he moves beyond object relations or usage in approaching transformations and evolutions in "O". In the transcendent position, for that moment, one must give up the presence of the object and look inward into one's own subjectivity. In this way, one goes beyond the defenses of all psychoanalytic theory against an unknown, inscrutable O.

Perhaps Ivy was trying, both despite and by means of her wounded object relating and object usage, to reach beyond, to reach toward moments of Grotstein's transcendent position in her search to meet her life in an I-thou rhythm of faith. Grotstein writes,

> It is the purpose of dreaming/phantasying [dreaming occurring during waking] to effect a mental transformation from the cosmic indifference of "O" to an acceptance of one's own personal, emotional, subjective response to "O" and to accept this response [this suffering] as one's legitimate portion of circumstance. (2004, p. 102)

Ivy feels reduced to an 'it,' a thing that makes no impact and is only impacted upon, and her dreaming is stifled in the face of this perceived implacability. But slowly, in our sessions and in the self-created container of time and sunlit spaces in her home, she seeks to hear her own dreaming again - her precious subjectivity. Yes, if she finds her rage, it may not change the Other, but it will change her relationship to the Other, which could make all the difference.

Ivy and I are slowly coming through, and I am moved and heartened for myself and for her by Eigen's words: "One works all one's life to have a heart, to be a person, to get it right or better, only to meet a heartless God who keeps demanding more heart. The miracle is there *is* more heart. [...] Not everyone discovers the heart that can't stop opening, but once discovered there seems to be nothing that can't be faced" (1998, p. 91).

Postscript: A Dream and a Poem

While I am writing this, grappling with the many faces of the welcoming object and the dawning of the *primacy of subjectivity*, I have the following dream:

> I am in a traditional wooden boat on a lake in a country in the Far East. I am with a couple who are tourists too but have invited me on this boat trip to show me the lake. I jump into the water to swim. I am unsure whether the couple do too. I dive down deep, down to the bottom of the lake. I am surprised that I am able to do this as I do not normally swim very well. I find that the whole sandy bottom of the lake, as far as I can see, is covered with small clay amulets loosely arranged in a pattern of hundreds of small circles. I feel a sense of joy but also of something numinous in this unexpected discovery. Many of the amulets in the circle I am focusing on are little open palms/hands. I pick up an amulet, and finding it is something different, perhaps a letter of a foreign alphabet, I discard it- I am more drawn to the hands. I very much want to take one with me, but I am unsure whether I am allowed to and whether it would be fair or ethical to do so. I wonder whether the couple have taken some or whether they would judge me if I did. I have to go up again. It is more difficult than I thought it would be. On the way up I discover that I am under a submerged roof, and I am somewhat anxious about not having enough breath to find the end of the roof and still get to the surface. I do eventually surface near the boat. I do not know whether I took a little hand amulet or not.

On waking, the precious little clay hands immediately remind me of the welcoming object. They remind me of the hands of a color image I have of a wooden figure of Mary of the Annunciation; I titled it "Saying Yes" and have cherished it for many years now. There is an unpolished humility in her rough wooden shape and her large, plain, open palms. She knows my broken processors, yet she has faith in Grace and has taught me a certain openness. Yet more recently, I had started wondering whether she is entirely adequate for the self I am becoming. Is she not too selfless, too innocent, too young, and too surrendered? Perhaps I need an image closer to Sharon Blackie's (2022) feisty Hags. The endless pattern of circles on the floor of the lake reminds me of Jung's Self, the organizing principle of the psyche, which tries to mediate O through a personal ego-Self relationship. The whole dream feels like a personal gift from my psyche. I take it to my analyst, who points out my ambivalence in taking something meaningful and precious to me that I really want. In the dream, I worry about whether it is 'right' and whether I will be judged. And I am unsure, in the end, whether I took it or not. It seems there are obstacles still - old patterns - in the way of surfacing with these open hands. Relevant to this paper, it seems the dream is integrating Mary and the Hags, showing me the value, if not necessity, of both the surrender in those hands and a feisty capacity to lay claim to my unapologetic subjective participation in transformation.

In the same week, I stumble upon this poem, *Song for Ishtar* by Denise Levertov (2010), and I laugh, at this most feminine version of an invitation to me/to Ivy to wrestle destiny from the jaws of fate, and because a postcard of Ishtar from the British Museum has been pinned to the noticeboard in my consulting room for more than a decade!

The moon is a sow
and grunts in my throat
Her great shining shines through me
so the mud of my hollow gleams
and breaks in silver bubbles

She is a sow
and I a pig and a poet

When she opens her white
lips to devour me I bite back
and laughter rocks the moon
In the black of desire
we rock and grunt, grunt and
shine

References

Blackie, S. (2022). *Hagitude: Reimagining the Second Half of Life*. San Francisco: New World Library.

Campbell, M. (2015). Psychic aliveness: on "being murdered into life." In S. Bloch & L. Daws (Eds.), *Living Moments: On the Work of Michael Eigen* (pp. 85–106). London: Karnac.

Eaton, J.L. (2015). Becoming a welcoming object: personal notes on Michael Eigen's impact. In S. Bloch & L. Daws (Eds.), *Living Moments: On the Work of Michael Eigen* (pp. 131–148). London: Karnac.

Edinger, E.F. (1992). *Transformation of the God-Image: An Elucidation of Jung's Answer to Job*. Toronto: Inner City Books.

Eigen, M. (1986). *The Psychotic Core*. London: Karnac.

Eigen, M. (1998). *The Psychoanalytic Mystic*. London: Free Association Books.

Eigen, M. (2011). *Faith and Transformation: Eigen in Seoul: Volume Two*. London: Karnac.

Eigen, M. (2018). *The Challenge of Being Human*. New York: Routledge.

Grotstein, J. (2000). Bion's "transformations in 'O'" and the concept of the "transcendent position". In P. Bion Talamo, S.A. Merciai & F. Borgogno (Eds.), *W.R. Bion: Between Past and Future*. Abingdon: Routledge.

Grotstein, J.S. (2004). 'The light militia of the lower sky': the deeper nature of dreaming and phantasying, *Psychoanalytic Dialogues, 14*(1), 99–118.

Grotstein, J.S. (2007). *A Beam of Intense Darkness: Wilfred Bion's Legacy to Psychoanalysis*. London: Karnac.

Hollis, J. (2006). *Finding Meaning in the Second Half of Life: How to Finally, Really Grow Up*. New York: Penguin Random House.

Jung, C.G. (2002). *Jung: Answer to Job*. London: Routledge.

Levertov, D. (1992). *New & Selected Essays*. New York: New Directions Books.

Levertov, D. (2010). Song for Ishtar Poem by Denise Levertov. https://www.poemhunter.com/poem/song-for-ishtar/.

Malater, E. (2015). Eigentime: time in the writing of Michael Eigen. In S. Bloch & L. Daws (Eds.), *Living Moments: On the Work of Michael Eigen* (pp. 51–63). London: Karnac.

Orange, D.M. (2010). *Thinking for Clinicians: Philosophical Resources for Contemporary Psychoanalysis and the Humanistic Psychotherapies*. New York: Routledge.

Popova, M. (2022). https://www.themarginalian.org/2022/11/02/anais-nin-d-h-lawrence/.

Rilke, R.M. (2007). https://slowmuse.wordpress.com/2007/05/01/rilke-pushing-through/.

Ulanov, A.B. (2005). *Finding Space: Winnicott, God, and Psychic Reality*. Louisville: Westminster John Knox Press.

Winnicott, D.W. (2005). *Playing and Reality*. Oxon: Routledge Classics.

Chapter 12

Music as Dreaming
Welcoming Absence through Music

Stephen Bloch

Introductory Comments

The intersection of psychoanalysis and music has highlighted the capacity of music to express and contain emotional states of mind. Many writers have emphasized music's particular potency in capturing profound and especially pre-verbal emotional experiences. Implicit in this view has been the critique that psychoanalytic discourse has privileged the visual, despite it being the "*talking cure*" and the apparent fact that it relies on listening. In combining this sense of music's mutative, affective potency with its relative neglect in the literature, one can suggest the possibility that the visual has been used defensively against the auditory. The visual may be a less intense, "cooler" sensory medium, in contrast to the raw and embodied immediacy of the auditory.

Significantly, neither of the founders of analysis had any particular interest in music. Freud described himself as "quite unmusical". Sabbadini (2006). Jung seems to have been averse to music, although he states that music deals with "deep archetypal material" (Tilley, 1980). He also felt that active imagination could be practiced in all sensory modalities. Of particular importance is the fact that he appears to be the first theorist to have suggested the idea of the "acoustic image" (Tilley, 1980).

The idea of an auditory image or symbol is fascinating but challenging to define precisely. In some ways, it seems contradictory because in the literature, images and symbols are mainly taken to be visual. To take a representative example, Samuels, Shorter, and Plaut (1988) state plainly that symbols "are captivating pictorial statements" (p. 145). In Hillman's post-Jungian writing, the sense of the visual basis of imagery also predominates.

Within the archetypal school, however, Casey writes, "An image is not what you see but the way you see" (Casey, 1974, p. 2). Similarly, one can suggest that an auditory image is not a sound in itself but more a channel through which we hear. It is the equivalent of a lens through which we apprehend experience. Music literally "sounds out" the implicit emotional dimensions, raising them to consciousness. It gives sonorous form to Bollas's notion of "unthought known." Similarly, an auditory symbol is neither a particular musical form nor a rhythmic or tonal sequence, but a symbolic resolution reached through an acoustic or auditory channel.

DOI: 10.4324/9781003322993-12

In this paper, two 20th-century minimalist musical works are used as a basis for exploring how an acoustic symbol may develop. The music has been selected for several reasons. Firstly, as will be shown, minimalist music has particular points of convergence with the analytic experience. Secondly, the works are significant because of how they explore the interface of words and music. Thirdly, in the sense that they concern themselves with the experience of absence, they allow insight into the earliest origins of the symbolic process.

The aim has been not to interpret the music psychoanalytically but to demonstrate how psychoanalytic insight can be expressed musically.

Minimalist Music and Analysis

Minimalist music is a genre of music in which musical phrases or figures are repeated over extended periods with only gradual, incremental changes. Typically, the music does not modulate in the way that more familiar Western music does. It does not use tension and release as a central musical device. It is music that "doesn't go anywhere" (Wildman, 2007, personal communication). The style is associated with American composers such as Philip Glass, Steve Reich, Terry Riley, and John Adams and emerged in the 1960s.

Minimalist music can be trance-like and fall into a new-age mindlessness. Reich, for example, acknowledged that some of his early work may be vulnerable to this criticism. However, "… later works demand intense listening and can be technically challenging. The crucial distinction depends on the understanding of the amount of repetitions and when change occurs" (Reich, 1988, p. 54).

Minimalist music provides an imaginal (acoustic) background to two significant aspects of the analytic process. Firstly, because it doesn't develop and resolve in the manner in which most Western music does, the experience can be disorientating and unsettling. One's usual sense of time collapses and expands, and this can foster regressive experiences. Indeed, some of the antipathies toward minimalist music may be due to the primitive affective states which are elicited by the music.

The second important link with analysis is that in the repetitive musical loops in minimalism, one is made conscious of the repeated experiential loops of analysis. These recursive loops are the musical counterparts of patients who state that they are "stuck records" and fear that they are boring the therapist (and themselves). There is also a link here to unwanted patients and themes of psychic deadness, including people who die with unheard music inside themselves. This type of music speaks, therefore, to the common analytic experience of themes repeated over and over, the complex running continually in the unconscious and making only slight incremental changes, seemingly untouched by linear time. This is a model of the psyche deepening not by elaborate interpretation, or, for that matter, the heroic myth, but by the experience of the eternal return of the major motifs in the analysand's life. It is, as Schwarz (1997) comments, the music of the "repetition compulsion," the need being to repeatedly revisit the "site of trauma", to work it through and gain mastery over it.

Steve Reich addresses this revisiting aspect in his minimalist work "The Desert Music", where he uses the following excerpt from a William Carlos Williams poem as the basis for a section in his composition:

> "...it is a principle of music
>   to repeat the theme. Repeat
>   and repeat again
>   as the pace mounts. The
>   theme is difficult
>   but no more difficult
>   than the fact to be
>   resolved." (From "The Orchestra", W.C. Williams, 2006)

Different Trains (Steve Reich)

Different Trains (1998) is a work for string quartet (Kronos Quartet) and tape. The taped portions are of short spoken phrases as well as train sounds such as whistles and sirens. The voices on the tape are of Reich's childhood governess, railway porters, and Holocaust survivors.

The project links the experience of Holocaust survivors with Reich's own childhood experience of traveling by train between New York and Los Angeles in order to visit his separated parents. The title, *Different Trains*, comes from his reflection that, had he been in World War II Europe, he would have been on trains transporting people to concentration camps.

Reich was interested in speech-generating musical ideas, and one can hear this in the way the sounds of the voices are developed and echoed melodically and harmonically. He transforms the cadences of the spoken word into melodic contours. In the work, he emphasizes the rhythm of the spoken phrases.

The work concerns itself with the experience of traumatic loss and absence. This is exemplified by the phrase in the third movement,

> "But today, they're all gone"

A train porter speaks the sentence. It becomes more unsettling in the realization that a Holocaust survivor could have spoken it.

Jesus' Blood Never Failed Me Yet (Gavin Bryars)

The work, *Jesus' blood never failed me yet*, by Gavin Bryars, is based on recording a homeless London tramp singing the remnants of a hymn. This motif is repeated repeatedly, while an accompaniment of strings, choir, and orchestra complements the tramp himself. The effect after listening to the full 74-minute CD is, at once, searing, redemptive, soothing, and haunting.

The original tape, a found object, was left over from a film about homeless vagrants in London. The composer copied this onto a continuous reel in a recording studio and left it running. He writes (1993, p. 4):

> I copied the loop and left the door of the recording studio open … while I went downstairs to get a cup of coffee. When I came back, I found the normally lively room unnaturally subdued. People were moving about much more slowly than usual, and a few were sitting alone, quietly weeping. I was puzzled until I realized that the tape was still playing and that they had been overcome by the old man's unaccompanied signing.

Bryars comments that he does not share the optimism of the tramp's faith but was touched by the poignancy and "humanness" of the singing. The London tramp and the words and melody themselves have never been traced. This suggests that the tramp created it himself.

Music as Dreaming

Schwarz (1997) approached Different Trains from a psychoanalytic perspective, understood the music as a "sonorous envelope", and showed how the work moves between linguistic and pre-linguistic sound. The sonorous envelope is a musical representation of the earliest experience of maternal containment. It may be involved in all musical experiences but is particularly significant in minimalist music.

In this paper, I will show how Bion's and Eigen's concepts of dreaming (and specifically the undreamable object) deepen our understanding of what occurs in the sonorous envelope. Bion's approach to dreamwork inverts the classical Freudian perspective. Rather than the psychoanalytic view that dream analysis facilitates the unconscious being made conscious, Bion sees dreamwork as the ongoing unconscious processing of conscious experience. Dreaming is the operation whereby experience is worked on psychologically so that it can be metabolized and absorbed; the dream digests psychic material. This allows recall, storage, and the linking of feeling/experience to images. The analyst "dreams" the patient in this sense of "doing psychological work" on the patients' unprocessed experience (Ogden, 2005). It is only when this dreaming operates that psychological growth occurs.

Ogden writes:

> Dreaming … must involve unconscious psychological work achieved through the linking of elements of experience (which have been stored as memory) in the creation of dream-thought. This work of making unconscious linkages – as opposed to forms of psychic evacuation such as hallucination, excessive projective identification, manic defense and paranoid delusion – allows one unconsciously and consciously to think about and make psychological use of experience. (Ogden, 2005, p. 47)

Similarly, Eigen writes:

> Waking life is dependent on dreamlife. Dreams store raw impacts and play a role in the work that makes them communicate. Dreamwork is continuous; it goes on while we are asleep or awake. Impressions from outside/inside are transformed by dreamwork and made available for further work. (Eigen, 2001, p. 46)

The operation of this dreaming occurs in the interactive field of the container and the contained. Bion uses the term "alpha function" to designate the metaboliz-ing operations that work on undigested sense impressions (which he termed beta-elements). Dreamwork-alpha acts on raw experience so that it may be thought of, symbolized, mourned, or learned from. Beta-elements cannot be linked or held in memory. They can only be evacuated.

> The alpha function operates on sense impressions, whatever they are, and on the emotions whatever they are, of which the patient is aware. (Bion, 1967, p. 111)

Without alpha, these sense impressions and emotions remain unprocessed, un-changed, and incoherent. The person in this state cannot sleep or wake up. The undigested beta-elements can be experienced as "foreign bodies in the mind" or "debris of which the mind wants to rid itself." When alpha has successfully oper-ated, experience is made "comprehensible and meaningful" (Bion, 1984, p. 111), and a symbol can develop.

Music can be regarded as dreaming, in the sense that it performs alpha work on raw emotional experience. Indeed, Bion described *beta*-functioning in musical terms when he wrote: "It is as if the word is a counterpart of the pure note in music, devoid of undertone/overtones" (Bion, 1992, p. 53). Moreover, Bion regarded al-pha elements as also operating in auditory (and olfactory) domains and wrote of the "auditory system with which is linked transformations such as music noise". In *Dif-ferent Trains* and *Jesus' Blood*, one can see the action of musical dreamwork-alpha on undigested experience, allowing it to be thought, remembered, and mourned.

The selected music demonstrates how music dreams and metabolizes raw emo-tional experience. In both *Different Trains* and *Jesus' Blood*, the music deepens the implicit unconscious emotionality of the voices. The musical working of the undigested voices draws out the full intensity and meaning of the experience of the Holocaust survivors and the London tramp. In this way, Bion's notion of the unconscious dreaming of the conscious can be experienced. Because the resolu-tion is happening musically (especially in *Different Trains*), Reich and Bryars are inverting the more common analytic direction where words contain the emo-tional experience. Here, the music carries out the containment and dreaming of the words. The words are the beta-elements; alpha functioning is completed by the music.

In *Different Trains*, the narrative fragments, indeed the fragmented narratives, are echoed by the string quartet. In some places, the rhythm, cadences, and emphasis of the words are imitated identically by the violins and, at crucial points, by the cello (that instrument whose range is equivalent to the human voice). The repetitive echoing and harmonizing create a visceral sense of the words being worked on psychologically and metabolized. Often, the music can only proceed once sufficient digestion of a phrase has occurred. The rhythm and cadences change at these intersections, allowing a new statement to be grappled with.

The repeated violin phrases create a sense of train rhythms. They can also sound like rocking, inconsolable sobbing, or the struggle to give form to pre-verbal emotion.

The train siren, which intermittently penetrates the sound of the string arrangement, evokes a howl or scream and elicits a feeling of loss or terror. At other times, low, sustained, almost drone-like cello notes create a sense of severity and grief.

Winnicott (1989, pp. 115–118) writes of a vanishing scream that has always been not experienced; "the great non-event of every session. The last scream just before hope was abandoned" (p. 118). Eigen comments that therapy provides the context in which this scream can be "felt and hope retrieved" (Eigen, 2002, p. 122) to heal the schism between psyche and soma. The therapist's alpha dreamwork, therapist as a welcoming object, facilitates this retrieval. It is a movement from screaming to dreaming. This movement is also experienced in the ceaseless train rhythm in Reich's work. Through this and the speech micro-melodies, there is a thawing of history, frozen stuck trauma time. This trauma time is a negative here and now, a -HN, so to speak. The discovery of the last scream enables the movement into linear chronological time. This scream can be heard in many musical genres. But particularly in the Blues and "keening" in Irish music.

Reich creates a feeling of intense turbulence throughout much of the work. *Different Trains* portrays a landscape of disorientated loss and shock. It is a psychological space existing before the more resolved mourning of a requiem can be expressed. *Different Trains* is a *proto-requiem* – communicating the process whereby undigested experience is worked with until more symbolized acceptance can be achieved in mourning. The possibility of mourning is suggested in the closing bars of the final movement.

The struggle that characterizes parts of *Different Trains* points to the strain of performing dreamwork on an experience that is so traumatically unbearable that it overwhelms the capacity to contain it. Eigen, in dealing with "the undreamable object", writes of "a dread of dreads that is not only unnamable but also undreamable" (Eigen, 2001, p. 47). It is as though the experience of traumatic loss bursts through an absorbing/symbolizing function. Here, "the very background of psychic life is damaged. Not only are there dreadful objects that cannot reach dreams, but there is no place to dream them" (Eigen, 2001, p. 47). If the mother cannot take the full impact of the infant's projective identification, the infant is thrown back on himself and reintrojects a "nameless dread" (Bion, 1984). The homelessness of Bryars' London tramp may be seen as characterizing this internal state of lack of containment. One can consider a trauma that is unbearable here because the other/mother cannot dream it.

Bryars' musical responses to the tramps' singing function as a containing reverie. He *participates* in the tramp's singing respectfully and empathically. This provides a musical image of non-intrusive holding reminiscent of Winnicott's "primary maternal preoccupation" (Winnicott, 1975), where the mother emotionally attunes to the infant's experience. The layered chordal accompaniment provides this sense of sustaining containment and locates the tramp's experiences on a larger time scale. For Winnicott, part of the mother's role is to hold the infant's experience across time, protecting the infant from the impingement of time external to the infant's reality (Ogden, 2005). Ogden also points out that "primary maternal preoccupation" is subjectless – the mother suspends her own needs in the service of the infant. Bryars' musical holding of the tramp's experience reflects this non-obtrusive attitude.

The minimalist style of the work, with its extended, recurring loops, highlights the crucial role echoing plays in analysis and the early mother-infant interaction. The echoing accompaniment reflects the singing tramp back to himself and is itself echoed in the endless cycles of the work. *Echoing* in the analytic context is an essential root of empathy and congruence. It is the sonic reflection by another which holds experience and allows it to be felt and experienced. The echoed patient knows that he has been heard more than merely seen. It also develops continuity in the analytic dyad and mirrors the crucial motifs of the analysand's life. In the mother-infant situation, echoing is a fundamental aspect of the mother's musical responsiveness to the infant. As a basic and ubiquitous reflex, it is a key feature of the acoustic language, the "motherese", which develops between mother and infant.

However, the music seems to drag and die out at points, exposing a void and emptiness. A bell sounding rescues the tramp from this experience, seemingly calling him back. Some listeners hear in the phrase "never failed Me yet" some defensiveness, self-reassurance, and some doubt. In the sense, however, that he has been heard (via Gavin Bryars on the CD), he has, in fact, not been "failed". Perhaps the redemptive blood is that of a containing reverie.

The tramp's experience is more coherent than the speech fragments of *Different Trains*. He does sing the full stanza, and the music is more soothing than the intensity of *Different Trains*. This may be because the experience he has been through is easier to meet, or, in that he is already singing, some alpha dreaming has already occurred. The work, in its entirety, does evoke a movement, in Eigen's words, "from catastrophe to faith" (Eigen, 1983). Faith here refers to the capacity to emerge from destruction and remain open to experience. There have been many subsequent renditions of this work, some from a few minutes to many hours, and Bryars himself recomposes parts at every performance. The extended versions more accurately carry the long-term aspects of mother-infant and analytic experience.

Peter Boutenoff (2021) has commented on this work: "It makes you wonder how at any given moment, there's something passing being said or sung, that if we cared enough to isolate it and love it, it could become exactly as beautiful". Here we have the aesthetic dimension of analytic experience, as emphasized by both Bion and Eigen. The prayer of the homeless man becomes a cry of the heart, the *lacrimae mundi*, archetypal in the sense of it being a shared, enduring human experience.

In this regard, Morton (2018) writes of Bryars' quest for the heart of humanity and quotes Beckett... ." The tears of the world are a constant quantity. For each one who begins to weep, someone else stops".

Ogden contrasts Bion's concept of container-contained with that of Winnicott's "holding", although both are different dimensions of the same experience. Bion's model is more dynamic in that the dreamwork processing of emotional experience occurs in a state of mutual interaction. The container and contained are "fiercely, muscularly in tension with one another" (Ogden, 2005, p. 105). Winnicott's "holding" involves a "continuity of being" in the empathic participation of the mother in her "gentle, sturdy wrapping of the infant" (Ogden, 2005, p. 105). The two musical works provide an arresting encounter with these two crucial analytic constructs. Reich's *Different Trains* exemplifies the intense interplay of container and contained. The Bryars' piece reflects the feeling tone of Winnicott's concepts of non-impinging "holding" and "continuity of being".

Music and Absence

The works explored above demonstrate a particular musical response to actual experiences of intolerable loss, abjection, and degradation. They can also refer to equivalent subjective experiences where absence and rupture predominate (see Eigen, 1996, 1999).

Winnicott locates these experiences at the earliest breaks in continuity of mothering, when the infant has not developed the capacity to deal with this gap. Bion describes this lack as "no-thing". Confronted with absence, or no-thing, or that which is internally absent (Bion, 1967), the infant must either tolerate frustration and develop psychologically, or deny frustration and evacuate experience. By tolerating frustration, thinking structures and symbolism develop.

In the glossary to his book *Psychoanalysis and Art*, Gosso (2001) provides the following formulation in discussing symbolism:

"No breast – therefore a thought"

Symbolism emerges in the awareness of and growing capacity to tolerate absence. This is facilitated by the maternal reverie, where dreamwork-alpha contains experience. Much of this containing and metabolizing by the mother may be done through the medium of music. Her musical responsiveness (through, for example, use of humming, repetition, variations in frequency, pitch, and emphasis) helps the infant develop a symbolic function. It is not only the infant's sounds that are at the root of music but more the mother's *acoustic responses* as she 'at-tunes' to and digests the infant's experience. The infant's experience of absence is mediated by the mother's sounds; as she helps process the experience of separation, she uses "music across absence" (Perera, 2006).

One can transcribe Gosso's formulation by writing,

"No breast – therefore a song"

Here, song would be the outcome of an auditory symbolic process. However, in the early stages of infant development, a song may be too sophisticated, and the attuned mother uses more primitive sounds and a musical responsiveness that is less complex. The music compositions presented here illustrate how the musical working through of absence provides a model of the maternal containment of primitive states of mind.

Reik was the first writer to highlight the importance of music in the analyst's awareness, providing the analytic correlate of the mother-infant situation. He used musical references as the basis for exploring his countertransference reactions. For example, he sometimes associated certain operatic themes with his patient's material.

More recently, Knoblauch (2004) has written about the musical aspects of therapeutic listening and response. For him, musical sensitivity is an important channel for the awareness of affect, and he suggests that this way of listening emphasizes understanding of shifts, particularly in rhythm and tone, but also in volume, emphasis, and tempo. The metaphoric model he developed is that of the therapist's harmonic accompaniment to the patient as a soloist. He focuses on patients who require pre-verbal responsiveness and are particularly sensitive to impingement. However, his insights also apply to other therapies and highlight a mode of listening that most therapists do intuitively.

In this harmonic accompaniment to the patient, the therapist can provide a dense, chordal responsiveness or a sparser, thinner response that hints and suggests meanings rather than making definitive statements. Variations in tempo can also create different shifts in the way a session develops. Close empathic attunement may be as basic as an octave interval or drone accompaniment. Confrontation can be seen as a dissonant harmonic response highlighting a particular communication. For Knoblauch, the musical genre that most closely approximates analysis is jazz. It is as though the patient states a theme that is then creatively responded to by the therapist, who keeps within the frame of harmonic and rhythmic rules. Following Knoblauch, one can imagine sessions that are essentially improvisations in the "key" of, for example, anger, envy, or regret. The therapist is 'playing' in Winnicott's sense of the word while keeping within the analytic frame and attitude. The jazz musician is also "playing" while grounded in tradition and within the structures of scales, harmony, and rhythm.

Eigen (2001, p. 82) emphasizes a background musical imagination when he writes, "deeply damaged people reach for something musical in the therapist, and hope that the latter will respond to something deeply musical in themselves". To be understood musically by an analyst is to be comprehended in an essential pre-linguistic, possibly *pre-visual way*. The patient seeks this empathic resonance, and there is often relief, and indeed joy, when the therapist knows a valued, crucial musical work.

There is a further way in which music is involved with absence. Rose (2004) points out that music is the "temporal art", whose meaning is based on its movement through time. Music moves toward us and away as it proceeds through linear time. As Colombier (2003) writes, "Music is the art whose object disappears almost at the same moment it appears, which brings it very close to the presence/

absence scansion" (p. 277). It is as though music confronts us with loss at the same time as it digests the experience. Conversely, it provides a containing presence while it is itself evoking absence and moving toward silence. This impermanent aspect of music must have been particularly significant before the relatively recent invention of recorded sound. Previously, music may have been experienced as the equivalent of Tibetan sand mandalas that disintegrate after construction. Holding this paradox represents the nothing in consciousness rather than letting it disappear into hallucinosis. The effect of music is to hold the opposites of presence and absence and, in so doing, to continually exercise and develop our capacity to mourn.

Concluding Remarks

In an interview with Regina Monte, Eigen (Eigen, 2006) cites the following statement of Bion's from Cogitations:

"I am his other self and it is a dream."

Eigen encourages rumination on the meanings embedded in this comment. One potential meaning is that we are dreaming about each other's experiences and digesting each other's trauma. Music and creativity can carry this function as this "dreaming other". The "dreaming other", as that process where psychological work is done on experience, is linked to analysis and creative endeavors such as art and music. Music has been shown to function as a "dreaming other" in two musical works. The themes explored in these works concern experiences of rupture and loss. This allows consideration of how music may be involved in the symbolization of absence in early infancy. The two musical examples discussed are significant because they are so direct and immediate in interacting with raw emotional experience. Other musical forms involve more sophisticated and developed emotional states of mind expressions. However, they may rely, in their basis, on the dreaming and metabolizing processes illustrated by these minimalist works. It can be helpful when listening to music to ask, "What state of mind is this music dreaming?" or "How is this music dreaming this experience?"

Music in mediating and digesting emotional impacts provides an imaginal base, a home for experience. It is as though Bryars' tramp personifies homeless, undreamt, and, therefore, unredeemed beta phenomena. The musical reverie dreams, holds, and locates unmetabolized dimensions of experience and moves them toward a symbolic resolution. The move is from absence to the emergence of the auditory symbol and the hearing of unrepresentable experiences through Eigen, Winnicott, and Bion.

Discography

Bryars, Gavin. *Jesus' Blood Never Failed Me Yet*, Point Music, 1993.
Reich, Steve. *Different Trains*, Nonesuch, 1988.

References

Bion, W.R. (1984). *Attention and Interpretation*. London: Karnac.

Bion, W.R. (1963). *Elements of Psychoanalysis*. London: Heinemann.

Bion, W.R. (1967). *A theory of thinking in Second Thoughts*. London: Heinemann, p. 111.

Bion, W.R. (1992). *Cogitations*. London: Karnac.

Boutenoff, P. (13, August 2021), Interview Lumnous Conversations on the Sacred Arts podcast. Accessed on 28 Dec 2022.

Bryars, Gavin – *Jesus' Blood Never Failed Me Yet*, CD, booklet notes.

Colombier, J.P. (2003). So you want to write a fugue. Wilfred R. Bion with Glen Gould in Lipgar R.M. and Pines, M. *Building on Bion; Branches*. London: Jessica Kingsley, pp. 253–284.

Eigen, M. (1999). *Toxic Nourishment*. London: Karnac.

Eigen, M. (2001). *Damaged Bonds*. London: Karnac.

Eigen, M. (2002). *Rage*. Middleton: Weselyan University Press.

Eigen, M. (2006). Interview with Regina Monte *Dharma Café* Website accessed 6 Jan 2023.

Morton, B. (2018). Anthem for the homeless: mystery at the heart of a contemporary classic. *The Guardian* June 20, 2018.

Ogden, T.H. (2005). *This Art of Psychoanalysis* London: Routledge.

Sabbadini A. (2006). On Sounds, Children and Identity and "A Quite Unmusical Man". *British Journal of Psychotherapy*, 14(2), 189–196.

Samuels, A., Shorter, B., & Plaut, F. (1986). *A Critical Dictionary of Jungian Analysis.* London: Routledge & Kegan Paul.

Schwarz, D. (1997). *Listening Subjects*. Durham and London: Duke University Press.

Symington, J., & Symington, N. (1996). *The Clinical Thinking of Wilfred Bion*. London: Routledge.

Rose, G.S. (2004). *Between Couch and Piano*. New York: Brunner-Routledge.

Wildman, C. (2007). *Music Therapist*. Cape Town.

Williams, W.C. (2006). The Orchestra Cited in CD liner notes; Steve Reich PHASES; A Nonesuch Retrospective, p. 36, Nonesuch Records, New York.

Winnicott, D.W. (1989). *Psycho-analytic Explorations*. Edited by C. Winnicott, R. Shepherd, M. Davis. London Routledge.

Chapter 13

Moving to Inner Lights

Ebru Salman

There are dimensions in which the soul is made of music. In which music is the raw material of creation.

Michael Eigen.

What Bion calls O, the eternal, non-sensuous ultimate reality, the absolute truth or meaning of an emotional experience, is internal. It is internal to external reality, and it is internal to our inner reality that is in the domain of K. O is the meaning that filters through the formal elements of the dream. That is a realm of internality beyond the semi-permeable boundaries of the finite aspect of human subjectivity marked by a "distinction-union structure" described by Eigen (1986, 2011). There is an ever-present gap between this and the finite human subject, insurmountable for the latter. I would like to call this gap, *void*. Bion, who was asking in a 1959 note in *Cogitations* (1992), "What is being resisted?" (p. 90), writes in *Transformations* (1965) that resistance comes about in the experiencing of this *immanence*: "Resistance operates because it is feared that the reality of the object is imminent" (p. 147). The human subject comes face to face with the *void* in "experiencing" reality, in "being that which is real" (ibid., pp. 148). *Après coup*, we are able to know some things partially, but in the here-and-now, the *void* is always there. In this encounter, the finite part of human subjectivity can feel like an object: "a cornered rat which a giant ['Lord Cat Almighty'] was nonchalantly aiming to club to death."[1] This is experienced in an "I-It" attitude toward the world that Martin Buber described. In this mode of relating, the "rat" can easily be reversed with the "cat," and the *void* can be done away with. In a note, Bion tape-recorded on 8 August 1978, in Dordogne, France, he suggests relating with O in what Buber termed the "I-You" attitude, where Bion writes, "the significant thing is not the two objects related, but the *relationship*—that is, an open-ended reality in which there is no termination" (1992, p. 371, original italics). In this note, 81-year-old Bion describes the "terrifying unknown" (ibid., p. 371) also as "some other love that is mature from an absolute standard ... the further extension to 'absolute love', which cannot be described in the terms of sensuous reality or experience" (ibid., p. 372).

DOI: 10.4324/9781003322993-13

I call the gap *void* with Rabbi Nachman's (1772–1810) teaching *The Torah of the Void* in mind, where he wrote on a concept in Lurianic Kabbalah, which Eigen (2012) refers to in *Kabbalah and Psychoanalysis* as in the creation of the world "God contracts to make room for the world" (p. 5). Nachman (1996) writes, "God, for Mercy's sake, created the world to reveal Mercy."

But as He wished to create
there was not a *where?*
All was Infinitely He,
Be He Blessed!

The light he condensed

sideways
thus was *space* made
an empty void.

In *space* days and measures

came into being.
So the world was created.[2]

His lines portray the creative quality of the gap. A similar idea exists in *Timeaus*, where Plato introduces a *third* kind to his priorly dual system of Forms ("that which always is and has no becoming," the eternal, unchanging, non-sensible, intelligible truth or reality) and particulars ("that which is always becoming and never is," the ever-changing sensible world, phenomena). One of the main ideas in his account is that "two things cannot be rightly put together without a third; there must be some bond of union between them. And the fairest bond is that which makes the most complete fusion of itself and the things which it combines" (Plato, 360 BC). In this story of creation, out of Necessity, the two worlds are bound by the Receptacle, "the nurse of all generation." Plato's descriptions of the Receptacle imply a *container* in which symbolization takes place. He refers to it as "space" and admits to its mystery, as its existence is "neither in heaven nor in earth." It is *Chora* in Greek in his text. There is a Chora Church in Istanbul, a Byzantine church dating back to the 4th century AD. On epithets on two mosaics at the entrance, Mary and Jesus are referred to, respectively, as "the Chora, the dwelling place, of the uncontainable God" (*he Chora tou Achoretou*) and "the land of the living" (*he Chora ton zonton*), the land of living things. Both the idea of "representation" through a tripartite structure in union in Plato's frame-work—"we may liken the receiving principle to a mother, the source or spring to a father, and the intermediate nature to a child" (Plato, 360 BC)—and "incarnation" through Trinity in what Bion calls "Christian Platonism" are what Bion (1965, 1970, 1992) saw psychoanalysis as a thing-in-itself within the same tradition.[3] This *void* was gradually obliterated in the institution of modern scientific methodology, with a claim to knowability—e.g., in the first edition of *Principia Mathematica* (1687), Newton had written that matter was active; matter pulled on itself other particles, and in the distance between them there was "vacuum." Upon receiving much criticism from both scientific and religious circles, he amended the General Scholium in the second edition (1713), saying that the interaction of two particles of matter happened via "ether" in the air and that air can sustain gravitational forces because of ether (Gurses-Tarbuck, 2022). The *void* exists in psychoanalysis under various formulations, like "transitional space" (Winnicott), "unknowable inside of the mother" (Meltzer), "contact-barrier" (Bion), "creative unknown" (Eigen), "creative emptiness" (Milner), and others. It can be discerned in Freud's conceptualization of the "primal scene" and in Klein's concept of the "depressive position."

I gather from my reading of Bion that he thinks the experience of the finite aspect of human subjectivity vis-à-vis the *void* is fundamentally *envy*. He describes the emotional state of "transformations in O" in *Attention and Interpretation* as "dread"—fear from a "frightful fiend," who close behind doth tread[4] (1970, p. 46). I think that the dread experienced in this state is, in Bion's view, "fear of envy, either [one's] own or another's," which he refers to in *Learning from Experience* (*LFE*) (p. 13).[5] Envy, in ourselves or others, is a part of lived reality that O is. In his later writing, Bion notes regarding O,

> Its existence as indwelling has no significance whether it is supposed to dwell in an individual person or in God or Devil; it is not good or evil; it cannot be known, loved or hated. It can be represented by terms such as ultimate reality or truth. The most, and the least that the individual person can do is to be it. (1965, pp. 139–140)

or "The problem, psycho-analytically, is easier to grasp if O represents ultimate reality, good and evil" (ibid., pp. 148–149); or "It is not possible to talk about 'god' unless one assumes it also means 'devil'" (1992, p. 371). I think he means bad is part of it, and it is beyond bad and good.

In *LFE*, Bion describes a psychotic patient who "as an escape from [experiencing] fear of envy, either his own or another's, … attempt[s] *to evade experience of contact with live objects by destroying alpha-function*" (p. 13, italics added). This leaves the personality "unable to have a relationship with any aspect of itself that does not resemble an automaton" (ibid., p. 13). He is describing a *de-animation*. In this, "Only beta-elements are available for whatever activity takes the place of thinking and beta-elements are suitable for evacuation only" (ibid., p. 13). About the "minute fragments" that accrue with the destruction or inhibition of the alpha-function—which sustains one's capacity for communication with himself and others and generates a sense of reality—Bion's conclusion in *Attention and Interpretation* is that they are the "proliferation of fragmented envy," that envy is split. (1970, p. 128) "If envy were to assume an aspect of whole object," he writes, "it could be seen as envy of the personality capable of maturation and of the object stimulating maturation" (ibid., p. 128). The word "maturation" in his use has the meaning of *becoming more real*, more *O happening*. He describes the splitting in question,

> The stimulating object is the breast (♀) or mouth (♂). They replace each other. The stimulating quality in turn replaces the stimulating object. A series of trans-formations is thus initiated, each a substitution for the previous one and each subject to splitting. (Ibid., p. 128)[6]

His proposition has reverberations with Money-Kyrle's (1968) theory of cognitive development and its failures based on "misconceptions" of the primal scene due to "emotional impediments"—in his words, a theory of the "interaction between our perception of truth and the will to distort it" (p. 211), and which is founded on Bion's (1962) notion of an innate pre-conception mating with a realization to form a concept. Meltzer (1978) underlines that for Bion, attacks are essentially attacks on linking, and "Envy, in Bion's view and in Bion's terms, would not be aroused either by container or contained but only by their successful (symbiotic) conjunction" (p. 379). A mysterious and generative mating is not tolerated.

My conceptualization of Bion's thinking is that one's emotional experience vis-à-vis the *void* can be what Bion (1970) describes as the "emotional matrix" from which springs an incremental splitting of an idea that was to be born (hence "becoming" is hindered), which is "envy and greed" (p. 127); or it can be what he compares that here with: "envy and gratitude".

> The idea that is nourished by love develops from matrix to function in Language of Achivement; from which it can be transformed into achievement. But if the idea is subjected to splitting it may split again repeatedly, each split growing and having to be split again. … The emotional matrix from which this springs is not envy and gratitude, but envy and greed. (ibid., p. 127)

It seems to me that with the term "envy *and* gratitude" (italics added), Bion refers to what he mentions at the beginning of this paragraph as "love". I think, he means here a love that is inclusive of envy[7], and I believe this is what he will refer to in the *Memoir* as "passionate love." I conceive that, in the emotional matrix of "envy and gratitude," the *void* is preserved, and through it, what Bion (1992) describes as "some other love that is mature from an absolute standard" (p. 372) is received. The "contact-barrier" (Bion, 1962), sustained by the operation of the alpha-function, is a *semi-permeable* membrane. The "distinction-union structure" (Eigen, 1986, 2011) rests, or rather, *moves* in this area of mental functioning.

Bion describes beta-elements in *Elements of Psycho-Analysis* (1963) as "aspects of the personality linked by a sense of catastrophe" (p. 40). At the same time, he speaks of beta-elements as "dispersed" (ibid., p. 40), which is in line with his earlier description of them in *LFE* (1962) in comparison to alpha-elements, which can link among themselves.[8] In *Elements* (1963), Bion seems to introduce a peculiar quality of linkage to these dispersed elements. They seem bound by death. In a footnote attached to the term "aspects of the personality linked by a sense of catastrophe," Bion writes, "There is a curious parallel in a description of R. B. Onians (Origins of European Thought, p. 369 C. U.P.) of the Greek ideas of the riddle and the sphinx" (p. 40). In *Origins of European Thought*, Onians (1951) illustrates the concept of 'bond', i.e., binding, as associated with magic in Ancient Greece (pp. 367–369), and in this context, he describes,

> The 'Sphinx' of the Theban legend can also now perhaps be better understood. She is usually explained as the 'Throttler', 'Choker', but was rather, I suggest, the 'Tight-binder', the meaning naturally indicated by *sphigho* and fitting, as we see, her character as of a death demon … It fits also the possibly later version of her as singing deadly riddles … The Greeks conceived of a riddle or trap of words difficult to deal with as a woven rush basket. (p. 369)

A death demon as a "tight-binder," her riddle as a "woven rush basket." No room for *void*.

Eigen (1995) highlights that, Freud (1937) thought the operation of the death instinct that is not bound by the life drive probably involved "some temporal characteristics … some alterations of a rhythm of development in psychical life which we have not yet appreciated."[9] (p. 288) Eigen (1995) writes, "The focus here is … timing and movement. The music of the psyche is off. A rhythmic warp results in structural alterations. Structure depends on rhythms" (p. 290). As Eigen notes, Freud did not localize this anti-development force in a structure in the psyche but saw it as an anti-growth tendency, in Eigen's words, "that cannot be pinned down. It is structural and atmospheric; it taints the very 'space' and 'air' the psyche breathes in" (ibid., p. 290). Like the "tight-binder" death demon, the Sphinx. The peculiar binding in "aspects of the personality linked by a sense of catastrophe" is paradoxically a fragmentation—"cemented in a fragmentary way," as Eigen (2011) puts it (p. 10). I think this species of 'binding' is the "unbinding" activity of the death drive, an "untying of sentient unities," which Eigen (1995, p. 281) describes with reference to Freud's (1920) *Beyond the Pleasure Principle*. "Untying of sentient unities" calls for the "reversal of alpha-function" (Bion, 1962, pp. 20–27), a –K activity that brings about "dispersal of the contact-barrier" and its replacement by a "beta-element screen." I imagine that the curious binding "by a sense of catastrophe" is attained by means of the dispersed fragments of the "beta-element screen," covering the *void* of unknowability, of our brokenness and dependency. In other words, covering the "crack" where "the light gets in,"[10] and, as I see it, also from where the light shines out. Our expressivity relies on the integration of the *void*.

In my experiences of observing improvised human movement, like in the practice of Authentic Movement[11], I noticed human movement can be both psychical and corporeal. Movement appears to be a liminal medium between the two aspects of human experience. In these observations, I also noticed that in a flow of impro-vised human movement, there were movements that were more animate, leaving their place to movements of less vitality, and those replaced again by movements that were more soulful and less, and so on. The term "animate movement" is com-monly used for the movement of living things, as different from the movement of non-living things. But my observation is that not all human movement is *animate*. We have a disposition for de-animation. Although I do not know any 'objective definition' for the kind of animateness I refer to, I have no doubt the readers rec-ognize its varying degrees in observable aspects of human movement. I think such animate movement of the human being is what makes up the Language of Achieve-ment, Bion (1970) describes as a conceptualization which establishes the inclusion of psychoanalysis into the domain of action[12]. I suggest our animate movement is the human activity that is the counterpart of what Bion (1991) calls "passionate love," describing it as "not only physical or mental, but a development of the fusion of both." From my view, drawing mainly on Bion, Winnicott, Eigen, and Meltzer[13], it is possible to think that animate human movement might be a liminal medium between the infinite and the finite, a means in "transformations" (Bion) of one to the other. Wave movement transmits energy and momentum.

The idea of movement as constitutive to creation and as enabling communica-tion between the worlds of Ideas (Forms) and particulars exists in *Timaeus*. When I read *Timaeus*, I thought it was another account of the internal world, like the Bible—a "probable tale," as Plato has Timeaus say in it. The Creator or Intellect (*Nous*) that creates the universe resembles the "alpha-function" (Bion); the com-position, form, and operation of the soul of cosmos with its "cognitive" powers resemble the "transitional space" (Winnicott). The creation of the soul of the cos-mos, with the establishment of intervals and ratios that look like rhythms, seems quite like a musical composition. Two intersecting circular motions come about. And the motion of the outer circle, Intellect calls "the motion of the Same" (that is, the motion of the realm of Forms, of eternity), and the motion of the inner circle, he calls "the motion of the Other or Diverse" (that is, the motion of the generated; here, of the generated planets); the latter is under dominion and regulation of the former. The movement of human beings, which is not limited to "circular motion" like that of the the soul and the body of the cosmos, goes awry in connection of their soul to their body—which resembles Bion's (1965, 1991) description of the "turmoil" experienced at the birth of an idea. In *Timeaus*, human beings' move-ment is corrected in so far as they are able to "follow the revolution of the Same and the Like within them" with the help of reason, which is a faculty of the soul that is immortal and has a capacity for the discretion of reality, comparable with, in my interpretation of Plato's text, "apprehension of beauty" in Meltzer's (1988) formulation. The soul's capacity for discretion of reality is described in *Timeaus* as a vibrational discretion capacity.

By the end of *Attention and Interpretation*, Bion opens the door to a deeper cham-ber in the psyche, where there is nothing, "no memory, desire or understanding," but a movement. An *undulation* between "patience" and "security" the analyst must endure in "becoming O." Patience, in experiencing an "uncertainty cloud" and in "suffering," and security, as a feeling of "safety and diminished anxiety," when "a pattern 'evolves'" (1970, p. 124). Eigen (1985) sees the central thrust of *Attention and Interpretation* as "faith in O". Juxtaposing this "faith" with Bion's description in *Elements* of the state at the origins of the self, in which "aspects of the personality [are] linked by a sense of catastrophe," he describes the most basic terms of Bion's discourse as a "movement between catastrophe and faith"—between catastrophe as an elemental term of our existence, and faith as "the primordial and developed response to catastrophe" (ibid., p. 326). Eigen saw that the heart of the matter was a movement; he writes, "Bion tries to tap into a dimension in which it is an innate part of the self's rhythm to fall apart and come together" (ibid., p. 322). For this to happen, it is necessary not to hold on to anything but rather "be true to more basic movements" (ibid., p. 322). Eigen (2002) later elaborates this basic rhythm along with rhythmic variations in Elkin, Winnicott, and Bion's works, which describe coming through destruction. He names it also as a "rhythm of rebirth," a "rhythm of breakdown-recovery," and a "rhythm of faith." This basic rhythm is fundamental to healthy mental functioning; it is vital for unconscious processing of affects (Eigen, 2002, 2004, 2005). "We have a musical psyche," says Eigen (2011, p. 123). "There *is* a musical core. Perhaps more than one" (ibid., p. 118). In Eigen's depiction of mental life, the rhythm of breakdown-recovery sustains *dream work*.

I consider the "basic movements" Eigen lays out and invites us to be more true to as animate. Animate, as in soulful. The word in Turkish for a living thing translates to English as 'that with soul.' *Zôon*, this would be in Plato's term. Soulful, and as such, "intelligent" (with *Nous*). Plato (360 BC) attributes intelligence to soul, and he describes the creative work of Intellect (Nous), the Craftsman, as quite artistic. In his account, the "circular movement" of the soul and the body of the cosmos is "most appropriate to mind and intelligence," "herself turning in herself" (ibid.). To me, this implies *reflexivity* and it implies *rhythmicity*—like of breathing, heartbeat, blood circulation, and circadian rhythms, which are essential for the capacity to go to sleep and to wake up—a capacity, in Bion's view, based on the operation of the alpha-function that sustains dream thoughts, unconscious waking thinking, dreams, contact-barrier, and consciousness as "a sense-organ for the perception of psychical qualities."[14] Human muscular-skeletal movement, from small gestures and facial expressions to larger movements and actions, is inextricably bound with these rhythms and other less observable rhythmical movements in the human be-ing. I referred to a varying degree of animateness in observable aspects of human movement. I think the quality of animateness I refer to ultimately emanates from an "attitude of faith," which Eigen brought out in Bion's work as the *psychoanalytic attitude* and expanded in his own. I see the role of the attitude of faith as analogous with the role of the soul's faculty of 'reason' in Plato's account of creation in *Timeaus*.

Eigen (1986) posits an awareness of self and other at the emergence of the self and he describes a constant oscillation of "distinction-union" with an "I-yet-not-I," an "otherness" constitutive to human subjectivity. This is experienced in infancy as a primordial experience of merger and separation with the mother. Eigen speaks of the "distinction-union structure" as "a kind of DNA-RNA of experience. Every micro-moment or 'cell' of experience is made of distinction-union tendencies" (2011, p. 1). Semi-permeable boundaries between self and other, between psyche and body, between parts of the personality, and between the finite and infinity are marked by this "distinction-union structure" (Eigen, 1986). Eigen's conceptualization leans on various psychoanalytic formulations and his clinical experiences, along with the triune doctrine of the Holy Trinity (three-yet-one in communion), other ancient texts comprising the idea of many-in-one or one-in-many, and physicist David Bohm's implicate-explicate orders (Eigen, 2011, pp. 2–3). In Eigen's view, the "co-constitutive nature of distinction-union tendencies" supports the basic rhythm of breakdown-recovery and affect processing. In pscyhosis, due to very early trauma, the basic trust that sustains the distinction-union oscillation is maimed. The rhythm of faith gets damaged or jammed and is replaced with an "interlocking of rigidity and fluidity," which permits neither unintegration (union) nor being defined (distinction) (Eigen, 1986). Bion (1962) seems to point to the same condition in a description, and it is relevant with circadian rhythms, or a warp in them: "As alpha-function makes sense impressions of the emotional experience available for conscious and dream thought, the patient who cannot dream cannot go to sleep and cannot wake up. Hence the peculiar condition seen clinically when psychotic patient behaves as if her were in precisely this state." (p. 7) For Eigen, in healthier functioning, the basic rhythm is the "pulse" of the living psyche; the psyche "breathes" (2002), and the distinction-union structure enables communication and communion with a "boundless, unknown support" (2009, 2011). Eigen speaks of a "soundless sound."

> There is soul music, inner music, akin to the music of the spheres. You can hear it. Yet it has no sound at all. Profoundly silent. Yet this silence sounds. It is deeply musical. Keats writes "spirit ditties of no tone". There are moments when this no tone is the inaudible tone of the universe. Poets often use words to communicate wordless realities. We speak of vibrating to one another, or a bell ringing inside, or my bell ringing your bell, or yours ringing mine. What is it that rings? You can hear it or almost hear it —by what sense? (2011, p. 118)

When Bion and Eigen met in New York in 1978, Bion asked him out of the blue if he knew the Kabbalah, the *Zohar*. Eigen had read bits of Kabbalah since his early twenties, and it was part of his lived background from early childhood. He said, "Well, I know it, but don't really *know* it." "I don't either, really know it," said Bion, reassuring him. "There was a pause," writes Eigen. "Then he looked at me and said, 'I use the Kabbalah as a framework for psychoanalysis'" (2012, pp. ix–x). Thirty-two years later, Eigen gave two seminars on Kabbalah and psychoanalysis, which he began by saying, "The heart of Kabbalah, the very heart of Kabbalah is the line: You will love the Lord your God with all your heart, with all your soul, with all your might" (Deuteronomy 6:5) (ibid., p. 1). On Bion's notion of faith in O, Eigen (2002) writes, "I think this faith has in it a love of life. It is passionate about living. It opens heart wide and cannot stop opening. It is a faith that is stronger than murder, that makes murder fruitful" (p. 738). Unbound death drive binds with the life drive; in so far as envy, the serpent, is integrated, "passionate love" appears.

In *Learning from Experience*, Bion was asking, "What receives and deals with love?" while speaking of the maternal breast as the supplier of love as well as milk. Bion held that this was ultimately "consciousness," as described by Freud as "a sense organ for the perception of psychical qualities," with which also the feeling of frustration is tolerated (1962, pp. 33–34). In *Attention and Interpretation*, he wrote, "The idea that is nourished by love develops from matrix to function in Language of Achievement from which it can be transformed into achievement" (1970, p. 127). In *Cogitations*, in a note where he sets about to draw some tentative hypotheses to "illuminate the normal process of development," (1992, p. 198) he describes a patient whose sessions had been dominated by envy, where the envy had "a disastrous efficacy in cutting the patient off from every—or what seemed to be almost every—source of vitalizing influence" (ibid., p. 199). Bion mentions at the beginning of this note that he previously wrote on "the minutely destructive fragmentation inflicted by the schizoid on his capacity for communication with himself and others as a part of destructive attacks on all links" (ibid., p. 198). He is now referring to, in the operation of the same mechanisms, "the severance of [the patient's] means of communication with the vitalizing influence," and he notes, "This is the true significance of the attacks on linking" (ibid., p. 199). It is as if the attacks on linking within the personality (destruction or reversal of the alpha-function) are actually *an attack on a communicative link with a vitalizing influence*. I think that the *intention* here is obliteration of the *void* that is a reality of lived human experience and that the *void* makes this communication possible. Bion identifies "two main routes" by which the individual can "maintain communication with the sources essential for healthy development." One of them is PS↔D, "a vital factor in the conversion of the unknown to the known" (ibid., p. 199). He does not clearly name the other "route" but mentions "projective identification" among the victims of the attacks. It is possible to infer from his theory that ♀♂ is the other route he considers here. The effects of the attacks are also manifested in the destruction of "ideogrammatic expression, sound (as the matrix of that specialized form, which in its maturity we recognize as music), and indeed the ideational counterpart of all the senses" (ibid., p. 199). In other words, isolation from the vitalizing influence hinders *expression*. About the "vitalizing influence," he says, he "cannot pretend to anything but a shadowy idea of" (ibid., p. 200). He will later call it "O." And in *Memoir* (1991), he writes, "'Passionate love' is the nearest I can get to a verbal transformation which 'represents' the thing-in-itself, the ultimate reality, the 'O', as I have called it, approximating to it" (p. 183). This is "some other love that is mature from an absolute standard.... which cannot be described in the terms of sensuous reality or experience, [for which] there has to be language of infra-sensuous and ultra-sensuous" (Bion, 1992, p. 372).

Bion (1991) differentiates "passionate love" from "sexual maturity," which is solely "physical maturity as in adolescence" and often used as a defense against O; "passionate love," he writes, is "not only physical or mental, but a development of the fusion of both" (p. 472). "The bloom on the cheeks of men or women can show that the pair in love are suffused by a reality which cannot be gainsaid," says Alice in the *Memoir* (p. 566). The character Bion is of the opinion that

> the suffusion on the faces of the pair might be traced to a fetus in contact with the walls of the uterus.... The fetus—the germ plasm itself for that matter— could be affected by the loving relationship between the parents.

and he asks, "Could not the blush on the bridal cheeks be communicated by a corresponding blush on the walls of the uterus and vice versa?" (ibid., p. 566). Bion, the writer, considers a thus "inherited" passionate love, about which "Priests [representative of the religious vertex in Bion's personality] would say that the Church had preached these matters for generations—even before there was a Christian church" (ibid., pp. 566–567). Inherited passionate love as such reminds me of the innate "alpha-element Oedipal pre-conception," Bion postulated in *Elements* (1963, p. 93). For Bion, from the emotional matrix of passionate love, develops the birth of an idea in corporeality.

Bion considers in *Memoir* "the possibility of a fetal mentality suitable to a watery, fluid environment" (1991, p. 551). "Blush," for him, stands for "the body itself might think," as in the line by John Donne: "Her pure and eloquent blood spoke in her cheeks" (ibid., p. 590). He refers to "auditory and optic pits," which develop in the first few weeks of embryogenesis, as receptive to sub-sonic sound waves and infra-visual light waves (ibid., p. 472). In the Glossary of *Memoir*, about the "pits," he writes, "Under psycho-analytic observation, many stages display the dominance of characteristics which, like those of seeing and hearing, appear to mark the character of the individual; they are signs which can reveal the 'direction' the individual is likely to take" (ibid., p. 646). In *Transformations*, Bion mentions the patient's "lights," which the psychoanalysts aim to know (1965, p. 37). It is unlikely of him to speak figuratively; I think he means an invisible light, the evolving O of the personality. Eigen (2012) relates O with *Ein Sof* in the Kabbalah; O might as well be a notation for *Or Ein Sof,* meaning *eternal light*. Bion (1991) seems to suppose an "archaically surviving system of auditory or optic pits" (p. 568) functioning in the "watery medium" of the living human body, and sensitive to "changes of pressure in the watery medium" and "feelings, 'emotions' of sub-thalamic intensity" (ibid., p. 563). He writes,

> When we abandon our liquid environment for a gaseous one we take our liquid with us. Like fish, we can still smell by cause of the mucus preserved in our respiratory passages by the glands that maintain our watery medium, although we have moved into a gaseous one ... The liquid environment which we take with

us or manufacture inside is useful for making it possible to see or smell, or even to provide for the germ plasm which we produce. (ibid., p. 502)

And he says, "'Unscientific' traces [of this system] can be discerned in the survival of terms like 'rhinencephalon.' ...Even physiologically there are traces in the 'extra-cellular fluid'[15] unpolluted by salt and other chemicals, as are the oceans" (ibid., p. 590). Eigen's notion of "psychic taste buds" points to such a system. Eigen (2005) writes, "somewhat analogous to the ability of animals to 'smell' or sense danger or nourishment, we have a latent capacity to evolve psychic taste buds" (p. 10). Eigen (2001) also, speaking of ecstasy, which is mainly experienced in "the soul's union with God," quotes the Bible: "the soul is in the blood"; he writes, "[Ecstasy] pervades the body, the inside and outside of the skin, the pulsing of organs ... [it] is in the senses, touching, hearing, seeing ... in the body's movements, muscles, mucus membranes, flow of breath and blood" (p. 3).

Frances Tustin's (1981) conceptualization of "traumatic psychological birth" based on her work with psychotic children involves that "tactile sensations of being in the 'watery medium' (Bion's term) [of the womb] appear to linger on and to be carried over into the child's earliest experience of the outside world" (p. 97). In normal development, in the sheltering of what she calls the "post-natal womb," where the infant is not exposed to separateness prematurely, a primary integration between "hard" and "soft" sensations and other fundamental integrations that evolve from it, including "a 'marriage' between 'male' and 'female' elements," take place (ibid., p. 101). Maternal capacity to bear states of ecstasy shared between herself and the baby in "a sublime sense of 'oneness',," as well as "to hold the infant together through intense bodily-cum psychological states of tantrum" is crucial for this basic integration (ibid., pp. 106–107). Clearly, the basic integrations Tustin describes are very significant for "cognitive development" in Money-Kyrle's account, or for "maturation" in Bion's view, or "emotional development" in Winnicott's. Too soon or too harsh "catapulation" of the infant from this essential womb-like state leads to "the development of massive autistic obstructions to painful realities, which have been experienced before the infant's neuro-mental apparatus was ready to stand the strain" (ibid., p. 98). Tustin notes that in the mother–infant interaction of the "post-natal womb," "bodily sensations are transformed into psychological experience through reciprocal and rhythmical activity between mother and infant," which she says is a "mysterious process" (ibid., 101). I think *kinesthetic and proprioceptive sensations* in the watery medium carried over to our gaseous environment may be of significance as well. Winnicott (1955) wrote in his letter to Bion,

A mother properly oriented to her baby would know *from [his] movements* what [he] need[s]. There would be a communication because of this knowledge which belongs to her devotion, and she would do something *which would show that the communication had taken place.* (p. 91, italics added)

Winnicott described this as "subtle communication which is the only basis for communication that does not violate the fact of the essential isolation of each individual."16 (ibid., p. 92) A subtle communication in movement that does not violate the essential isolation of the individual but lets him or her know that the communication has taken place. Perhaps the "sheltering of the post-natal womb" (Tustin) serves primarily the integration of the *void* as an essential aspect of lived human experience because it is experienced as functional.

The auditory pit is the first rudiment of the internal ear. The internal ear has the cochlea, dedicated to hearing, and it has the vestibular system, dedicated to balance—which is related to kinesthesia and proprioception. What Bion calls the "optic pit" is the optic cup that is part of the diencephalon and gives rise to the retina of the eye. And like the internal ear, there is a "binocular" functionality in the retina of the eye.[17] Other than the two types of cells dedicated to vision, there is a third type of cell that entrains circadian rhythms. These photosensitive cells contain melanopsin and give electrical signals when they perceive light. They are related to sleep and mood (Canbeyli, 2021). This is interesting, considering how significant sleep and dreaming are for consciousness as "a sense organ for perception of psychical qualities." The earth's movement around the sun dictates sleep on us. A circular movement, "herself turning in herself," that eventuates in a rhythm of day and night, light and dark, is fundamental for consciousness.

I think that the "K link" in *Learning from Experience* is not the same as the "K," that is, "transformations in K," in *Attention and Interpretation*. The K link in *LFE* (1962), which Bion called the "psycho-analytic function of the personality" and described in detail in terms of a "mating" relationship of a ♀ and ♂, that operates dreaming and thinking, bifurcates in *Transformations* (1965) into "transformations in K" and "transformations in O." The stem K link in *LFE* has within it, though inchoately, the notions of faith and negative capability, which Bion will put forth in *Attention* (1970). He writes in *LFE*, "Tolerance of doubt and *tolerance of infinity* are the essential connective in $\male^n$ [growing ♂] if K is to be possible" (p. 94, italics added). Also, I think the "painful feeling" in the K link he describes poetically in *LFE* is a part of the "suffering" he underlines in *Attention* (pp. 19, 124) and of the experience of "faith": "The question 'How can x know anything?' expresses a feeling; it appears to be painful and inhere in the emotional link that I represent by x K y" (1962, p. 48). Relatedness with a non-sensuous reality is like a rising full moon in Bion's work; it becomes more and more central in his thought as the latter grows. I believe the branching in K in *Transformations* into "transformations in K" and "transformations in O" derives from this development in his thought. In *Attention*, he portrays the ♀♂ relationship as inadequate for "transformations in O" and as functional in "transformations in K," which depend on a background of sensuous experience. By the end of reading *Attention,* one cannot help but think, "Did he abandon the ♀♂ theory of dreaming?" My reception from his writing is that he did not, but it has transformed.

Bion (1970) considers "dreams that float into mind unbidden and unsought and float away again mysteriously" and "thoughts that also come unbidden, sharply, distinctly, with what appears to be unforgettable clarity, and then disappear leaving no trace by which they can be captured" as in the domain of "transformations in O" (p. 70). To differentiate them from "memory" as a conscious attempt to recall, he refers to them here as "dream-like memory." They are "the memory of psychic reality" and thus "the stuff of analysis," (ibid., p. 70) he writes—which reminds his wording in *LFE*, "the stuff of life itself," where he cautions readers on the animate-ness of psychic reality (1962, p. 14). For Bion, psychic reality is the animate reality. Dreaming appears to be in the realm of "transformations in O" in his framework of *Attention and Interpretation*, not in the realm of "transformations in K." Here, he rephrases his theory of dreams as "the dream is the *evolution* of O where O has evolved sufficiently to be represented by sensuous experience" (1970, p. 70, original italics). And he goes on to speak about the "experience" of the analytic session as "material akin to the dream," that "the dream and the psycho-analyst's working material both share dream-like quality" (ibid., pp. 70–71). At this level of unknowability we leaped to or descended into, the analytic session, the patient, the analyst herself, the interpretation are all "aspects of the 'evolved' O," like the dream.[18] Who is the dreamer? In this respect, I get a similar meaning from my read-ing of Bion with what Grotstein (2007) articulated as "to have our O, our godhead incarnate us" (p. 37). I cannot verbalize anything about the dreamer, but I can conjecture dreaming as a mysterious incarnation of non-sensuous meaning (Plato's Forms or the godhead) represented by sensuous experience—both in "concreteness of psychic reality," which Meltzer often underlines with reference to Klein, that we are familiar with in dreams and in the ordinary concreteness of corporeality. This seems succinctly phrased by Eigen (2011) as: "We are the unknown responding to itself" (p. 5).

In *Attention and Interpretation*, it seems as if Bion abandoned the ♀♂ model for dreaming, but I think his title for Chapter 12, "Container and Contained Trans-formed," implies the model underwent a transformation. I will suggest an expan-sion in his formulation of the aim of psychoanalysis at the end of the book.

> What is required is not the decrease of inhibition but a decrease of the impulse to inhibit; the impulse to inhibit is fundamentally envy of the growth-stimulating objects. What is to be sought is an activity that is both the restoration of god (the Mother) [♀, *void*, represented in Plato's *Timeaus* as the Receptacle] and the evo-lution of god (the formless, infinite, ineffable, non-existent) [♂, non-sensuous meaning], which can be found only in the state in which there is NO memory, desire and understanding. (Bion, 1970, pp. 128–129)

Becoming is letting dreaming be and accepting being an *offspring* of this couple. And as Bion (1965, 1970) writes, the agency of the finite aspect of our subjectiv-ity, of "the person of the analysand" in Bion's words, does not reside in a deci-sion to let be. Consent to "incarnation" or "becoming reality," notes Bion, is in the domain of "a particular part of the analysand, namely his 'godhead.'"[19] The agency of the person of someone in "being O," "being the real self," resides, in

Bion's view, in the careful study of "lies", how one lies in thought and action, and their reduction.

Eigen's work illuminates and illustrates our capacities for *Attention* on O, a "soundless sound," "spirit ditties of no tone," and *Interpretation* (action) that follows. Practicing is a human activity of love.

> Sometimes, I say to a patient at the end of sessions, "Love thyself." A mix of Polonius, Socrates, oracle, and therapist? Can I be sure of what I mean, how deep, how real, how banal, how suspect, how cautionary? At times, love is direct, immediate, palpable reality. Sometimes, saying it creates it, calls it into being. Perhaps I or someone or something in me senses it, a dim, urgent background presence, and naming births it. At such moments, saying "Love thyself" is an act of faith, and faith a kind of birth. (Eigen, 2011, pp. 38–39)

Notes

1 Bion's description, in his autobiography *The Long week-end* (1982, p. 262), of how he felt in the battle of Amiens, on 8 August 1918—the day, he writes in the *Memoir* (1991, p. 257), his soul "died."
2 Italics are in the English translation by Z. Schacter.
3 The two are not identical, as Bion indicates in *Transformations* (1965, pp. 138–139). Karahan (2016) writes on this distinction with respect to Byzantine Orthodoxy; she brings out that Christian fathers and theologians were resorting to Platonic terms to elucidate their view and there were similarities between their apophetic theology (*apophasis*, "negation") and Platonism, but these differed. The 4th century Cappadocian fathers, Basil of Caesarea, Gregory of Nazianzus, and Gregory of Nyssa, who developed the apophatic theology that shaped Byzantine Orthodoxy and held that "God's essence is unknowable and ineffable, beyond human words, language, and perception" (ibid., p. 214), advised "to seek God through direct experience of God's energies" (ibid., p. 213). Karahan's article (2016) illuminates a lineage from St. Paul, who articulated this *via negativa* with his reference "To an unknown god" (Acts 17:23) to the Cappadocian fathers to Pseudo-Dionysus the Aeropagite, 5th or 6th-century Greek theologian and philosopher, who used the term "the truly mysterious darkness of unknowing," which influenced the 14th-century anonymous author of *The Cloud of Unknowing*, a text of Christian mysticism. Meltzer (1983) notes in *Dream-Life* (p. 70) that *The Cloud of Unknowing* is one of Bion's sources in his use of the term "uncertainty cloud" in *Elements* (1963, p. 42). St. John of the Cross was among those who were influenced by this 14th-century text, and Bion (1965) resorts to his description of the "dark night of the soul" to describe what he means by "becoming O" (pp. 158–159). Bion appears to view, rather than what he calls the "configuration" of "Forms" that he relates to Plato, the "configuration" of "Incarnation" which he relates with "Christian Platonism," Meister Echart and the Blessed John Ruysbroeck, as descriptive of "being O" (1965, pp. 138–141).
4 Like one that on a lonesome road

> Doth walk in fear and dread;
> And having once turned round walks on,
> And turns no more his head;
> Because he knows a frightful fiend
> Doth close behind him tread.
> —From The Rime of Ancient Mariner by Coleridge, quoted by Bion (1970, p. 46)

5 Meltzer (1978) interprets the "frightful fiend", Bion refers to in *Attention and Interpretation*, as the "–K link" and I agree with his interpretation. Bion, in his exposition of the –K link in *Learning from Experience* (1962), markedly relates it with envy (pp. 96–97).

6 ♀ and ♂ are signs Bion uses to denote a "container" and a "contained."

7 As the rest of the rest of the paragraph implies: "The idea is split over and over again and is felt to produce a quantity of splits—'mental faeces'. Envy and gratitude, on the other hand, stimulate a desire for gain, but enable the individual to establish a good relation between what has been gained and that which has enabled him to gain it. The repudiation of the debt owed to his 'predatory' personality, and the need to continue repudiating it, exclude the other parts of the personality from activity." (Ibid., pp. 127–128)

8 Ogden's (2005) metaphor for beta-elements depicts well their "dispersed" quality: "They might very roughly be compared with 'snow' on a malfunctioning television screen in which no single scintillation or group of scintillations can be linked with other scintillations to form an image or a meaningful pattern" (pp. 45–46).

9 Freud in "Analysis terminable and interminable" (1937), quoted in Eigen, 1995, p. 288.

10 With reference to the lyrics in Leonard Cohen's song, *Anthem*, "There is a crack, a crack in everything. That's how the light gets in."

11 A form of expressive movement practice and therapy developed by Mary Starks Whitehouse in 1950's, based on Jungian psychology, where his technique of "active imagination" is applied in movement. It was further developed by dance and movement therapists Joan Chodorow and Janet Adler.

12 See Bion, 1970, pp. 116–124 for his elaboration of exclusion of psychoanalysis from the domain of action, and his description of and references to the Language of Achievement in the following chapter, pp. 125–129.

13 In this paper, I present some of Eigen's and Bion's ideas and formulations that make this line of thinking possible, touching briefly on Winnicott. Meltzer's psychoanalytic theory of two-tiered language development (1975), his theory of dreaming extending Bion's (1983), his concepts of "apprehension of beauty," "aesthetic conflict," "combined object" (1986) also feed into my view.

14 Freud refers to consciousness as a "sense organ for the perception of psychical qualities" in *Interpretation of Dreams* (1900). This conceptualization becomes particularly significant in Bion's theory of dreams, quoted by him in *LFE* (1962).

15 "Found in blood, in lymph, in body cavities lined with serous (moisture-exuding) membrane, in the cavities and channels of the brain and spinal chord, and in muscular and other tissues." (*Encylopaedia Britannica* online).

16 Winnicott (1955) wrote this letter to Bion the day after listening to his presentation of his paper "The differentiation of the psychotic from the non-psychotic personalities" at the British Psychoanalytical Society in 1955 (published 1957). Eshel (2022) illuminates a very possible influence of Winnicott with this letter in Bion's recognition of the significance of the early maternal environment's failure to receive these subtle communications, which appears in Bion's following work (i.e., Bion, 1958, 1959, 1962), which remained not formally acknowledged by Bion. Having read Winnicott's letter, I think Bion's thought was inoculated at the start with a significant but not formally acknowledged contribution from Winnicott, which seems to have influenced him to formulate projective identification as communication, "an extremely primitive species of link between the patient and the analyst" (Bion, 1958, p. 146), which will be an important basis of his later work. Also, Winnicott's term "devotion" he uses in this letter, and throughout his work with the concept of the "ordinary devoted mother," may have been influential in Bion's (1962) conceptualization of the "mother's capacity for reverie" as effective in development when it is associated with "love" for the child and his father (p. 36).

17 To borrow here Bion's term "binocular" with its loaded meaning in his theory seems adequate. In Bion's (1962) description, the alpha-function, by proliferating alpha-elements,

produces the "alpha contact-barrier," which is an entity that both separates the unconscious and the conscious and forms the unconscious. "[T]he conscious and the unconscious [are] thus constantly produced together [and] function as if they were binocular, therefore capable of correlation and self-regard" (p. 54).

18 In *Attention and Interpretation* (1970), Bion describes "objects of awareness" as "aspects of the 'evolved' O," where he writes, "A term that would express approximately what I need to express is 'faith'—faith that there is an ultimate reality and truth—the unknown, unknowable, 'formless infinite'. This must be believed of every object of which the personality can be aware: the evolution of ultimate reality (signified by O) has issued in objects of which the individual can be aware. The objects of awareness are aspects of the 'evolved' O and are such that the sensuously derived mental functions are adequate to apprehend them." (1970, p. 31). In this frame of reference, he refers to the patient, the analyst himself, and the interpretation, each as "an evolution of O" (ibid., p. 27).

19 "It is not the same for the 'godhead' to consent to incarnation in the person of the analysand as for the analysand to consent to 'becoming' god or the 'godhead' of which 'god' is the phenomenological counterpart. The latter, at any rate, would seem to be closer to insanity than mental health" (Bion, 1965, p. 148).

References

Bion, W.R. (1958). On arrogance. *International Journal of Psychoanalysis, 39*, 144–146.

Bion, W.R. (1962/2005). *Learning from experience*. London: Karnac.

Bion, W.R. (1963). *Elements of psychoanalysis*. London: Heinemann.

Bion, W.R. (1965/1991). *Transformations*. London: Karnac.

Bion, W.R. (1970). *Attention and interpretation*. London: Tavistock.

Bion, W.R. (1982/1986). *The long week-end*. London: Free Association Books.

Bion, W.R. (1991). *A memoir of the future*. London: Karnac.

Bion, W.R. (1992). *Cogitations*. (F. Bion Ed.). London: Karnac.

Canbeyli, R. (2021). Talk on night-day rhythms on *Açık bilinç* [Open consciousness] hosted by G. Guzeldere on Açık Radyo. 07.27.2021. <https://acikradyo.com.tr/podcast/229773>.

Eigen, M. (1985). Toward Bion's starting point: between catastrophe and faith. *International Journal of Psychoanalysis, 66*, 321–330.

Eigen, M. (1986/2004). *The psychotic core*. London, New York: Karnac.

Eigen, M. (1995). Psychic deadness: Freud. *Contemporary Psychoanalysis, 31*, 277–299.

Eigen, M. (2001). *Ecstasy*. Middletown: Wesleyan.

Eigen, M. (2002). A basic rhythm. *Psychoanalytic Review, 89*, 721–740.

Eigen, M. (2004). A little psyche-music. *Psychoanalytic Dialogues, 14*, 119–130.

Eigen, M. (2005). *Emotional storm*. Middletown: Wesleyan.

Eigen, M. (2009). *Flames from the unconscious*. London: Karnac.

Eigen, M. (2011). *Contact with the depths*. London: Karnac.

Eigen, M. (2012). *Kaballah and psychoanalysis*. London: Karnac.

Eigen, M. (2023). MEigenworkshop, Yahoo group, private.

Eshel, O. (2022). Bion's long road toward intuiting the patient's suffering: 'theoretical' versus 'clinical' Bion. *Contemporary Psychoanalysis, 58*, 46–76.

Grotstein, J.S. (2007). *A beam of intense darkness*. London: Karnac.

Gurses Tarbuck, D. (2022). *Bilim tarihi sohbetleri* [Conversations on history of science] on Açık Radyo. 03.07.2022. <https://acikradyo.com.tr/podcast/232973>.

Karahan, A. (2016). Byzantine visual culture: Conditions of "right" belief and some Platonic outlooks. *Numen, 63*, 210–244. Leiden: Brill.

Meltzer, D., Bremner, J., Hoxter, S., Weddell, D. & Wittenberg, I. (1975/2008). *Explorations in autism: A psychoanalytical study*. London: Karnac.

Meltzer, D. (1978). *Kleinian development*. London: Karnac.

Meltzer, D. (1983). *Dream-life*. London: Karnac.

Meltzer, D. & Williams, M.H. (1988). *The apprehension of beauty*. London: Karnac.

Money-Kyrle, R. (1961/2014). Cognitive development. In M. H. Williams (Ed.), *Man's picture of his world and three papers* (pp. 209–227). London: Karnac.

Nachman of Brazlav. (1996). From *the Torah of the void*. (Z. Schacter, Trans.). In C. Milosz (Ed.), *A book of luminous things. An international anthology of poetry* (pp. 269–270). New York: Harcourt Brace & Company.

Plato. (360 BC). *Timaeus*. (B. Jowett, Trans.). Retrieved from <http://classics.mit.edu/Plato/timaeus.html>

Ogden, T.H. (2005). Foreword. In A. Ferro (Ed.), *Seeds of illness, seeds of recovery* (pp. ix–xii). East Sussex: Brunner-Routledge.

Onians, R.B. (1951/2000). *The origins of European thought*. Cambridge: Cambridge University Press.

Tustin, F. (1981/2013). *Autistic states in children*. New York: Routledge.

Winnicott, D.W. (1955). Letter to Wilfred R. Bion, 7 October 1955. In R. Rodman (Ed.), *The spontaneous gesture. Selected letters of D. W. Winnicott* (pp. 89–93). Cambridge, MA: Harvard University Press.

Chapter 14

Seer, Mystic, Sage

Luminous Presence in the Work of Michael Eigen

Paul DeBlassie III

Terrorizing emotions, relationships, and dreams can assault the psyche with angst, despair, spiritual emptiness, and madness, or, as stated by Plato's *Socrates on the Oracle of Delphi*, "The greatest blessings come by way of madness, indeed of madness that is heaven-sent." (Plato, 1952, pp. 244a–245a) There is a sense, surge, and deluge of chaotic and dread-filled states that grab hold and take us under stormy currents of emotion, mind, and soul. And then, by sheer perseverance and heaven's blessings, archetypal and potentially transformative realities reveal themselves as a "shock of grace" (Eigen, 1998, p. 118). Without such spiritually transformative moments, psychotherapy stops short and falls flat. Depth psychotherapy, faithful to the ancient Greek etymology of psyche as soul and therapeia as healing, is akin to ancient Asklepion mystery rites where the patient entered the temple, lay down, dreamt, and experienced transformative encounters with luminous images and symbols. Thus, for a therapist as a devotee of soul healing, rigid and dogmatic understandings of unconscious drives, objects, and relational nuances must be shed in order to invite transformative mystic encounters and luminous presence/s that provide entrance into higher and deeper orders of meaning, healing, and transformation – an infusion of grace.

In the words of William James, "Perhaps every religious person has the recollection of particular crises in which a director vision of the truth, a direct perception, perhaps, of a living God's existence, swept in and overwhelmed the languor of the more ordinary belief" (James, 1985, p. 61). Thus, psychoanalytic sensitivity to the illuminative presence of mystic realities opens the way for a particular nurturance of healing and growth within what can be a subtle but definite register of spiritual sensitivity within the human psyche. It is an attunement to what Corbin (2000), pioneer of archetypal metapsychology, calls the *mundus imaginalis*, the world of spirits, archetypal dimensions, and what he refers to as "inner intelligence" (p. 10). It is an interior realm of "Image that can be qualified as a symbol ... a primordial phenomenon (*Urphaenomen*). Its appearance is both unconditional and irreducible and it is something that cannot manifest itself in any other way in this world" (p. 11). Such intelligences, images, and moments of truth open doors to what Eigen in *Kabbalah and Psychoanalysis* (2012) writes of as a passionate love of God, "... an absolute kernel of uplift and affirmation" (Eigen, 2020, p. 15), an illuminative

DOI: 10.4324/9781003322993-14

presence that generates blessings by way of the madness inherent in psychological suffering.

The illuminative presence of Demeter, one of many archetypal images and realities, is surfacing on to the mystic white screen of my mind as I write. This feels like a moment akin to what Grotstein (2007, pp. 74–75) calls "summoning the muse ... an internal ineffable presence." Demeter is the Lady of the Golden Blade; She Who Makes all Things Wither and Die or Grow and Flourish. She sheds light on the psychic reality of the felt withering and dying of the malnourished self, threatened dissolution of fragments of being—madness. As I write, She, Demeter, whispers in my ear, perhaps what Reik (1983) wrote of as the third ear, that Her coming is an imaginal luminous presence to guide this exploration of psychoanalytic mindstuff, overwhelming, undreamable, unbearable, yet pregnant with generativity.

She kindles awareness of the mundus imaginalis, what seers, mystics, and sages through the ages have referred to as the spiritual world. My third eye opens, an ageless and interior/imaginal counterpart to psychoanalytic hearing with one's eyes (Khan, 1974). I do my best to listen and see as She sends imaginary metabolizations of Eigen's inspiration, recounting St. Paul's moment of grace as psyche transported by the ineffable (Eigen, 1993, p. 167). On his way to Damascus, Saul of Tarsus was struck by a light brighter than the sun, rendering him blind for a time before his sight was restored outwardly and inwardly. It was a shock of grace so profound that mad-minded Saul was transformed into Paul, apostle of the consciousness of love as patient, kind, and rejoicing in truth—blessing by way of madness.

And now, the moment's vital spark (Winnicott, 1964, p. 27), a microshock of grace, lights up a continuity of thought about blessings and grace sensed within Eigen's work. The spark leaps from Demeter's two flaming torches, destruction and generativity, and illuminates the ineffable quality of madness' birthing blessing. It speaks to the welcoming luminous presence at work within the therapist/patient encounter, a stabilizing grace in the midst of damaged bonds, unbearable experiences, and undreamable objects (Eigen, 2000). Then, with the sensibility of Grotstein (2007), we're struck by a beam of intense darkness, and what Marlan (2008) calls the black sun, and Eigen (2016, p. 24) further elucidates from the Kabbalah as "'a spark of impenetrable darkness' flashing from the depths of infinity." Within the therapeutic context, the creative flash of understanding emanates as an energy of an archetypal sage, insight paradoxically facilitated by a "stripping away of mind ... generative zero state or radical openness to Freud's free floating attention ... so that the intuition of psychic reality builds" (Eigen, 1998, p. 75).

Thus, the illuminative realm of seer, mystic, and sage opens psychic senses to a "mystic-genius aspect of self" (Eigen, 1998, p. 16), welcoming illuminative objects (Eaton, 2015), Bion's godhead (Bion, 1984, 1995), and the "infinite presence at one with O" (Grotstein, 2007, p. 77). Psychoanalytic mystic openness nourishes the subtle sensitivities of the seer's third eye, the sage's third ear, and the psychoanalytic therapist's openness to the mystic unknown (Eigen, 1998, p. 11). It is the ineffable intuition of the instant (Bachelard, 2013). Ever evolving, the work of

Eigen explores the complexities of psychoanalytic understanding of self, other, and everyday life that coalesce into "…the great light and creative darkness, pointing to experience that uplifts and transforms" (Eigen, 2016, p. 25).

And so, at the heart of sensitivity to the imminent yet transcendent process of psychic evolution – without which therapy falls flat, reside the archetypes of the seer, mystic, and sage. They, as Grossmark (2021) profoundly writes of Eigen, generate wild thoughts and compassionate feelings, free associations, liminal reveries, and yieldedness to what one patient I have seen for decades describes as "moments of blinding clarity that touch and forever change the soul."

Crisis, Illuminative Mind, and the Seer

> So you have chosen to study Divination, the most difficult of all magical arts. I must warn you from the outset that if you do not have the Sight, there is very little I will be able to teach you. – Professor Trelawney in J.K. Rawling, *Harry Potter and the Prisoner of Azkaban.*

Eigen's illuminative sensibilities usher us behind the scenes of daily life and into the explosive stuff of the unconscious, the psychic underworld teeming with both destructive and generative energies. Oh, and they are wonderfully dangerous! There is nothing quite like beginning, living through, and ending one's day in the illuminative mystic as it deepens via sleep and dreaming. Just this week, in a nighttime visionary state, I was visited in my study by a poltergeist, an independent imaginal energy from what Jung penned as the collective unconscious and what Eastern and Western mystic traditions have referred to as the spiritual world.

The adolescent phantom proved so frightening, her enacted message so blinding yet illuminating, that I found myself propelled into a world of unobscured perception, shedding light on what had been hidden from consciousness. The poltergeist dramatized the dynamic of a particular patient I am seeing, the tell in the elements of her dress that were similar to my patient's. This proved to be a critical clarification regarding what was at play during a time of crisis in therapy. In treatment the next day, my psychoanalytic attitude honed, and I was with the patient in a manner that was better, truer, and simply more helpful as the result of the otherworldly visitation. I am reminded of the role of seers in ancient Greece as curing madness in their capacity of "…diviner, healer, and purifier" (Flower, 2008). Thus, the sharpened blade of Demeter cut through my limited consciousness into Bion's O, "…an ultimate reality and truth" (Bion, 1977, p. 31). At the core, the centerpoint of my visceral encounter with the infinite, lay the capacity to sense and see in a moment of crisis, with soul-piercing clarity, an evolving psychic reality. It further kindled an appreciation and nurturance of hard-won psychoanalytic seeing. It honed my ability to yield to, be open to, and evolve into metamorphoses of sightedness that craft a therapist's soul within the therapeutic encounter. In Eigen's words, "The vicissitudes of faith involve the struggle not only to know but in some way be one's true self…" (Eigen, 1993, p. 127).

How I felt the impact of these words some twenty years ago when first reading them. Caught in a personal and professional maelstrom, I wrestled with angels and demons. The church I had identified with and within which I treated patients in emotional/spiritual crises was crumbling. I had lost sight, my lens for religious seeing having been shattered. Disorientation set in as news reports of emotional and sexual trauma inflicted by clergy on innocents emerged. Then, amid all the ecclesiastical wrongdoings reported on national and international news sources, Sixty Minutes news magazine broke loose with extensively investigated coverage of the sexual scandal of the archbishop of my archdiocese. Patients flooded my office, sufferers of religious faith violated and traumatized. Secrets had been kept, abuse perpetrated. The conventional religious world, as so many knew it, was being cut through by Demeter's sword, the blade exposing the complexities of truth and lie, good and bad, and what had been a mediator of religious meaningfulness.

Distraught, unable to catch my spiritual breath, I entered into what centuries-old Western religious texts have called the dark night of the soul. Night after night witnessed a descent into the underworld of dreams and nightmares, dramatizing obscured dark truths behind the scenes of the ecclesia. Finally, one morning after yet another night of fitful sleep, I opened Eigen's recently released, *The Psychoanalytic Mystic*, then a new volume (now well-worn) on my bookshelf. I read, "... the repeated breakdowns the psyche endures in face of its inability to process its own experiencing ... psychotic agonies that the immature psyche can not process" (Eigen, 1998, p. 96). It resonated and cut to my core. I was incensed! My psyche was not immature! I can process this religious crisis! I *will* process one of the most profound agonies of my adult years! Eigen's words cut to the psychological quick. Umph!

Well, tale be told, time brought me to my proverbial knees, and I re-entered deep psychological care. Delving deeply into my feelings and nightmares (no, not dreams ... these babies were high-voltage sleep time nightmares), my therapist and I withstood seven years of doubting, wrestling, failed attempts, and quick glimmers of hope. Finally, at the seventh year of soul work, blaring nightmares morphing into dreams and their whispers, we found sabbath, rest, and a journey's completion emerging. A dream voice spoke by the end of the seventh year: "The time has come to live, to go forward in your own way on your own path."

Little did I know what that would mean – all that it would entail – the dream's guidance and understanding yielding to what in our decades-old study group I have often heard Eigen refer to as "understanding, but open understanding." It is an evolving complexity of nuances of experience and meaning, emerging layer after layer over days, months, and years. Another dream came on the night of my final therapy session. In the nighttime vision, I was a ferryman rowing soul after soul across a dark lake during the witching hour, the time of traveling between worlds. We traversed an underworld dimension of shadows and spirits. Person by person, I rowed from one shore to the other. Each person would disembark and step onto a path into a dark forest where a soft glow shone, an illuminative presence in the distance. And then, a voice spoke, "One by one, you are to take them." Now, nearly two decades since that vision, I continue to row. It is an open-ended journey of crisis and illumination along the path of deep psychological seeing that continually sheds light on the complexities of becoming human, making one's way from shore to shore, one life revolution/evolution to another.

Madness, Magic, and the Mystic

Follow your inner moonlight. Don't hide the madness. – Allan Ginsberg

Evolutions of illuminative presence birth what Eigen (1998) quotes from a patient's letter as practical magic: "The *best* in analysis approaches practical magic" (p. 43). My own patients have described psychoanalytic therapy as miraculous, to which I've added, "It is, but it's a hard work miracle." How close Freud (1930) came to affirming the reality of the illuminative mystic with the phrase "oceanic feeling" (p. 68). For years, I wrestled with his having stopped short of affirming the phenomenology of the transcendent and its potential to facilitate psychoanalytic transformation. In my early years, as Eigen has often recounted for himself in his lectures, many other psychological writers moved my psychic sensibilities more than Freud, especially James and Jung. Then one night three decades ago, during a psychoanalytic conference at the World Trade Center in New York, I acutely felt the deadening effect of psychoanalytic metapsychology sans openness to illuminative/mystic realities. That night, a vivid dream, the visual details evaporating upon awakening, left the remembrance of an indelible and illuminative voice: "Freud touched the face of God."

I awakened in tears, heartened by the dream to not succumb to despair/madness in my calling as a depth psychologist. Yet I knew that to survive professionally, I had to go my own way. I had to listen and learn but not fall prey to psychoanalytic allegiance or obeisance, a deadening dynamic. Eigen often states that to survive and thrive, we learn, pick up a few things, and then swerve. We go our own way and walk our own path. Georg Groddeck, oft mentioned by Eigen in lectures, carved his own psychological path with the proclamation, "Become who you are!" (Will, 1987, p. 170). Groddeck replied to those asking for his blessing to organize a society of devotees:

> Disciples like their master to stay put, whereas I should think anyone a fool who wanted me to say the same thing tomorrow as I said yesterday. If you really want to be my follower, look at life for yourself and tell the world honestly what you see. (Groddeck, 1951)

Bion affirmed this truth to self in noting that the psychoanalytic mystic sees things as they are, "…through the deception or camouflage of words and symbols" (Grotstein, 2007, p. 129). This individual path of the illuminative presence of the psychoanalytic mystic has been nurtured by Eigen's work. Jung also affirmed it, as he expressed relief that he was Jung and not a Jungian. Eigen assuredly has faced professional criticism for seeing things as he sees them, Grossmark (2021) noting,

...there was some caution in my psychoanalytic group about his work – was it 'wild' – was it 'spiritual' – was it not 'psychoanalysis.' Like Bion, he is intrepid in the psychic hell holes he will enter, and also like Bion appreciates beauty at the same time ... he is undoubtably a psychoanalyst – and a wise, compassionate, one at that.

Eigen, as a senior sojourner into deep realms of mind and heart, one who, in the words of Ginsburg, follows his own inner moonlight, proffers mental and spiritual openings for seekers of soul nourishment. He encourages us to courageously venture onto the wild, wise, potentially maddening, yet always illuminating paths of the psychoanalytic mystic.

How much struggle, ups and downs, and all-arounds there are in forever discovering one's illuminative path. Walking my own path of truth to the unconscious has meant remaining a depth psychologist and not a psychoanalyst. After completing my residency in clinical psychoanalysis at Northwestern University School of Medicine, an illuminative nightmare shook me to the core. It dramatized the horror ahead for me in adhering to one psychoanalytic school and becoming a card-carrying zealot of a particular ideology. In the nightmare, I desperately struggled to breathe as the collar and cloak of the clergy cut off my air supply, psychoanalysts surrounding me awaiting my ordination. Shocked, I awakened, knowing that the path of what the Greeks called *psyche therapeia*, a life of devotion to the soul, was my calling, but not as an ordainee. I remain, now forty years later, an independent depth psychologist on my own path of practicing devotion to and healing for the soul.

To this day, archetypal inspiration from illuminative dreams resonates and lingers. They were birthed years after wrestling with what was and was not viscerally experienced meaningfulness within the pluralistic realms of the mystic unconscious. As I confided, inherent in my struggles was that Freud never acknowledged the generative reality of the mystic. Ah ... but then, as illuminative dreaming clarified, he did not need to write about it! Whether in this life or in his passing, he touched it! *Freud touched the face of God!* Never will I forget the mystic words. The living reality of illuminative presence was touched by Freud despite cultural, scientific, and literary constraints. Perhaps he unconsciously feared his own inner madness if he dared to go beyond his already revolutionary empirical convictions. Who's to say? However, I do know that the dream message came as a welcoming luminous presence in a time of professional distress.

A few years after my dream, Eigen's work on the mystic within psychoanalysis flew onto the contemporary psychoanalytic scene. It propelled contemporary depth metapsychology into an openness of exploration of transcendent experience within the therapeutic encounter. I had read all of James and Jung, been in Jungian analysis, and appreciated the insights and inspirations of the budding field of transpersonal psychology. Eigen's work, however, was for me akin in its soul-quickening nature to another *spiritus rector*, the writings of 16th-century philosopher, priest, hermetic occultist, pantheist, and heretic, Giordano Bruno. In what some might consider his psychoanalytically heretical dialectics, Eigen's ideas and inspirations quickened my sensitivity to the workings of the depth psychological mystic. It was and is a wellspring of soul magic not plumbed in more classical, ego, and object-oriented psychoanalytic ideologies or various streams of thought within transpersonal psychology.

I understand the reluctance of psychoanalytic forebearers, contemporary theorists, and clinicians to venture too far into generative religious experience. By and large, references to the transcendent and sacred are notably absent in psychoanalytic discourse. It is understandable since, along with academic reservations, yielding to the illuminative mystic can prove terrifying. As Eigen notes, "Mystics themselves, while enjoying oceanic feelings, sometimes were … left terrified by the onset of a numinous awakening. They were overturned, and shaken to their core" (Eigen, 1998, p. 190).

Moonlight, it is said, can drive us to madness. During nights on call during my clinical residency at Northwestern School of Medicine, the full moon swamped the outpatient crisis center with a deluge of lunacy, incipient psychosis unraveling by the minute. It was madness chomping at the psychological bit for release, set loose as patients howled in back wards and screamed of persecutory voices in their heads. Yet, moonlight also causes things to grow. For one of my Jungian psychoanalytic sessions in Chicago with Arwind Vasavada in his apartment overlooking the University of Chicago, I was accompanied by my wife, Kate. Arwind and I had agreed that, for many reasons, it might prove meaningful and potentially helpful.

After introductions, we dropped into the illuminative world of dreams (Kate, to this day – forty years later – a prolific dreamer). By session's end, Arwind commented, "Your energy, Paul, is like the sun, Kate's the moon. And, in India, we revere the fact that certain plants grow only by the light of the moon." I was left stunned (still stunned) — a Lacanian, Zen, Eigen moment of awakening. It shook me, the subtle moonlight in our marriage at times maddening. Yet, with the resonance of Arwind's illuminative words and presence, our marriage's magical and intimate nature remains an ever-evolving relational and mystic wonder, for which I am grateful.

Eigen (2020) speaks of his own long-term marriage and how another psychoanalytic mystic, Bion, told him, "You should get married. Marriage isn't what you think it is. It's really two people speaking truth to each other, mitigating the severity to yourself." Eigen said, "I guess it was not as bad as I feared with my primitive thoughts of horrors" (p. 114). Primitive horrors, madness, and the moonlight magic of the psychoanalytic mystic pave the path of an illuminative understanding that lets "…psychic reality speak in a way that others may hear and feel it, love their lives a little more, appreciate the privilege of grappling with human difficulties" (p. 68).

The Sage and the Illuminative Numinous

> The test of a true sage is the ability to call forward the deepest parts of ourselves and awaken riches that lie dormant within. – Michael Eigen. *Flames from the Unconscious.*

Back to Demeter, diviner and arbiter of the deadening and enlivening, we go. She is but one of a plethora of archetypal images speaking to the pluralistic reality that "God is everywhere ... shifting numinous densities that characterize the influence of ancient gods on changing fortunes" (Eigen, 2007, p. 18). The sacred speaks as an intuitive surge, a psychoanalytic moment of cerebral/visceral insight, the inner sage urging us to knock on heaven's door. We feel the vibration, which yogis refer to as the subtle shift of *prana* from the base of our spine to the seventh chakra, the *sahasrara*, the crown chakra at the top of the head, that directly connects to archetypal wisdom and self/other knowledge. It's what I playfully tell patients is the "hot off the psychic press stuff." It is pure illumination, the archetypal energy of the sage. Eigen (1998) celebrates as he intones, "Let us call God *jouissance* ... the heavens, the earth, living beings – all creating is *Jouissance* creating" (p. 134). The pluralistic nature of the illuminative numinous is here, there, within, and without. Illuminative presence leaves no room for that which numbs and deadens, meta-psychologies that may have at one time served a purpose but no longer do. When illuminative spirit enters the front door, dogmas go out the back, states the old adage. According to the sagely guidance of Western and Eastern mysticism, the spirit blows where it will and cannot be constrained or dogmatized. It is that in which we live, move, and have our being.

The sagely proclamation of life manifest as psyche is referenced by Hillman in *An Introductory Note: Carus and Jung* to *Psyche: On the Development of the Soul* (Carus, 1970). Prophet, psychologist, and sage, Carl Gustav Carus, is one whom Jung (1970), in the epilogue of *Mysterium Coniunctionis,* affirmed as having first championed a mystic and holistic psychology of the unconscious. Carus (1970) wrote of the unconscious as that spiritual energy that expresses life and nature it-self, "... an expression of spiritual reality, observation (*Beobachtung*) for the sake of insight (*Schau*)" (p. 10). Sensitivity to the working of psychospiritual energies, often quite subtle, kindles the experience of an illuminative presence within psy-choanalytic encounters and draws us into what Eigen (2020, p. 156) calls "un-known boundless support."

Jung deemed the welcoming presence of generative spiritual energy within the nonlinear, ever-evolving psychoanalytic encounter integral to the soul's individua-tion. It harkens to what Emmanuel Ghent (1990) described as a "deep rooted need for transcendent experience ... an intense creative drive" (pp. 202–203). Thus, the destructive/generative blade of Demeter, archetypal energy within the self and the psychoanalytic relationship, facilitates the quickening of attunement to the perpet-ually self-renewing jouissance of the inner sage. This whisper, voice, and rumbling of interior wisdom opens what Cataldo (2019, p. 124) describes as an "...analytic holding place for religious experience … forces or structures that shape us which transcend the dyad and which engender movement toward self-expression, authenticity, and mutual recognition."

Now a seasoned depth psychologist of forty years, the deadening aspects of now dry metapsychologies continue to be cut away by the Lady of the Golden Blade, Demeter. What at one time enlivened but no longer does, I am free to shed. As I let go of worn-out perspectives and feeling states, *mana* rains from the heavens. It is a source of daily, infinite, and enlivening transformations. It is soul inspiration and sagely wisdom through the writings of one who Wikipedia (2022) states has allowed "…for the role of mysticism in the therapeutic process."

Ah! Far more than a *role* for me is psychoanalytic mysticism. Eigen's work, at one time a psychoanalytic lifeline, has now become a daily psychic happening, an ongoing soul immersion into new and changing wavelengths of psychoanalytic seeing, hearing, and living. It is ever-evolving sagely insight that begets a constantly developing appreciation of the complexities of human experience and the infinite manifestations of illuminative presence. It is sustenance.

Conclusion: An Evolving Omega Point

In our weekly study group, Eigen frequently references Chardin (2008) in *The Phenomenon of Man*, the ebb and flow and eventual convergence of ongoing life complexities into an essential and sustaining omega point of unification of soul, spirit, and nature.

In Eigen's words, "If I do not draw from the Holy Spirit on a daily basis, I become a semi-collapsed version of myself" (Eigen, 1998, p. 163). Thus, at the core of the work of Michael Eigen "…is a luminous affirmation of the wonder of human experience" (Eaton, 2015, p. 134). He sensitizes psychoanalytic soul seekers to the presence of the luminous: the archetypes of the seer that conjures insight, the mystic that opens pathways to ongoing experience and knowing, and the sage that facilitates evolving insights into self and others. In all, the psychoanalytic inspiration of Eigen's work stimulates what he calls Holy Spirit openings, an experience of the inexhaustible unconscious expounded upon by Carus, expanding transformations of self vis-à-vis Chardin, and archetypal reverberations of the Ultimate Reality – Bion's O (Bion, 1995) and what Eigen himself circumambulates about as a "mystic light" (2001, p. 35), a welcoming and luminous presence that awakens riches lying dormant within.

References

Bachelard, G. (2013). *The Intuition of the Instant*. Evanston, IL: Northwestern University Press.

Bion, W.R. (1995). *Attention and Interpretation*. New York: Routledge.

Bion, W.R. (1977). *Seven Servants*. New York: Jason Aronson.

Bion, W.R. (1984). *Transformations*. London: Karnac.

Carus, C.G. (1970). *Psyche: On the Development of the Soul.* Thompson, CT: Spring Publications.

Cataldo, L.M. (2019). Where God is Between Us: Religious Experience, Surrender, and the Third in Clinical Perspective, *Psychoanalytic Perspectives,* 16:2, 113–133.

Corbin, H. (2000). Mundus Imaginalis: Or the Imaginary and the Imaginal. In B. Sells (Ed.). *Working with Images: The Theoretical Base of Archetypal Psychology* (pp. 70–89). Woodstock, CT: Spring Publications.

de Chardin, P.T. (2008). *The Phenomenon of Man.* New York: Harper Perennial Modern Classics.

Eaton, J.L. (2015). Becoming a Welcoming Object: Personal Notes on Michael Eigen's Impact. In S.Bloch & L.Daws, *Living Moments: on the work of Michael Eigen* (pp. 131–148). London & New York: Routledge.

Eigen, M. (1993). *The Electrified Tightrope.* Northvale, NJ: Jason Aronson Inc.

Eigen, M. (1998). *The Psychoanalytic Mystic.* London & New York: Free Association Books.

Eigen, M. (2000). *Damaged Bonds.* London: Karnac.

Eigen, M. (2001). *Ecstasy.* Middletown, CT: Wesleyan University Press.

Eigen, M. (2007). *Feeling Matters.* London: Karnac.

Eigen, M. (2016). *Image, Sense, Infinities, and Everyday Life.* London: Karnac Books Ltd.

Eigen, M. (2019). *Dialogues with Michael Eigen: Psyche Singing.* London & New York: Routledge.

Flower, M.A. (2008). *The Seer in Ancient Greece.* Berkeley: University of California Press.

Freud, S. (1930). Civilization and its discontents. In *Standard Edition* (Vol. 21, pp. 64–145). London: Hogarth Press.

Ghent, E. (1990). Masochism, Submission, Surrender: Masochism as a Perversion of Surrender. *Contemporary Psychoanalysis,* 26, 108–136.

Groddeck, G. (1951). *The World of Man.* (V.M.E. Collins, Trans.). London: Funk & Wagnall's.

Grossmark, R. (2021). *Editorial Review for Eigen in Seoul Volume Three: Pain and Beauty, Terror and Wonder.* London & New York: Routledge.

Grotstein, J.S. (2007). *A Beam of Intense Darkness: Wilfred Bion's Legacy to Psychoanalysis.* London & New York: Routledge.

James, W. (1985). *The Varieties of Religious Experience.* Cambridge, MA & London: Harvard University Press.

Jung, C.G. (1916/1960). General Aspects of Dream Psychology. In G. Adler & R.F. Hall (Eds. & Trans.), *Collected Works* (Vol. 8, pp. 237–280). New York, NY: Pantheon.

Jung, C.G. (1970). *Mysterium Coniunctionis.* Princeton, NJ: Princeton University Press.

Khan, M. (1974). *The Privacy of the Self.* Madison, CT: International Universities Press, Inc.

Marlan, S. (2008). *The Black Sun: The Alchemy and Art of Darkness.* College Station, TX: Texan A&M University Press.

Plato. (1952). *Plato's Phaedrus.* Cambridge: Cambridge University Press.

Air Currents

For M.E.

> What a relief to let the heart open
> while seeing a gull
> unfurl and adjust its wings to the currents
>
> What a relief to break out of confinement
>
> speak my mind
> or lie as a corpse and imagine myself a warrior
> with outstretched arms
>
> Rachel Berghash 2022

Index

Note: Page numbers followed by "n" denote endnotes.

For Product Safety Concerns and Information please contact our EU
representative GPSR@taylorandfrancis.com
Taylor & Francis Verlag GmbH, Kaufingerstraße 24, 80331 München, Germany

www.ingramcontent.com/pod-product-compliance
Lightning Source LLC
Chambersburg PA
CBHW050645280326
41932CB00015B/2793